P9-BZS-816

Making Social Science Matter presents an exciting new approach to the social and behavioral sciences. Instead of trying to emulate the natural sciences and create a kind of general theory, Bent Flyvbjerg argues that the strength of the social sciences lies in their rich, reflexive analysis of values and power – so essential to the social and economic development of society. Moving beyond the purely analytic or technical, Flyvbjerg compares the theoretical study of human activity with real-world situations and demonstrates how the social sciences can become relevant again in the modern world. Powerfully argued, with clear methodological guidelines and practical examples, *Making Social Science Matter* opens up a new future for the social sciences, freed from an inappropriate and misleading comparison with the natural sciences. Its empowering message will make it required reading for students and academics across the social and behavioral sciences.

BENT FLYVBJERG is Professor of Planning, Department of Development and Planning at Aalborg University, Denmark. He is the author of numerous publications in twelve languages, most recently *Rationality and Power: Democracy in Practice* (1998).

Making Social Science Matter

Why social inquiry fails and how it can succeed again

Bent Flyvbjerg

Translated by Steven Sampson

CAMBRIDGE UNIVERSITY PRESS
Cambridge, New York, Melbourne, Madrid, Cape Town, Singapore, São Paulo,
Delhi, Tokyo, Mexico City

Cambridge University Press
The Edinburgh Building, Cambridge CB2 8RU, UK

Published in the United States of America by Cambridge University Press, New York

www.cambridge.org
Information on this title: www.cambridge.org/9780521772686

© Bent Flyvbjerg 2001

This publication is in copyright. Subject to statutory exception
and to the provisions of relevant collective licensing agreements,
no reproduction of any part may take place without
the written permission of Cambridge University Press.

First published 2001
13th printing 2011

Printed in the United Kingdom at the University Press, Cambridge

A catalogue record for this publication is available from the British Library

Library of Congress cataloging in publication data

Flyvbjerg, Bent
  Making social science matter: why social inquiry fails and how it can succeed
again / by Bent Flyvbjerg; translated by Steven Sampson.
    p. cm.
Includes index.
ISBN 0 521 77268 0 (hardback)   0 521 77568 x (paperback)
1. Social sciences–Philosophy.   I. Title.
H61.F6144 2001
300'.1–dc21   00–023608

ISBN 978-0-521-77268-6 Hardback
ISBN 978-0-521-77568-7 Paperback

Cambridge University Press has no responsibility for the persistence or accuracy
of URLs for external or third-party internet websites referred to in this publication,
and does not guarantee that any content on such websites is, or will remain,
accurate or appropriate.

In memory of
Regina Flyvbjerg
née Krakauer

A mind that is stretched to a new idea never returns to its original dimension.
Oliver W. Holmes

Contents

Acknowledgments

I wish to thank the many persons, organizations, and institutions who helped make this book possible. Special thanks must be given to Alan Wolfe, of Boston University, for encouraging me to translate the original Danish version of the book into English, resulting in this expanded, revised, and updated edition. I also wish to thank Hubert and Stuart Dreyfus, of the University of California at Berkeley, for their patience in interviews and discussions where I first tried out ideas that later became central to the book. Steven Lukes invited me to present my thoughts on power to faculty and students at the European University Institute in Florence, where both he and they gave me valuable feedback. C. Roland Christensen, Harvard's godfather to the case method, never failed me with support on my trek to understand and employ the case approach in research and teaching.

Thanks are due as well to the organizers, lecturers, and participants in the National Endowment for the Humanities Summer Institute, "The Idea of a Social Science, 40 Years Later," held at the University of Missouri, St. Louis, June–July 1998. James Bohman and Paul Roth generously invited me to sit in on the Institute. This provided me with the right impetus at the right time for finishing the book.

Several years ago, in preparing a paper outlining the ideas that would eventually develop into this text, I benefited from comments by Daniel Bell, Richard Bernstein, John Friedmann, Hans-Georg Gadamer, Anthony Giddens, Alasdair MacIntyre, Lisa Peattie, Martin Wachs, and Aaron Wildavsky.[1] My colleagues at Aalborg University, Finn Kjærsdam and Hans Gullestrup, read large portions of a first draft of the book, and their comments were invaluable in helping improve the original Danish version. For their help at various stages in the process, I also wish to thank Erik Albæk, Johannes Andersen, Robert Beauregard, Inger Bo, Peter Bogason, Irene Christiansen, Peter Munk Christiansen, William Connolly, Mitchell Dean, Raphaël Fischler, Henrik and John Flyvbjerg, John Forester, Gary Gutting, Maarten Hajer, Gorm Harste, David Hoy, Margo Huxley, Andy Jamison, Martin Jay, Karsten Friis Johansen, Ib

Jørgensen, Torben Beck Jørgensen, Terry Kelly, Peter Lassman, Bruno Latour, Seymour Mandelbaum, James Miller, Peter Miller, Thomas Osborne, Morten Rugtved Petersen, Jørgen Primdahl, Tim Richardson, Neal Richman, Stefan Rossbach, Joseph Rouse, Bish Sanyal, Arpád Szakolczai, James Throgmorton, and Oren Yiftachel. Two anonymous Cambridge University Press reviewers provided highly useful comments for preparing the final version of the typescript.

The theoretical and methodological considerations in the book were developed hand in hand with empirical studies in which theory and method were put to the test and refined. I wish to thank the many persons and organizations who have placed their experiences, time, and archives at my disposal in these studies. After having developed the book's approach in a European and Anglo-Saxon context, Fred Lerise and Tumsifu Nnkya, of the University of Dar es Salaam, and Jørgen Andreasen, of the Danish Royal Academy of Fine Arts, gave me the unique opportunity to learn in-depth about the pros and cons of the approach in a development setting.

Anni Busk Nielsen provided precious help in acquiring the literature on which this study is based. Lilli Glad and Dorte Madsen expertly transformed my many drafts into readable manuscripts.

The writing and translation of the book was made possible by grants from the Danish National Research Council, the Danish Social Science Research Council, the Cowi Foundation, and the North Jutland University Foundation. The work was also supported by the Fulbright Commission, the Carlsberg Foundation, the Denmark-America Foundation, the Egmont H. Petersen Foundation, Knud Højgaard's Foundation, and by a Christian and Ottilia Brorson Travel Grant. Finally, Aalborg University and its Department of Development and Planning provided generous support.

The translation of the book from Danish into English was carried out by Steven Sampson in collaboration with me. Not only did Steven Sampson once again produce a translation of clear, readable prose; he also suggested helpful improvements in the original text. Sarah Caro and Elizabeth Howard, senior editors at Cambridge University Press, provided valuable help in seeing the book through the printing process.

Finally, I cannot thank my family and friends enough for their love and care.

I apologize to anyone I have forgotten to mention here. Responsibility for any errors or omissions in this book remains mine alone.

1   The Science Wars: a way out

Plato is dear to me, but dearer still is truth.   *Aristotle*

Physics envy and pre-Kantian shamans

When the May 1996 issue of the journal *Social Text* appeared, an issue
devoted to the understanding of "Science Wars," the editors became
targets in these "wars" in ways they had not imagined. The issue included
a bogus article by New York University mathematical physicist Alan
Sokal, who feigned an earnest reflection on the political and philosophical
implications of recent physics research for cultural studies.[1] Sokal re-
vealed the hoax himself, and it immediately became a hotly debated issue
in academic and popular media around the world.[2] The appearance of the
article was not only taken as a sign of shoddy scholarship by the *Social
Text* editors but as an exposé of cultural studies and social science in
general. For instance, Nobel prize-winning physicist Steven Weinberg
used the hoax to identify what he calls a fundamental "opposition"
between natural and social scientists, especially regarding what Weinberg
sees as dangerous anti-rationalism and relativism in social science and
cultural studies.[3] Those on the other side of the "wars" countered by
criticizing Sokal and calling Weinberg and like-minded natural scientists
"pre-Kantian shaman[s]" repeating the "mantras of particle physicists,"
with their "reductionist view of science."[4]

The year before Sokal's hoax, the "wars" had raged over the scientific
status of a high-profile US National Opinion Research Center study,
which had been launched as a "definitive survey" of sexual practices in
the United States.[5] Here, too, doubts were raised not only about the
status of scholarship of the study in question, but of sociology and social
science as such. The study had received the doubtful honor of becoming
the topic of an editorial in *The Economist* under the heading "74.6% of
Sociology is Bunk."[6] In *The New York Review of Books*, Harvard biologist
and statistician R. C. Lewontin criticized the researchers behind the

1

study for believing what people said when filling in the survey questionnaires on which the study builds. "It is frightening," Lewontin wrote, "to
think that social science is in the hands of professionals who are so deaf to
human nuance that they believe that people do not lie to themselves [and
to others] about the most freighted aspects of their own lives."[7] Lewontin
concluded his review by warning social scientists that in pretending to
a kind of knowledge that it cannot achieve, "social science can only
engender the scorn of natural scientists."[8] Other social science critics
participating in the debate talked of "dumbed-down" sociology and
social scientists' "physics envy."[9] The authors of the NORC study re-
sponded in kind by calling Lewontin's review "professionally incompe-
tent" and motivated by an "evident animus against the social sciences in
general."[10] The authors also observed that the notion that an economist
or a sociologist should review work in population genetics, one of
Lewontin's fields of competence, "would properly be greeted with de-
rision."[11] While one might well agree with the latter point, the authors'
use of name-calling instead of substantive arguments in their attempt to
refute Lewontin's criticism, leaves us wondering, not about the validity of
this criticism, but about what it is regarding natural and social science
that makes it fairly common practice for natural scientists to review social
science, whereas the opposite is less common.

Good or bad?

However entertaining for bystanders, the mudslinging of the Science
Wars is unproductive. The Wars undoubtedly serve political and ideological purposes in the competition for research funds and in defining
what Charles Lindblom and Michel Foucault have called society's "truth
politics."[12] Judged by intellectual standards, however, the Science Wars
are misguided. In this book, I will present a way out of the Wars by
developing a conception of social science based on a contemporary
interpretation of the Aristotelian concept of *phronesis*, variously translated
as prudence or practical wisdom. In Aristotle's words *phronesis* is a "true
state, reasoned, and capable of action with regard to things that are good
or bad for man."[13] *Phronesis* goes beyond both analytical, scientific knowledge (*episteme*) and technical knowledge or know-how (*techne*) and involves judgments and decisions made in the manner of a virtuoso social
and political actor. I will argue that *phronesis* is commonly involved in
social practice, and that therefore attempts to reduce social science and
theory either to *episteme* or *techne*, or to comprehend them in those terms,
are misguided.

By introducing *phronesis* into the discussion of what social science is and can be, we will see that Lewontin and others are right, albeit perhaps not for the reasons they believe, when they say that social science has set itself an impossible task when it attempts to emulate natural science and produce explanatory and predictive, that is, epistemic, theory. We will also see, however, that this conclusion does not imply the oft-seen image of impotent social sciences versus potent natural sciences, which is at the core of the Science Wars. This image derives from the fact that both types of science tend to be compared in terms of their epistemic qualities. This book will argue that such a comparison is misleading. The two types of science have their respective strengths and weaknesses along fundamentally different dimensions, a point which Aristotle demonstrated but which has since been forgotten. At present, social science is locked in a fight it cannot hope to win, because it has accepted terms that are self-defeating. We will see that in their role as *phronesis*, the social sciences are strongest where the natural sciences are weakest: just as the social sciences have not contributed much to explanatory and predictive theory, neither have the natural sciences contributed to the reflexive analysis and discussion of values and interests, which is the prerequisite for an enlightened political, economic, and cultural development in any society, and which is at the core of *phronesis*. This should also be the core of social science if we want to transcend the current malaise of the Science Wars.

Virtue lost

Aristotle, the philosopher of *phronesis* par excellence, never elaborated his conception of *phronesis* to include explicit considerations of power. Hans-Georg Gadamer's authoritative and contemporary conception of *phronesis* also overlooks issues of power.[14] Yet as Richard Bernstein points out, if we are to think about what can be done to the problems and risks of our time, we must advance from the original conception of *phronesis* to one explicitly including power.[15] Unfortunately, Bernstein himself has not integrated his work on *phronesis* with issues of power. Nor, to my knowledge, has anyone else. I will argue that in modern society, conflict and power are phenomena constitutive of social and political inquiry. And I will develop the classic concept of *phronesis* to include issues of power.

   Aristotle, in arguing that natural and social science are and should be different ventures, discusses the three intellectual virtues, *episteme, techne*, and *phronesis*. Whereas *episteme* is found in the modern words "epistemology" and "epistemic," and *techne* in "technology" and "technical," it is indicative of the degree to which thinking in the social sciences has allowed itself to be colonized by natural and technical science that we today do not even have a word for the one intellectual virtue, *phronesis*, which Aristotle saw not only as the necessary basis for social and political inquiry, but as the most important of the intellectual virtues. *Phronesis* is most important because it is that activity by which instrumental rationality is balanced by value-rationality, and because such balancing is crucial to the sustained happiness of the citizens in any society, according to Aristotle. In what follows we will redress the imbalance between the intellectual virtues by submitting the concept of *phronesis* to a current reinterpretation in terms of the needs of contemporary social science. The goal is to help restore social science to its classical position as a practical, intellectual activity aimed at clarifying the problems, risks, and possibilities we face as humans and societies, and at contributing to social and political praxis.

A brief overview

Based on a critique of cognitivism and naturalism, Part one of the book shows why social science never has been, and probably never will be, able to develop the type of explanatory and predictive theory that is the ideal and hallmark of natural science. Chapter two demonstrates that context and judgment are irreducibly central to understanding human action. On this basis, following works by Hubert Dreyfus, Pierre Bourdieu, and Harold Garfinkel, chapters three and four explore the question of whether a theory of context and judgment is possible. The answer to this question is negative and the conclusion is that social science emulation of natural science is a cul-de-sac; mainstream social theory and social science methodology stand in need of reorientation.

Part two is an attempt at such a reorientation based on *phronesis*. Chapter five introduces Aristotle's original thoughts on the subject and explores the relationship between *phronesis* and social science. The following chapters then develop the concept of *phronesis* on three fronts to make for a more contemporary interpretation. First, chapter six takes its point of departure in Aristotle's insight that case knowledge is crucial to the practice of *phronesis*; on this basis the chapter clarifies the status and uses of case studies in social science. Second, based on works by Michel Foucault, Jürgen Habermas, and Friedrich Nietzsche, chapters seven and eight elaborate the classical conception of *phronesis* to include considerations on power, thus expanding the classical concept from one of values to one of values and power. Third, chapter nine further refines the approach by developing a set of methodological guidelines for doing what I call "phronetic social science." Chapter ten contains illustrations and examples of such an approach, while Chapter eleven sums up the perspective of the book.

My aims with this book are simply to call attention to a central problem in the social sciences and to outline a possible answer. I see the problem – the fact that the social sciences have not had the type of theoretical and methodological success that the natural sciences have – as fairly well defined and well documented. The answer, however, seems less clear, and I do not think there is a single answer. My own attempt at an answer – phronetic social science – should be considered only one attempt among many possible. It should also be seen as only a first step that will undoubtedly need further theoretical and methodological refinement, just as it will need to be developed through further practical employment in social-science research.[16] Despite such qualifications, I hope the reader will agree that given what is at stake – social sciences that can hold their own in the Science Wars, in the academic community, and in society at large – the attempt at reforming these sciences is worth making.

Part one

Why social science has failed as science

2 Rationality, body, and intuition in human learning

> Our task is to broaden our reasoning to make it capable of grasping what, in ourselves and others, precedes and exceeds reason.
>
> *Maurice Merleau-Ponty*

Context is central to understanding what social science is and can be. This chapter asks, "What role does context play in human knowledge and skills?" Philosophy of science and epistemology typically pose questions such as: "What is knowledge?"; "What can we know?"; "Under what conditions can we know that we know?" Here we will approach the question of knowledge by asking the more dynamic question: "How do people acquire knowledge and skills?" It is by addressing this question that we begin to understand the problem of context.

The intention here is not to outline and analyze all possible ways in which people acquire knowledge and skills, nor shall we review the many schools and theories that exist in this area. Rather we will deal with a single phenomenology of human learning as formulated by Hubert and Stuart Dreyfus.[1] This particular phenomenology has been chosen because it is especially useful for understanding the linkage between knowledge and context, and because it directly addresses the question of whether knowledge about human activity can be context-independent. The answer to this latter question is decisive for an understanding and response to two fundamental epistemological questions in the study of human activity: "Are theory and epistemology possible in social science?" "Can social and political science be scientific in the same sense as is natural science?"

The first part of the chapter reviews the phenomenology of human learning, the so-called Dreyfus model. We will then discuss the model's implications for social science.

Competence and virtuosity in human learning

Some years ago in the United States, an experiment was conducted on a group of paramedics. Video films were made of six persons administering cardiopulmonary resuscitation (CPR) to victims of acute heart failure. Five of the six were inexperienced trainees just learning CPR, while the sixth was a paramedic with long experience in emergency life-saving techniques. The films were shown to three groups of subjects: paramedics with practical experience, students being trained in this field, and instructors in life-saving techniques. Each subject was asked the following question: "Who of the six persons shown in the films would you choose to resuscitate you if you were the victim of such an accident?" Among the group of experienced paramedics, 90 percent chose the one experienced paramedic from the films. The students chose "correctly" in only 50 percent of the cases. Finally, and perhaps surprisingly, the instructors in resuscitation had poorer results than either the experienced paramedics or the students, choosing the experienced paramedic in only 30 percent of the cases.[2]

What form of rationality led the instructors to achieve such a poor performance? And what mechanisms lay behind the experienced paramedics' well-developed ability to choose correctly? These questions will be dealt with in the following discussion.

Detailed phenomenological studies of human learning indicate that people pass through several phases or levels in the learning of skills, where "skills" are understood to range from the technical to the intellectual; e.g., building a house, being socially adept, analyzing a text. Various studies, all after the degree of detail, have divided the learning process into a varying number of such levels. The Dreyfus model operates with five levels in the human-learning process:

(1) Novice
(2) Advanced beginner
(3) Competent performer
(4) Proficient performer
(5) Expert

They are levels, say Dreyfus and Dreyfus, because in phenomenological terms they consist of recognizable, qualitatively different ways of acting and performing in the process of learning a given skill. Individuals at a given level do better than individuals at the previous level. Not all people achieve the highest level in a given field. Some fields, such as chess, guitar playing, or surgery, are characterized by only a small fraction of novices becoming experts. In other areas, such as bicycling and driving, a large number of novices reach the expert level. Let us examine the levels one at a time.

1. Novice

As a novice, the individual experiences a given problem and a given situation in a given task area for the first time. During instruction the novice learns what various objective facts and characteristics of the situation are relevant for the performance of the skill. The novice learns to recognize these facts and characteristics when they appear. On this basis, the novice also learns rules for action. Facts, characteristics, and rules are defined so clearly and objectively for the novice that they can be recognized without reference to the concrete situation in which they occur. On the contrary, the rules can be generalized to all similar situations, which the novice might conceivably confront. At the novice level, facts, characteristics, and rules are not dependent on context: they are context-independent.

Let us take, for example, someone learning to drive a car. The student driver learns facts about speed and shifting gears, and he or she learns the rule that when the speed exceeds a certain level, you must shift gears. Both the fact (speed) and the rule (gear shift at certain speed) are independent of the concrete situation. In principle, shifting gears is executed as the same type of logical information process as within a digital computer. Later on, when the novice has shifted gears many times and has achieved a higher level in the learning process, the gear shift situation is recalled as analogous to prior situations. Shifting gears now occurs by reflex, without direct use of context-independent facts and rules.

Novices judge their skills by evaluating how well they follow the rules they have learned. When novices have learned a handful of rules for a given skill, however, performing the skill becomes so complex and demands so much concentration that it impedes continued improvement of performance. For example, the ability to speak and to listen to advice declines in relation to the number of rules which the novice learns and must remember to use. The first rules are necessary for gaining initial experiences, but the rules quickly become a barrier to the learning process and must be put aside in order for the novice to advance.

2. Advanced beginner

The beginner advances from the first level in the learning process by achieving real-life experience, in contrast to the often deliberative and protected learning situations of the first level. Via these further experiences, the advanced beginner learns to recognize relevant elements in relevant situations. Recognition occurs because the advanced beginner sees similarities in relation to prior examples of the same situation. Gaining experience consists in a cumulative recognition of similarities. Recognition is concrete and dependent on context, and it is precisely context which plays the decisive role, for it is context which becomes increasingly more important as one proceeds up the levels of the learning process.

For the advanced beginner, the basis for action may contain elements which are both situational and context-independent. A driver at the advanced-beginner level can thus shift gears on the basis of both the concrete situation of the motor sounds and the context-independent rule of speed, and will in fact use both indicators according to the specific situation. In this sense, situational behavior involves knowing when to bend or ignore the rules. A good chess player recognizes especially strong or especially weak positions in a concrete situation without use of context-independent rules. And there is no one who needs to combine facts and rules to identify the smell of freshly brewed coffee, Dreyfus and Dreyfus say. Personal experience via trial-and-error is more important than context-independent, explicit, verbally formulated facts and rules.

3. Competent performer

With more experience, the number of recognizable elements, which an individual sees in a concrete situation, becomes overwhelming. The individual lacks a feeling of what elements are important. In other words, the individual is unable to prioritize. At this stage, individuals learn from themselves and from others to apply a hierarchical, prioritizing procedure for decision-making. By first choosing a goal and a plan with which to organize the information about the concrete situation, and then processing only those factors relevant to achieving the goal and plan, the individual can simplify his or her task and obtain improved results.

A professor of nursing explains the problems her interns had with making the transition from the initial, rule-based levels in the learning process to the kind of prioritizing behavior and overview which characterizes competence:

I give instructions to the new graduate, very detailed and explicit instructions: when you come in and first see the baby, you take the baby's vital signs and make the physical examination, and you check the I.V. sites, and the ventilator and make sure that it works, and you check the monitors and alarms. When I would say this to them, they would do exactly what I told them to do, no matter what else was going on . . . They couldn't choose one to leave out. They couldn't choose which one was the most important . . . They couldn't do for one baby the things that were most important, and leave the things that weren't as important until later on . . . If I said, you have to do these eight things . . . they did those things, and they didn't care if their other kid was screaming its head off. When they did realize, they would be like a mule between two piles of hay.[3]

Via goals, plans, and the setting of priorities, the student nurses learn to deal with a smaller set of key factors instead of the total knowledge about the actual situation. The competent nurse, in contrast to the beginner, does not go automatically from patient to patient in a preset sequence, but continually evaluates the patients' need for attention and care and arranges his or her routine according to these evaluations. The performer's behavior "flows" and becomes better adapted to the concrete situation.

Selecting a plan is not simple, and not without problems for competent performers. It takes time and requires deliberation. There are no objective procedures for choosing a plan similar to the novice's context-independent choice of facts and application of rules. Besides, the choice of plan has wide-ranging consequences for actions and results in a way which the choice of other elements seldom has. The lack of *terra firma* for the choice of plan, combined with the competent performer's need to have a plan, produces a new, important relationship between performer and surroundings: a relationship of involvement. The novice and the advanced beginner have only limited responsibility for the consequences of their actions, these actions being predetermined by learned elements and fixed learned rules. Excluding a gross error, a bad result will therefore appear as having been caused by inadequately specified elements and rules. Actions and results will thus stand in an external relation to the beginner: they can be justified and given a rational explanation in relation to objective facts and abstract rules. Competent performers, on the other hand, are personally involved in their actions. The competent performer, after having struggled with the problem of selecting a plan, feels responsible for the consequences of the choice precisely because selecting a plan cannot be done objectively, but must nevertheless be carried out in order to be able to act competently. Hence, the actions of the competent performer comprise an element of interpretation and judgment. As we shall see, the ability to make these judgments becomes crucial at the upper levels of the learning process. It is this ability, according to Dreyfus and Dreyfus, which constitutes the core of true human expertise.

Cognitivists and others who conceive of thinking as logical information-processing and analytical problem-solving concern themselves mainly with the kind of thinking processes which take place at the "competent performer" stage. Herbert Simon is a leading exponent of this view. In his attempt to understand how people select plans, goals, and strategies, Simon and his colleagues have convincingly illustrated how people confronted with unknown tasks in unfamiliar situations act as analytical problem-solvers. The cognitivists, however, tend to generalize these results as being valid for all intelligent behavior. People are generally seen as problem-solving beings who follow a sequential model of reasoning consisting of "elements–rules–goals–plans–decisions."[4] It is this model which the cognitivists have attempted to simulate in computers and in various problem-solving models, in "expert systems" and in artificial intelligence. Their extrapolation yields good results when the models are applied to well-defined tasks with well-defined solutions. The cognitivists have had much less success, however, when the tasks and solutions are less well-defined. According to Dreyfus and Dreyfus, the poor results reflect the lack of evidence for the cognitivists' assertion that humans can act intelligently only by acting as analytical problem-solvers. There are other kinds of intelligent behavior, assert Dreyfus and Dreyfus, which appear especially among those individuals who are either very proficient or experts in their fields.[5]

In many of our daily activities, we can see phenomenologically that humans do not exclusively act as conscious problem-solvers, i.e., choosing goals, plans, and combining elements according to rules for reaching goals. When we ride a bicycle, recognize faces on the street, or talk to our neighbors, we do not appear to be solving problems. Of course, we may be operating unconsciously as logical information-processors and problem-solvers, but as we will see, this does not have to be the case and there is no evidence to support this claim. The fundamental error of the cognitivists is that they exclude any other possibility.

In contrast to the competent performer, genuine human experts exhibit thinking and behavior that is rapid, intuitive, holistic, interpretive, and visual and which has no immediate similarity to the slow, analytical reasoning which characterizes rational problem-solving and the first three levels of the learning process. On the contrary, it seems that there is a fundamental and qualitative jump from analytical problem-solving to genuine, human expertise. This jump must be made in order for someone to be really adept at performing a given skill. Stuart Dreyfus, the main architect behind the five-level model for human learning, is a competent chess player. However, he has remained at the "competent" level and cannot improve because he finds himself unable to make the qualitative jump to the next level of "proficiency," and he says he will never become an "expert." Dreyfus elaborates on the possible causes:

I was always good at mathematics and took up chess as an outlet for that analytic talent. At college, where I captained the chess team, my players were mostly mathematicians and mostly, like me, at the competent level. At this point, a few of my teammates who were not mathematicians began to play fast chess at the rate of five or ten minutes a game, and also eagerly to play over the great games of the grandmasters. I resisted. Fast chess was no fun for me, because it didn't give me time to figure out what to do. I found grandmaster games inscrutable, and since the record of the game seldom if ever gave rules and principles explaining themselves, I felt there was nothing I could learn from the games. Some of my teammates who through fast chess and game studying acquired a great deal of concrete experience have gone on to become masters.

As I look around at my mathematical academic colleagues, most of whom play chess and none of whom have gotten beyond my own competent level, I see how our view of chess as a strictly analytic game has cut us off from absorbing concrete chess experience. While students of mathematics and related topics predominate in the population of young people enthusiastic about chess, you are as likely to find a truck driver as a mathematician among the world's best players. You are more likely to find an amateur psychologist or a journalist. In a way I am glad that my analytic approach to chess stymied my progress, because this helped me to see that there is more to skill than reasoning.[6]

When I asked Stuart Dreyfus in an interview where in the body a chess player feels that a move is right, he told me, "in the whole body. In the pit of the stomach."[7] It is similar, says Dreyfus, to asking where do you feel you are hungry when you are hungry. "You can't say that your brain thinks it is hungry," continues Dreyfus, "you experience your whole body as craving and the chess player has the same type of experience."[8] Dreyfus explains in the interview that when chess players play one-second-a-move chess, they describe a strange sensation that their hand is playing and they are not. "Their hand is just moving pieces as fast as it can and they almost feel as if their detached brain looks down at their hand playing chess," says Dreyfus, "so the whole body is even in that picture."[9]

Stuart Dreyfus touches here on two important general points. First, an exclusive use of analytical rationality tends to impede further improvement in human performance because of analytical rationality's slow reasoning and its emphasis on rules, principles, and universal solutions. Second, bodily involvement, speed, and an intimate knowledge of concrete cases in the form of good examples is a prerequisite for true expertise. We will return to these factors repeatedly in the following chapters.

Doctors and nurses say that experiences from working in an emergency ward are important for developing skills in clinical practice. The emergency room's patients are often acute cases with a broad range of different problems. Often there is no time to retrieve all the information one might want about the patient, and doctors on night duty will often not be able to obtain immediate aid from their more experienced colleagues. Doctors and nurses in an emergency room are therefore forced to think on their feet, i.e., to act quickly and to utilize spontaneously their experiences from similar, prior situations. Thinking on their feet contributes to the development of intuition and judgment; prerequisites for becoming a good clinician. The emergency room situation contrasts with a ward for internal medicine, for example, where the doctor has more time, the patients have been there longer, the case histories are more detailed, the illnesses less acute and the outcomes more predictable.

4. Proficient performer: beyond analytical rationality

In the first three levels, the performer of a given skill has made a conscious choice of both goals and decisions after having reflected thoroughly over various alternatives, if the individual has not simply followed rules. Dreyfus and Dreyfus call this procedure the "Hamlet model" of decision-making.[10] In contrast to this model, decision-making for the proficient performer is more continuous and is not sequential in the same way. Proficient performers tend to be deeply involved in their actions and have evolved their perspective on the basis of prior actions and experiences.

This perspective enables certain key features of a situation to stand out, while others recede into the background. New actions and experiences change the predominant features, plans, and expectations, and with it the actions. No objective choice or conscious evaluation of appropriateness takes place, which is the case in selecting elements, rules, and plans. The choice is simply made, that much is clear phenomenologically speaking. And this seems to happen because the proficient performer has experienced similar situations earlier. Via spontaneous interpretation and intuitive judgment the memory of these situations generates plans corresponding to plans which have worked before. Similarly, memory of earlier situations releases expectations about actions, which correspond to those actions carried out in similar situations earlier.

The proficient performer understands and organizes her or his tasks intuitively, but intermittently continues to reflect analytically over what will happen. Elements and plans from the performer's experiences, which appear as intuitively important, are evaluated and combined analytically with the help of rules for reaching decisions about the most appropriate actions. Deep intuitive involvement in performance thus interacts with analytical decision-making.

To use one of Dreyfus and Dreyfus's examples, a proficient marketing manager keeps herself oriented about the market situation for her product by reading and listening to everything in her area, from formal reports to gossip in the field. One day the manager can intuitively decide that a problem or sales possibility exists, and that a new sales strategy should be considered. The manager then initiates a study of the situation and may even take great pride in carrying out a sophisticated scientific market analysis, while overlooking the equally important ability to be able to identify the existence of the problem or possibility intuitively; this despite the fact that it was the manager's intuition which led to the marketing study being initiated in the first place.

5. Expert[11]

The proficient performer gradually achieves intimate experience from different situations, all of which touch upon the same goal and the same perspective, but which demand different tactical decisions. The proficient performer then perhaps achieves a level in which it is not only situations, which are recognized intuitively, but also – synchronically and holistically – the relevant decisions, strategies, and actions. According to Dreyfus and Dreyfus, this is the level of genuine, human expertise and is characterized by effortless performance. It is the level of virtuosity.

Expert soccer players assess the moment for dribbling or the possibility to score a goal by the entire visual situation in front of them, together with the sensations in their bodies releasing memories of earlier situations, where dribbling or attempts at scoring have succeeded. There is nothing which indicates that soccer players utilize general rules to combine various facts about their own and their opponent's positions, movement, speed, etc., and then select a course of action on this basis. Intuitive, holistic, and synchronous action is now at the center.

In normal, familiar situations, real experts do not solve problems and do not make decisions. They just do what "works." This does not mean that experts never think consciously, nor that they always do the right thing. When there is time, and when much is at stake, experts will also deliberate before they act. Their deliberation, however, is not based on calculated problem solving but on critical reflection over the intuition, which the expert applies. Even after this reflection, there will remain situations where the expert's decisions do not work. Unforeseen events may occur. And when one expert confronts another in competition, as in a championship chess or tennis match, only one of them can win.

Compared to rational decision-making, intuitive decision-making has been neglected as an object for scientific study, perhaps because science tends to emphasize analytical rationality as its own tool. Ultimately it is a question of what constitutes science, and whether it is possible to study phenomena such as intuition and synchronicity scientifically. Yet, we are familiar with most of these phenomena in their nonscientific form – seeing what needs to be done in an instant – when we perform in a craft, a sport, or making music.

Where science does not reach, art, literature, and narrative often help us comprehend the reality in which we live.[12] Freud, who in many ways was a pioneer for research into human learning, thus saw writers as "valuable allies . . . [who in] their knowledge of the mind . . . are far in advance of us everyday people, for they draw upon sources which we have not yet opened up for science."[13] The late Danish novelist Hans-Jørgen Nielsen described virtuoso expertise in soccer and used a label for the virtuoso soccer player, which says it all: "soccer angel" (*fodboldengel*). Here are some "angels" in action:

We get a free kick, just within the other team's penalty zone, just to the right of the goal, and I take it, self-assuredly waving the others off, with the seductive movement which means that I and no one else knows what needs to be done. The opponents stand up in a wall in front of me in order to block a shot aimed at the goal, as I perhaps also had first thought, but suddenly, Franke stands next to them, far to the right, like an extension of their wall. This has happened during my approach, while everything is focused on me, and I keep running toward the ball as if to kick directly. When I get to it, I instead kick it in a very flat arc, over the defensive wall, and the ball would have taken the turf a few meters behind it. In the same moment, Franke has made his way around and has rushed toward the place where it would have landed. It never does, he catches it in the air with his right leg, half-gliding it into the goal with his left. No one else is able to grasp what has happened before he lifts his arms.

Soccer players tend to have this kind of thing with them from home, working on it over and over again during training. Franke and I have perhaps done something similar before, but never practiced it as something specific in this way, we don't exchange a word before I take the free kick, not even a telling glance, everything happens during the run-up, completely natural, he just stands there where he stands, I just play him like he has to be played when he has positioned himself where he has suddenly positioned himself, the thought doesn't even become anything we are so aware of that it can become clear for us in advance. It is a shared knowledge, from the perspective of the bodies and the eyes, ready to become reality, and it is prior to our being able to speak about it as a language and an ego . . . It lies prior to, or outside, sentences which must contain an I, you, he, she, it, in themselves . . .

Standing there, first genuinely surprised, then intensely happy, knowing right then and there that this very moment in the grey, luminous May evening, the teammates just away from me in a bunch around Franke . . . it is precisely this moment I will always remember . . . The fantastic thing is that the goal was successful in precisely this nonchalant, effusive way. This is what surprises me, and Franke, too; in any case he opens the bunch around him ever so slowly, comes toward me, while we eye each other, and gives me a little slap on the arm, like a receipt.[14]

Experts operate from a mature, holistic well-tried understanding, intuitively and without conscious deliberation. Intuitive understanding comes primarily from experiences on one's own body and is in this way at one with the performer. Experts do not see problems as one thing and solutions as something else; they do not get anxious about the future while they act; they do not make plans. Their skills have become so much a part of themselves that they are no more aware of them than they are of their own bodies.

It is important to emphasize that when Dreyfus and Dreyfus use the word "intuition" they do not mean some kind of guesswork, irrationality, or supernatural inspiration, as the cognitivists often describe it, usually as a preface to a critique. For Dreyfus and Dreyfus intuition is a property which each individual uses in everyday life. The cognitivists, limited as they are to explanations in terms of rule-based processes, can explain only *competent* human performance. They are so far unable to integrate humans' *expert* performances into their models. Take something as mundane as riding a bicycle. Someone able to ride a bike has not formulated a set of rules, which, if followed, can teach somebody else to ride a bicycle. How could we, for example, "teach" the difference between nearly falling and the need to lean over in order to turn a corner? How do we explain the best response to being off balance? Bicyclists can bicycle because they have the necessary know-how, achieved via practical experiences, invariably accompanied by a few childhood scrapes and bruises. Experience cannot necessarily be verbalized, intellectualized, and made into rules. Therefore, the cognitivists have a difficult time understanding it.

Sitting at a computer, a virtuoso secretary "is one" with the machine and does not think over what finger does what on the keyboard. A virtuoso car driver is one with the car. If an American attempts to drive in a left-hand-drive country such as England, however, the experience is one of stepping backwards in the learning process: formerly effortless, unreflected driving becomes stiff and dependent on the conscious deliberations and decisions of the beginner. It becomes a problem to make a right turn or to drive through a rotary. The same happens to hospital doctors who transfer to a new unfamiliar ward. Hence, there exist rotation arrangements as part of training young doctors. Studies of pilots' learning processes indicate that novice pilots "fly their planes," while as experienced pilots "they fly." The separation between person and machine, subject and object disappears.

One scientific domain, which puts virtuoso expertise into sharp and instructive contrast with rational competence, is the area of "artificial intelligence" and "expert systems." The field so far has been strongly procedural and rule-bound because both artificial intelligence and expert systems must be programmed.[15] When designers of expert systems seek to replicate in their systems the decisions of professionals such as doctors, geologists, chemists, pharmacologists, and stockbrokers, these

professionals have a difficult time explaining to the system designers
what they are doing in terms of specific procedures and rules. Donald
Schön has described the problem: "When [the professional practitioner]
tries, on rare occasions, to say what he knows – when he tries to put his
know*ing* into the form of know*ledge* – his formulations of principles,
theories, maxims, and rules of thumb are often incongruent with the
understanding and know-how implicit in his pattern of practice."[16]

The Dreyfus model enables us to understand why: virtuosos simply do
not use rules. They recognize thousands of cases directly, holistically, and
intuitively on the basis of their experience. In the preface to the revised
paperback edition of their *Mind over Machine*, on the basis of experience
from neural networks, Dreyfus and Dreyfus downgrade the importance
of storing memories and recognizing similarities. Instead, because of her
or his experience, "the expert holistically *discriminates* among classes of
situations and *associates* with these classes appropriate responses" (emphasis in original).[17] The rules for expert systems are formulated only
because the systems demand it. They are characteristics of the systems,
but not of the real experts. Research shows that heuristic expert systems,
being rule-based, are unable to go further than level three in the learning
process. The heuristic systems cannot make the qualitative jump to levels
four and five and therefore never become as skillful as human experts.
This conclusion also applies when the systems are compared with the
behavior of the same experts who gave the rules to the system builders. In
this sense, the term "expert systems" is a misnomer. In terms of the
Dreyfus model they are no more than "competent systems." Only in
areas which are context-independent, which can be strictly separated
from daily understanding and from change, and which have well-defined
problems with clear rules for their solution, only in these rare areas, and in
tasks where brute computational number crunching can solve problems,
will expert systems succeed as well or better than human experts. Tests of
existing expert systems support this conclusion.

Rationality, irrationality, arationality

The five levels in the learning process can be briefly summarized as
follows.

(1) Novices act on the basis of context-independent elements and rules.
(2) Advanced beginners also use situational elements, which they have
    learned to identify and interpret on the basis of their own experience
    from similar situations.
(3) Competent performers are characterized by the involved choice of

goals and plans as a basis for their actions. Goals and plans are used to structure and store masses of both context-dependent and context-independent information.

(4) Proficient performers identify problems, goals, and plans intuitively from their own experientially based perspective. Intuitive choice is checked by analytical evaluation prior to action.

(5) Finally, experts' behavior is intuitive, holistic, and synchronic, understood in the way that a given situation releases a picture of problem, goal, plan, decision, and action in one instant and with no division into phases. This is the level of true human expertise. Experts are characterized by a flowing, effortless performance, unhindered by analytical deliberations.

The Dreyfus model contains a qualitative jump from the three first to the fourth and fifth levels. The jump implies an abandonment of rule-based thinking as the most important basis for action, and its replacement by context and intuition. Logically based action is replaced by experientially based action.

Dreyfus and Dreyfus provide several conceptual and empirical examples to illustrate the validity of their model. They also describe how the results of recent research in human learning fit with it. They conclude that intelligent action consists of something other than calculated, analytical rationality, even though we often hear the opposite. From the perspective of the Dreyfus model, analytical rationality is a limited rationality: it is appropriate to the lower levels in the performance of a skill, but not to high-level performance.

The best performances within a given area require a qualitatively different expertise based on intuition, experience, and judgment. As yet, there exist no computer programs which have succeeded in capturing and simulating this expertise. Intuition is the ability to draw directly on one's own experience – bodily, emotional, intellectual – and to recognize similarities between these experiences and new situations. Intuition is internalized; it is part of the individual. Existing research provides no evidence that intuition and judgment can be externalized into rules and explanations, which, if followed, lead to the same result as intuitive behavior. Such externalization is possible only for analytical rationality, that is, for those skills which characterize the lower levels in the learning process.

That conventional rationality is not the ultimate outcome of human learning processes does not mean, however, that one necessarily ends in irrationality. Research in learning processes indicates that the conventional opposition between rationality and irrationality is inadequate for an understanding of what actually happens when individuals understand and act. In order to bridge this gap, Dreyfus and Dreyfus invoke the concept "arational." The word "rational," from the Latin *ratio*, means to calculate or reason. Rationality in the West has become identical with analytical thinking, that is, with conscious separation of wholes into parts. Arational behavior, in contrast, connotes situational behavior without the conscious analytical division of situations into parts and evaluation according to context-independent rules. Dreyfus and Dreyfus link increasing levels of skill acquisition with a relatively declining level of analytical rationality: "competent performance is rational; proficiency is transitional; experts act arationally."[18] In the present context, the interesting point is that the Dreyfus model and "arationality" accord a central importance to context in the development of knowledge and skills. As will be shown in the next chapter, this has radical implications for social science.

The Dreyfus model can be criticized for being slightly mechanistic and insensitive to issues of creativity, innovation, and power.[19] However, such weaknesses do not detract from our use of the model in the current context. The argument in the following chapters is based on only a single property of the model, and this property is convincingly established in its original form; namely, the qualitative jump from the model's first three stages to the two last stages, that is, from rule-based, context-independent to experience-based, situational behavior. Other properties of the model are irrelevant for our purposes.

On closer examination, the qualitative difference between rule-based and experience-based behavior shows itself to have radical consequences, in that every rule-based, rational mode of conceiving of human activity – be this activity scientific, practical, or didactic – collapses when confronted with the Dreyfus phenomenology. This is the model's critical and deconstructive perspective, a perspective which caused Jürgen Habermas, after having heard Hubert Dreyfus present the model to him at Frankfurt University, to exclaim, "you are talking about skills like hammering and playing chess, but what you really want to do is undermine Western society." To which Dreyfus replied, "you are right, that's exactly what it comes to."[20]

The Dreyfus model shows how the rational mode of thinking is inadequate for comprehending the total spectrum of human activity, both in relation to human everyday activities and to rare virtuoso performances. Instead, the rationalist perspective focuses on those properties of human activity by which humans most resemble machines or Weberian bureaucrats: rule-based deliberation based on formal logic.

The Dreyfus model has not only critical implications, however. Its additional value – which in this context is more important – is constructive.

The model makes clear that what we could call the "rational fallacy" does not lie in the rationalists' emphasis on analysis and rationality as important phenomena. These *are* important, also according to the Dreyfus model. Rather, the rational fallacy consists of raising analysis and rationality into the most important mode of operation for human activity, and allowing these to dominate our view of human activity: so much so that other equally important modes of human understanding and behavior are made invisible. The Dreyfus model does not present a situation of "either rationality or intuition" but of both of them in their proper context: the position of intuition is not beyond rationality but alongside it, complementary to it, and insofar as we speak of experts, above rationality. The model specifies that what is needed in order to transcend the insufficient rational perspective is explicit integration of those properties characteristic of the higher levels in the learning process which can supplement and take over from analysis and rationality. These properties include context, judgment, practice, trial and error, experience, common sense, intuition, and bodily sensation.

Context, experience, and intuition

In the introduction to this chapter I described a study in which a group of paramedics had been asked, "who would you choose to revive you if you had been victim of an accident?" The experienced paramedics, that is, the practitioners, knew what was good for them and chose the experienced rescuer even though this individual appeared in only one of the six video films shown. Practical experience consists precisely in an individual's ability to readily recognize skill and virtuoso expertise. Teachers in rescuing life were especially unable to identify the expert paramedic, they were even worse than the group of inexperienced trainees.

After the review of the Dreyfus model we can understand why. The teachers attempted to identify a competent rescuer by looking for individuals who best followed the rules the teachers themselves had taught their students in CPR. The teachers' concept of "good" resuscitation technique was simply to follow the rules. They tended to identify the inexperienced students on the films as "good" because, as novices, they closely and consciously followed the rules they had learned. Being novices, the students could do little else. In 70 percent of the cases the teachers could not identify the experienced rescuer because this individual, being truly experienced – an expert – had gone beyond rule-based behavior.

The example would be trivial if the problem of the dominance of rule-based rationality over practical experience pertained only to teaching in the health sector or only in the United States. Regrettably, the pervasiveness of the rational paradigm to the near exclusion of others is a problem for the vast majority of professional education, and especially in practical fields such as engineering, policy analysis, management, planning, and organization. All are professions where practical skill occupies central importance but has been threatened by epistemic science and didactics. Law is an exception. The practice of law cannot be decontextualized to the same degree as other disciplines and has therefore never been made "scientific" to the same extent.

As for the teachers in heart–lung resuscitation, the rule-based, rational mode of thinking generally constitutes an obstacle to good results, not because rules and rationality are problematic in themselves, but because the rational perspective has been elevated from being necessary to being sufficient, even exclusive. This has caused people and entire scholarly disciplines to become blind to context, experience, and intuition, even though these phenomena and ways of being are at least as important and necessary for good results as are analysis, rationality, and rules. In part, this is the problem Nietzsche points to when he stresses that "the growth of consciousness becomes a danger"; the faculty of consciousness may marginalize those faculties making true human expertise possible.[21] It is also one reason that Nietzsche is highly critical of central tenets in the thought of Socrates who regarded explicit rational understanding as the highest human accomplishment. "Socrates was a misunderstanding," Nietzsche writes, "rationality at any cost . . . in opposition to the instincts, has itself been no more than a form of sickness."[22] As an antidote to Socrates, Nietzsche suggests that the central task for human beings is not the Socratic one of making knowledge cerebral and rational but instead one of making it bodily and intuitive. In Nietzsche's own words what is central is "the task of *incorporating* knowledge and making it instinctive," a task Nietzsche regrets "is only beginning to dawn on the human eye and is not yet clearly discernible"[23] (emphasis in original). The Dreyfus model helps make this task clear.

The conclusion that rationality may endanger sensitivity to context, experience, and intuition is important for teaching, and teaching can be directly compared with the model for human learning. However, the conclusion also applies to scientific research, even though it demands a more complex argumentation. In the following two chapters, I will deal with the implications of arationality to social science, using the conclusions from this chapter to evaluate social science theory and methodology. We will see a whole gamut of key scientific notions collapses when subjected to the model's critical perspective. Then the constructive perspective creates the point of departure for the development of an alternative concept of social science, one based on context, judgment, and practical knowledge.

3   Is theory possible in social science?

> If I was told anything that was a *theory*, I would say, No, no! That does
> not interest me.
>
> *Ludwig Wittgenstein*

What are the implications of the previous chapter's phenomenology of
human learning for social science? This question will be the focus of this
and the following chapter. In addressing the question, one confronts yet
another, which is as old as the very concept of science itself, and which
continually reappears in discussions of the scientific enterprise: can the
study of humans and society be scientific in the same manner as the study
of natural objects? Can we speak of a unified science, or should natural-
science inquiry and social-science inquiry be viewed as two basically
different activities?

The history of science shows these questions to be both difficult to
answer and controversial. The controversy is due partly to the fact that
besides having fundamental methodological consequences, these questions touch on sensitive factors such as the status of social science in
relation to natural science, as well as what the philosopher Richard
Bernstein calls, "Cartesian anxiety," that is, the fear of ending in relativism and nihilism when one departs from the analytical–rational scientific
tradition that has dominated Western science since Descartes.[1]

The Dreyfus model and the work of Michel Foucault and Pierre
Bourdieu are a useful starting point for discussing the question of a
unified science, and for grappling with the problem of relativism.[2] In the
previous chapter we noted that the Dreyfus model has both a critical and
a constructive perspective. Here the focus is on the critical, deconstructive perspective. Using the Dreyfus model, we will see that the study of
social phenomena is not, never has been, and probably never can be,
scientific in the conventional meaning of the word "science"; that is, in its
epistemic meaning.[3] We will also see that it is therefore not meaningful to
speak of "theory" in the study of social phenomena, at least not in the
sense that "theory" is used in natural science. The constructive perspective will then be taken up in chapter five, where we will start developing an

alternative approach to social science. Let us begin, however, by briefly examining the natural-science model as an ideal for the study of society. And let me underline at the outset that the concepts of natural science and theory that I develop below are ideal types. I employ the ideals, not to describe actual natural science and actual theory, but to bring out differences and similarities between the ideal types and actual science.

The theoretical ambition

The natural-science model has been, and continues to be, an ideal shared by several traditions in the study of human activity, such as positivism, functionalism, structuralism, cognitivism, and neopositivism. Although it has now been argued that the ideal does not even work for the natural sciences, and even though the natural sciences and the technologies they have generated have shown themselves to be far more costly and hazardous locally and globally than assumed just a few decades ago, it is easy to understand why the natural-science ideal over time has been so attractive to so many scholars. There is a logical simplicity to the natural science paradigm, and the natural sciences' impressive material results speak for themselves: these sciences certainly have an undeniable basis as a means by which we have attempted to achieve mastery over nature, technology, and over our own conditions of life. In this interpretation advances in natural-science research and technological progress are founded upon a relatively cumulative production of knowledge, the key concepts being explanation and prediction based on context-independent theories. The consequence of this knowledge production is a strong, prestigious position for natural science in society.

In this sense, it is not surprising that many who study human affairs have attempted to imitate the natural science paradigm. This was the case with the founder of positivism, August Comte, but it is just as true for figures such as Sigmund Freud and Karl Marx. In the *Paris Manuscripts*, Marx thus expresses his faith in a future unified science: "natural science will in time subsume the science of man just as the science of man will subsume natural science: there will be *one* science"[4] (emphasis in original). Freud, too, early in his career, was as optimistic as the young Marx. Freud's declared goal was "to furnish a psychology that shall be a natural science: that is, to represent psychical processes as quantitatively determinate states of specifiable material particles, thus making those processes perspicuous and free from contradiction."[5] Later on, Freud continued to view the natural sciences as an ideal worth striving for, but he became more skeptical about how far one could go in approaching this ideal within psychology and psychiatry. "I always envy the physicists and mathematicians who can stand on firm ground," Freud later said, "I hover, so to speak, in the air. Mental events seem to be immeasurable and probably always will be so."[6]

Lesser thinkers than Marx and Freud have looked, and continue to look, to the natural sciences as their ideal for the study of human activity. If anything, the idealization of the natural sciences has become more pronounced since Marx and Freud. This applies not only to positivism and critical rationalism, but also to areas of research not normally associated with the natural science model. The fact that Marx and Freud erred in their ambitions about developing their sciences into natural sciences is perhaps not so interesting today. But the general question of whether the natural science model is an appropriate ideal for the study of human activity remains timely. The question remains: must the "science of man" be different from natural science?[7]

The natural sciences are relatively cumulative. Thomas Kuhn's famous phenomenological evolutionary scheme for the natural sciences contains long periods with stable normal science; that is, periods with a generally accepted mode of conducting research.[8] The researcher's work in such periods consists according to Kuhn in what he calls "puzzle solving" within the framework of a common, accepted "paradigm." The stable periods of normal science are at times broken by periods of radical instability and "revolutionary" change. After a time, change leads to a new paradigm, to cumulative replacement in which the old paradigm becomes superfluous.

Periods with scientific revolutions are a consequence of periods with stable, normal-science research, in that it is via the daily normal "puzzle solving" that the anomalies and contradictions appear which gradually undermine the original paradigm. The resulting crisis continues until the anomalies and contradictions can be explained within a new paradigm; that is, until researchers experience "the pieces suddenly sorting themselves out and coming together in a new way," to use Kuhn's words.[9] The result is a new paradigm around which there is again general agreement and on the basis of which normal-science research can again be conducted.

Kuhn's now-classic description of the research process was criticized for introducing an element of relativism within the natural sciences and in the theory and history of science, a critique which has recently been restated by physicist Steven Weinberg.[10] Kuhn apparently activated the Cartesian anxiety of natural scientists and of philosophers and historians of science. A similar critique and anxiety has been directed at Foucault, Derrida, and other nonessentialist thinkers. The matter is far from settled, but it is clear for most observers, that even though natural-science theory, following Kuhn, can not be seen as entirely so constant and cumulative as previously assumed, there is still room for a degree of stability and progress for these sciences, also in a Kuhnian interpretation. Therefore the ambition has continued to be to emulate the natural-science model in the study of human affairs, especially as regards the development of theory which is typically seen as the pinnacle of scientific endeavor.

Hermeneutical stumbling blocks

Since Kuhn's *The Structure of Scientific Revolutions*, natural science has been further relativized via what could be called the "universality of hermeneutics," argued by scholars as diverse as Paul Feyerabend, Richard Rorty, Harold Garfinkel, Hans-Georg Gadamer, Jürgen Habermas, Anthony Giddens, and, since the late 1970s by Kuhn himself. Kuhn, for example, says:

> What I as a physicist had to discover for myself, most historians learn by example in the course of professional training. Consciously or not, they are all practitioners of the hermeneutic method. In my case, however, the discovery of hermeneutics did more than make history seem consequential. Its most immediate and decisive effect was instead in my view of science . . . [T]he term "hermeneutic" . . . was no part of my vocabulary as recently as five years ago. Increasingly, I suspect that anyone who believes that history may have deep philosophical import will have to learn to bridge the longstanding divide between the Continental and English-language philosophical traditions.[11]

Whereas hermeneutics according to Wilhelm Dilthey and, in part, to Max Weber was regarded as an activity linked only to the study of human activity, it is now argued that the natural sciences are also historically conditioned and require hermeneutic interpretation. In other words, the natural science ideal can not even be found in the natural sciences themselves. Natural scientists, too, must determine what constitutes relevant facts, methods, and theories; for example, what would count as "nature." These determinations are made on the basis of a common interpretation of what constitutes scientific work. Interpretation tends to occur implicitly, but is, nevertheless, interpretation. It is acquired as tacit practical skills and conventions via training in the actual performance of scientific activity.

Possession of these skills is a requirement for being able to undertake scientific work at all, and performance occurs without reflection. One can produce and reproduce objective results from these skills, but one cannot argue objectively for the skills. Methodology is not a universal theoretical rationality and can never be argued to be so because one ends in infinite regress: how does one argue theoretically for the practical skills one uses to formulate a theory? How does one determine scientifically what science is?

The answer is that one cannot. Methodology is a concrete practical rationality. In this sense, the natural sciences are just as lacking in objectivity as the social sciences. This has led Richard Rorty and others to conclude that the two branches of science are not essentially different. It must be concluded, however, that despite the argument of the universality of hermeneutics and despite the common conditions in the form of epistemological relativism, which is argued to be valid for both natural and social sciences, it can be phenomenologically demonstrated that the natural sciences are relatively cumulative and predictive, while the social sciences are not and never have been. In other words, on the basis of the universality of hermeneutics, it is incorrect to underplay the differences between natural and social sciences, as do Rorty, Bernstein, and Giddens.[12]

Recent developments in the argument that the natural-science ideal cannot even be found in the natural sciences are the "chaos" and "complexity" theories and the break with determinism, as elaborated, for example, by the Nobel Prize winner, Ilya Prigogine. In some interpretations, this development runs counter to the assumption that science will eventually describe nature's universal laws. Complexity, chance, irreversibility, time, and evolution have made their entry into physics and have led to debates as to whether this prototype of natural science can be epistemic in the classical Aristotelian sense.[13] Convergence between the natural and social sciences on the basis of seeing both as dealing with complex systems has been argued by, for instance, the Gulbekian Commission on the Restructuring of the Social Sciences, of which Prigogine is a member.[14] Following this view, some have thought that a unified social and natural science is possible, analogous to the argument of the universality of hermeneutics, because natural sciences reveal themselves to have the same nonepistemic status as social sciences, and not because the social sciences can become epistemic like the natural sciences. We may agree with this argument insofar as the natural sciences' foundation now seems epistemologically more complex than previously thought. But the existence of an identity between social and natural sciences on one point does not necessarily mean that they are the same. One cannot overlook the difference in results between the natural and the social sciences. Epistemic vocabularies have worked successfully in relation to their own intentions within particular domains in the natural sciences with no parallel in the social sciences. However, the fact that the epistemic vocabularies have worked effectively in some areas does not necessarily mean that such vocabularies are universal, or that the Great Book of Nature can be written in the language of mathematics, as Galileo asserted. Neither argument is sufficient for making the case of a possible unified thinking of the natural and the social sciences.

The social sciences do not evolve via scientific revolutions, as Kuhn says is the case for the natural sciences. Rather, as pointed out by Hubert Dreyfus, social sciences go through periods where various constellations of power and waves of intellectual fashion dominate, and where a change from one period to another, which on the surface may resemble a paradigm shift, actually consists of the researchers within a given area abandoning a "dying" wave for a growing one, without there having occurred any collective accumulation of knowledge. Not paradigm shifts but rather style changes are what characterize social science: it is not a case of evolution but more of fashion. Foucault poses the question of whether it is reasonable at all to use the label "science" for this kind of activity. Even the expression "body of knowledge" is too pretentious for Foucault: "let us say, to be more neutral still . . . body of discourse."[15]

The social sciences have always found themselves in a situation of constant reorganization, characterized by a multiplicity of directions. It is not a state of crisis in a Kuhnian sense, that is, of a period with competing paradigms located between periods with normal science. The condition of the social sciences has been termed "pre-paradigmatic," if we remain in the Kuhnian terminology. The social sciences have always been in this state and as a result are neither relatively cumulative nor relatively stable. Why are the social sciences characterized by such instability? Is it immanent, or can it be transcended? Why have the social sciences not been able to develop predictive theory to the same degree as the natural sciences?[16] These are the questions which we will now attempt to answer.

Pre-paradigmatic sciences

To maintain that the study of humans and society finds itself in a preparadigmatic stage is to imply that a coming "maturation" of the social sciences will produce a more desirable paradigmatic stage characterized by normal science. It is argued that the study of human society is somewhat younger than the natural sciences; the social sciences have not benefited from the same resources as has the study of nature; their object of study – human activity – is more complex; their conceptual apparatus and research methods need to be more refined; and with more time for further development and refinement, there should, in principle, be nothing in the way of the social sciences achieving the same paradigmatic stage as the natural sciences, becoming cumulative, stable, and predictive. This is the essence of what is here called the "pre-paradigmatic argument."

It follows from this line of thinking that there is a fundamental distinction between normal and non-normal science, a distinction which cuts across the boundary separating the study of human affairs on the one hand and the study of nature on the other. In *Philosophy and the Mirror of Nature*, Richard Rorty expounds this argument when he discusses the relationship between *Geistes-* and *Naturwissenschaften*:

> The line . . . is not the line between the human and the nonhuman but between that portion of the field of inquiry where we feel rather uncertain that we have the right vocabulary at hand and that portion where we feel rather certain that we do. This *does*, at the moment, roughly coincide with the distinction between the fields of the *Geistes-* and the *Naturwissenschaften* but this coincidence may be *mere* coincidence.[17]

According to the pre-paradigmatic argument, both the natural and the social sciences may find themselves in periods where they are cumulative, stable, and predictive, and both may also experience periods with confusing and incorrect predictions. The immature state of social science on which this argument is based has nothing to do with fundamental properties of human beings or of social science. For example, even though political scientists may disagree as to what constitutes "the political," while physicists seem to be in more agreement as to what constitute physical phenomena, this state of affairs does not necessarily have to remain permanent. According to the pre-paradigmatic argument, there is nothing in principle which prevents political scientists from being able to reach agreement concerning the political domain, nor physicists from again disagreeing as to the basic categories of nature, as they did when quantum theory first appeared.

The pre-paradigmatic argument is seductive. First because it entails a high degree of methodological clarity for the study of human activity, where, following the argument, it models itself on the natural sciences' well-developed and well-tested methodology for theory development. Second, the natural sciences have had inordinately great success with their methodology. Could the social sciences achieve similar results if they developed their research methods sufficiently far along the natural science path? Yes, the argument goes. It is therefore not surprising that the pre-paradigmatic argument is popular among many social scientists. The argument tends to constitute the conventional wisdom within positivist and neopositivist thinking in the social sciences and it is also a key element in various types of functionalism.

Belief in the pre-paradigmatic argument provides the basis for a good portion of optimism within social science. But the fact remains that today's natural-science-modeled social sciences are no more "normal" and have no more predictive success than their seemingly less sophisticated predecessors. After more than 200 years of attempts, one could reasonably expect that there would exist at least a sign that social science has moved in the desired direction, that is, toward predictive theory. It has not. And when the social sciences are compared with relatively new natural sciences such as meteorology and biology, which also struggle with especially complicated objects of study, it can be seen that the latter exhibit slow, but relatively cumulative, progress. These relatively new natural sciences have evolved ever more complex theories which account for an increasing range of phenomena, while social science typically seeks to develop theories pertaining to one class of phenomena and then abandons these for theories which include another. The social sciences appear unable to demonstrate the kind of progress which is supposed to characterize normal science.

The difference between the natural and social sciences seems to be too constant and too comprehensive to be a historical coincidence, as the pre-paradigmatic argument and the Richard Rorty of *Philosophy and the Mirror of Nature* would have it. We may thus be speaking of so fundamental a difference that the same research procedure cannot be applied in the two domains. It is this argument which is put forth by hermeneutics and phenomenology.

Dead objects, self-reflecting humans

The hermeneutic-phenomenological argument takes its point of departure in a critical difference between natural and social sciences: the former studies physical objects while the latter studies self-reflecting humans and must therefore take account of changes in the interpretations of the objects of study. Stated in another way, in social science, the object is a subject.

Anthony Giddens, basing himself on Peter Winch's discussion of hermeneutics in social science, expresses this difference as follows:

The technical language and theoretical propositions of the natural sciences are insulated from the world with which they are concerned because that world does not answer back. But social theory cannot be insulated from its "object-world," which is a subject-world.[18]

Two types of self-interpretations appear in what Giddens calls the "double hermeneutic."[19] First are the self-interpretations among those people the researchers study. According to hermeneutics and phenomenology, these self-interpretations and their relations to the context of those studied must be understood in order to understand why people act as they do. Hermeneutics is here closely connected to Max Weber's *verstehen*, which emphasizes understanding as distinct from explanation. The second aspect of the double hermeneutic concerns the researchers' own self-interpretations. Just as the people studied are part of a context, research itself also constitutes a context, and the researchers are a part of it. The researchers' self-understanding and concepts do not exist in a vacuum, but must be understood in relation to this context. Context both determines and is determined by the researchers' self-understanding.

Following the double hermeneutic, the question of what are to be counted as "relevant" facts within a given discipline – for example, political facts within political science or social facts within sociology – is determined by both the researchers' interpretations and by the interpretations of the people whom the researchers study. In the hermeneutic–phenomenological argument, this means that the study of society can only be as stable as the self-interpretations of the individuals studied. And inasmuch as these interpretations are not constant, the study of society cannot be stable either. The natural sciences, say the practitioners of hermeneutics, do not have a corresponding problem because their objects of study are not self-interpreting entities: they do not talk back. Giddens has later come to see the double hermeneutic as part of a more general condition of modernity's mode of functioning in what he calls the "institutional reflexivity of modernity" which Giddens now sees as modernity's "tendency to continually react back upon itself and generate (to some extent unpredictable) new processes of change."[20]

Harold Garfinkel's ethnomethodology is especially interesting in relation to the second part of the double hermeneutic. The ethnomethodologists assert that the basic skills which researchers in the social sciences must possess in order to carry out their work are just as situational, just as dependent on the context, as the interpretations of the people whom the researchers study. People's daily activities, regardless of how trivial they may seem, and the researchers' work within the sciences, are both objects of the ethnomethodologists' scrutiny. Garfinkel describes the field of ethnomethodological inquiry like this:

No inquiries can be excluded no matter where or when they occur, no matter how vast or trivial their scope . . . Procedures and results of water witching, divination, mathematics, sociology – whether done by lay persons or professionals – are addressed according to the policy that every feature of sense, of fact, of method, for every particular case of inquiry without exception, is the managed accomplishment of organized settings of practical actions.[21]

In accordance with Kuhn, the ethnomethodologists assert that the researchers' basic skills and work cannot be derived from general logical and methodological rules for scientific rationality. Basic skills must be seen as an internal affair within a given research area, as an "ongoing, practical accomplishment" which cannot be generalized theoretically or methodologically:

[A] leading policy [of ethnomethodology] is to refuse serious consideration to the prevailing proposal that efficiency, efficacy, effectiveness, intelligibility, consistency, planfulness, typicality, uniformity, reproducibility of activities – i.e., that rational properties of practical activities – be assessed, recognized, categorized, described by using a rule or a standard obtained outside actual settings within which such properties are recognized, used, produced, and talked about by settings' members. All procedures whereby logical and methodological properties of the practices and results of inquiries are assessed in their general characteristics by rule are of interest as *phenomena* for ethnomethodological study but not otherwise. [Emphasis in original][22]

Because researchers' background skills are internal in relation to their activity, ethnomethodologists contend that researchers must explicitly account for their procedures in producing knowledge. This is seen by the ethnomethodologists as especially important in the study of society, because here researchers' production of knowledge is an important part of human activity and can therefore not be left out as study object.[23] It is precisely here that the ethnomethodologists see a breakdown in the possibility for objective social sciences. A formalization and theorization of the researchers' background skills into genuine rules of research is thus necessary for this objectivity, say the ethnomethodologists. However, such formalization is not possible because the researchers' basic skills are situational. Infinite regress again sticks up its ugly head: how does one formalize the skills, which make formalization possible?

With the help of the Dreyfus model described in the previous chapter, we can formulate the hermeneutic–phenomenological argument more concisely than either Giddens or Garfinkel has done. Acquisition of researchers' basic skills is no different from acquisition of other skills. Researchers do not need to be able to formulate rules for their skills in order to practice them with success. On the contrary, studies show that rules can obstruct the continuous exercise of high-level skills. There is nothing which indicates that researchers at expert level – those who have achieved genuine mastery in their field – use mainly context-independent rules or traditional rationality in their best scientific performances, even though they might depict it as such when they get around to writing their scholarly articles or memoirs. The same is true for other professionals: clever businessmen, eminent doctors, pilots with "the right stuff," inspiring teachers, instinctual financiers, skilled shoemakers, and prize-winning journalists. And this use of tacit skills instead of rules also applies to everyday activities. Anthony Giddens could benefit here from using the concept "practical consciousness" which he has developed in another context, to reinforce his double hermeneutic and the hermeneutic–phenomenological argument, but apparently has not.[24] It is precisely the kind of "tacit skills" referred to by Giddens and others which characterizes the highest levels of the learning process. Tacit skills are that level on which expert researchers operate.

Opposed to this view stands the rationalist view, which builds upon Plato's and Kant's theories that the human brain works on the basis of rules. Skills are therefore seen as rule-based, and development from beginner to expert level is explained in terms of the development of more and better rules. Whereas the beginner uses the rules consciously, the expert uses them unconsciously, but in the rationalist view both are instances of rule-based behavior.

No genuine proof exists as to the validity of either the hermeneutic or the rationalist view. Introspection does not help, in that both camps agree that regardless of what happens with human experts, it happens unconsciously. Existing experiments do not clearly point in one or the other direction. However, the documented failure of cognitivism and artificial intelligence to simulate human intelligence on the basis of rules can be taken as an indication of the limitations of the rationalist view. The attempts to develop artificial intelligence can in this sense be seen as the litmus test of the two views.[25] The cognitivists' project's lack of success when faced with the Dreyfus model's ability to account for the transition to the effortless, intuitive performance of experts means that on empirical and practical grounds, we must currently opt for the Dreyfus model over the cognitive model.

For the moment, then, we must assume that the researchers' basic skills, as with other high-level skills, cannot be described theoretically in terms of objective rules. And inasmuch as the study of human affairs, according to the ethnomethodologists, requires such a description in order to become normal science, it follows that the social sciences are incapable of achieving scientific status in this sense.

This apparently convincing argument is problematized, however, by Michel Foucault in *The Order of Things*.

Meaning-giving and meaninglessness

In *The Order of Things*, Foucault states that the study of individuals and society, what he calls the "human sciences," understands human beings in a dual manner, as both constituting what counts as facts in these sciences and at the same time as an object for theoretical and empirical research.[26] Foucault turns the perspective from the self-interpretation in the double hermeneutic of those being studied and the researchers doing the studying to humankind's double role as both meaning giver (subjects, who give things meaning by deciding what counts as an object) and as the "meaningless" objects of study, whom the subjects study and on whom meaning is rendered.[27] If one wishes to understand human knowing, it is necessary to understand both poles of this duality, says Foucault. According to Foucault, however, this attempt to understand what makes understanding possible drives the study of human activity into an "essential instability." Hence, the human sciences

find themselves treating as their object what is in fact their condition of possibility. They are always animated, therefore, by a sort of transcendental mobility. They never cease to exercise a critical examination of themselves. They proceed from that which is given to representation to that which renders representation possible, but which is still representation. So that, unlike other sciences, they seek not so much to generalize themselves or make themselves more precise as to be constantly demystifying themselves . . . [28]

Briefly summarized, Foucault's argument contains three elements. First, he points out that the study of human society since Kant has been characterized by a meaning giver and object duality, and that this duality has been an obstacle to the development of stable and objective human sciences. For Foucault, no science can objectivize the phenomenon which makes it possible. Stability cannot be achieved when that phenomenon which is the locus of inquiry (human activity) is both subject and object of science. Second, Foucault argues – with the help of his "archaeological" method – that the meaning giver and object duality is characteristic of the human sciences only in a specific historical period, and that it is therefore not necessarily irrevocably connected with every form of human science.

Finally, at the time when *The Order of Things* was published (1966), Foucault believed that the problems of the human sciences were solvable. Like many French intellectuals, Foucault at this time saw structuralism – as formulated by Claude Lévi-Strauss, Jacques Lacan, Noam Chomsky, and others – as a promising research program for overcoming the historically specific meaning giver and object duality and achieving a new era of objective, stable, and cumulative human sciences. As is well known, however, the hopes of Foucault and many others were dashed. The reason for the failure of structuralism has been made clear by Foucault himself in his works subsequent to *The Order of Things*. Structuralism, despite its high hopes and ambitious promises, was not up to the task of creating objective human sciences any better than was behaviorism, cognitivism, or other schools in the study of human activity.[29]

The question of whether something more fundamental in social science prevents normal science (in the Kuhnian sense) from developing therefore remains stronger than ever. We will see that Foucault is wrong in his assertion that the meaning giver and object duality characterizes the human sciences only during a specific historical period. We will see this by addressing the question: "What are the problems for *any* theoretical study of human activity modeled after the natural sciences?" We will address this question with the help of Hubert Dreyfus and Pierre Bourdieu.

4   Context counts

[P]ractice has a logic which is not that of logic.   *Pierre Bourdieu*

The deadly paradox of social theory

Hubert Dreyfus and Pierre Bourdieu argue that the study of individuals and society can never be "normal" in the Kuhnian sense because of the relationship between ideal scientific theory on the one hand and human activity on the other. The limitation on "normality," according to Dreyfus and Bourdieu, lies not in the historically contingent definition of "man," as Foucault asserts, but more generally, in problems with establishing theories about the social world which parallel natural-science theories; and more specifically, for social science in problems with explaining and predicting social activity using abstract, context-independent elements. Let us examine Dreyfus's and Bourdieu's argument from its foundation.[1] The argument is clearer than other arguments about the status of the social sciences and it has wide-ranging consequences for our understanding of what these sciences can and cannot be.

Dreyfus's first step is to make clear what he understands by ideal "theory." He goes back to Socrates, whom he regards as the founder of that unique intellectual activity called theorization. Ideal theory is viewed by Dreyfus as having six basic characteristics that can never be fully realized, but can be approached to varying degrees. Socrates introduced and argued for the first three of these when he said that a theory must be (1) explicit, (2) universal, and (3) abstract. It must be *explicit* because a theory is to be laid out so clearly, in such detail, and so completely that it can be understood by any reasoning being; a theory may not stand or fall on interpretation or intuition. Second, a theory must be *universal* in that it must apply in all places and all times. Third, a theory must be *abstract* in that it must not require the reference to concrete examples.

Descartes and Kant supplemented Socrates' three criteria with two more. A theory must also be (4) *discrete*, that is, formulated only with the aid of context-independent elements, which do not refer to human interests, traditions, institutions, etc. And it must be (5) *systematic*; that is, it must constitute a whole, in which context-independent elements (properties, factors) are related to each other by rules or laws.

Finally, modern natural science has added further a criterion of ideal theory: that it must be (6) *complete and predictive*. The way a theory accounts for the domain it covers must be comprehensive in the sense that it specifies the range of variation in the elements, which affect the domain, and the theory must specify their effects. This makes possible precise predictions. Today, it is especially this last criterion which is the hallmark of epistemic sciences. We will see that even disciplines like biology, which are not completely epistemic and depend on context-dependent theory, have ways of approaching the ideal of prediction that do not appear available to social science disciplines.

The six criteria characterize an ideal type of scientific theory. The argument that follows is not dependent on scientists – natural or social – ever really succeeding in constructing ideal theory. The argument also does not ignore the fact that context-dependence is known, not only in social science, but in natural science, too, for example in evolutionary biology (see the section below on science of the second order). The argument only requires that the theories, which approach this ideal, do not refer to shared basic interpretations, metaphors, examples, etc.; i.e., that they are context-independent and predictive. The difference between predictive and nonpredictive theory is so consequential that it would be better not to use the same term to denote the two. In other words, if we choose to call one of the two "theory," the other should be excluded from this designation. In the argument that follows, the term "theory" refers to predictive theory. We will see that even though prediction requires special preconditions and is relatively rare even in parts of the natural sciences, prediction is the criterion which most clearly helps us distinguish between natural and social sciences.

Just as ideal natural science explains and predicts in terms of context-independent elements which can be abstracted from the everyday world – mass and position in physics, for example – the study of society, insofar as it attempts to follow natural science, must also abstract such elements from the context-dependent activities of human beings in order to subsequently explain and predict those activities in terms of formal relations (rules or laws) between the abstracted elements. It is on this basis that Noam Chomsky seeks out general syntactic elements and formal transformational rules for explaining everyday speech, and that Claude Lévi-Strauss abstracts the exchange of objects between individuals and groups and formalizes their role in social interaction.

Dreyfus and Bourdieu argue that this approach, which has been successful in many parts of the natural sciences, cannot succeed in the study of society. The reason, says Dreyfus, has to do with the central importance of context in human social life:

Insofar as the would-be sciences [social sciences modeled upon the natural sciences] follow the ideal of physical theory, they must predict and explain everyday activities, using decontextualized features. But since the context in which human beings pick out the everyday objects and events whose regularities theory attempts to predict is left out in the decontextualization necessary for theory, what human beings pick out as objects and events need not coincide with those elements over which the theory ranges. Therefore predictions, though often correct, will not be reliable. Indeed, these predictions will work only as long as the elements picked out and related by theory happen to coincide with what the human beings falling under the theory pick out and relate in their everyday activities.[2]

Dreyfus's point is that the phenomena, which a theory selects as relevant via the theory's logic, are not necessarily identical with those phenomena selected as relevant by those people covered by the theory. Dreyfus states further, that this is the case because the context is excluded, the very context in which human beings select those everyday phenomena, whose regularities the theory attempts to explain and predict. The key question is: why does the exclusion of context cause the theory to collapse?

If Dreyfus is right he has identified a fundamental paradox for social and political science: a social science theory of the kind which imitates the natural sciences, that is, a theory which makes possible explanation and prediction, requires that the concrete context of everyday human activity be excluded, but this very exclusion of context makes explanation and prediction impossible. It is in confronting this paradox that Pierre Bourdieu enters the picture.

A question of style

In *Outline of a Theory of Practice*, Bourdieu presents a reflection on scientific practice, which "will disconcert both those who reflect on the social sciences without practicing them and those who practice them without reflecting on them."[3] Bourdieu's analysis is centered on Lévi-Strauss's theory of gift exchange. Lévi-Strauss's theory consists of several formal, reversible rules for the exchange of gifts. The theory appears to be the type of theory described by the six criteria cited above; that is, it seeks to explain and predict actual exchanges of gifts. Bourdieu, however, in a chapter called "The Objective Limits of Objectivism," argues that Lévi-Strauss's exchange theory cannot accomplish this task. Bourdieu's point is not that of hermeneutics, phenomenology, or ethnomethodology, considered in the previous chapter. Thus he does not assert that Lévi-Strauss's theory does not account for the subjective factors (*verstehen*) in gift exchange. This would not be a valid critique in the line of argument we are following here. Bourdieu's point is more fundamental, and more devastating. He argues that Lévi-Strauss's abstractions are fundamentally incorrect because no kind of gift exchange would take place if exchange were perceived as the simple, reversible operations described by Lévi-Strauss's theory. The argument hinges upon the decisive role of timing and tempo for human expertise identified in chapter two. In this connection, let us quote Bourdieu at length:

"Phenomenological" analysis and objectivist analysis bring to light two antagonistic principles of gift exchange: the gift as experienced, or, at least, meant to be experienced, and the gift as seen from outside. To stop short at the "objective" truth of the gift, i.e. the model, is to set aside the question of the relationship between so-called objective truth, i.e. that of the observer, and the truth that can scarcely be called subjective, since it represents the official definition of the subjective experience of the exchange; it is to ignore the fact that the agents practice as irreversible a sequence of actions that the observer constitutes as reversible . . . [E]ven if reversibility is the objective truth of the discrete acts which ordinary experience knows in discrete form and calls gift exchanges, it is not the whole truth of a practice which could not exist if it were consciously perceived in accordance with the model. The temporal structure of gift exchange, which objectivism ignores, is what makes possible the coexistence of two opposing truths, which defines the full truth of the gift . . . The difference and delay which [Lévi-Strauss's] model obliterates must be brought into the model not, as Lévi-Strauss suggests, out of a "phenomenological" desire to restore the subjective experience of the practice of the exchange, but because . . . the *interval* between gift and counter-gift is what allows a pattern of exchange that is always liable to strike the observer and also the participants as *reversible*, i.e. both forced and interested, to be experienced as irreversible.[4]

This cannot be the whole argumentation for the importance of context, however. Theoretical researchers do not need to worry about how the exchange is perceived, or whether the exchange must be misperceived in order to take place. They are concerned only with explaining and predicting exchange. The fundamental step forward in this argument is that the context, which is excluded and must be excluded in the theory, does more than add the necessary meaningful (*verstehen*) perception or experience of exchange to the formal theoretical skeleton. Context, sequence, tempo, and rubato in the gift exchange determine what counts as a gift at all. Of this Bourdieu states:

The observer's totalizing apprehension substitutes an objective structure fundamentally defined by its *reversibility* for an equally objectively *irreversible* succession of gifts which are not mechanically linked to the gifts they respond to or insistently call for: any really objective analysis of the exchange of gifts, words, challenges, or

even women must allow for the fact that each of these inaugural acts may misfire
. . . In every society it may be observed that, if it is not to constitute an insult, the
counter-gift must be *deferred* and *different*, because the immediate return of an
exactly identical object clearly amounts to a refusal (i.e. the return of the same
object).[5]

The context for an event studied by a researcher thus determines whether
the event should at all count as a relevant event for the study. For
example, returning a gift, which one has just received, is not the same as
gift-giving, but a rejection or negation of gift-giving, an insult. Hence
Bourdieu concludes that "[it] is all a question of style, which means in
this case timing and choice of occasion, for the same act – giving, giving in
return, offering one's services, paying a visit, etc. – can have completely
different meanings at different times."[6]

The rules are no game

As Dreyfus notes, however, the problem for social studies is not the
hermeneutic–phenomenological problem: it is not simply a problem that
the researchers lack a theory of how to determine what counts as an event
or act ("gift-giving" in Lévi-Strauss's theory). This problem is no larger
than physics not having a theory for the classification of images from a
bubble chamber. The problem in the study of human activity is that every
attempt at a context-free definition of an action, that is, a definition based
on abstract rules or laws, will not necessarily accord with the pragmatic
way an action is defined by the actors in a concrete social situation. Social
scientists do not have a theory (rules and laws) for how the people they
study determine what counts as an action, because the determination
derives from situationally defined (context-dependent) skills, which the
objects of study are proficient and experts in exercising, and because
theory – by definition – presupposes context-independence. Here, the
concepts "proficient" and "expert" are used in the sense set forth in
chapter two.

Stated in another way, most people find themselves at the "proficiency" and "expertise" levels in using the skills necessary to manage
their everyday activities and normal social interaction. And proficiency
and expertise exist by virtue of context and judgment, as we have seen.
Moreover, while context is central for defining what counts as an action,
context must nevertheless be excluded in a theory in order for it to be a
theory at all. It is this contradiction which punctures the aspirations of the
social sciences to become normal sciences in the Kuhnian sense. Bourdieu uses the words "virtuoso" and "excellence," for what Hubert and
Stuart Dreyfus call "expertise." And even though habits, traditions, and

social role patterns are important phenomena, Bourdieu argues directly against the possibility of a rule-based "Book of Appropriate Conduct:"

Only a virtuoso with a perfect command of his "art of living" can play on all the resources inherent in the ambiguities and uncertainties of behaviour and situation in order to produce the actions appropriate to each case, to do that of which people will say, "There was nothing else to be done," and do it the right way. We are a long way, too, from norms and rules: doubtless there are slips, mistakes, and moments of clumsiness to be observed here as elsewhere; and also grammarians of decorum able to state (and elegantly, too) what it is right to do and say, but never presuming to encompass in a catalogue of recurrent situations and appropriate conduct, still less in a fatalistic model, the "art" of the *necessary improvisation* which defines excellence . . . The fact that there is no "choice" that cannot be accounted for, retrospectively at least, does not imply that such practice is perfectly predictable, like the acts inserted in the rigorously stereotyped sequences of a rite; and this is true not only for the observer but also for the agents, who find in the relative predictability and unpredictability of the possible ripostes the opportunity to put their strategies to work. But even the most strictly ritualized exchanges, in which all the moments of the action, and their unfolding, are rigorously foreseen, have room for strategies: the agents remain in command of the *interval* between the obligatory moments and can therefore act on their opponents by playing with the *tempo* of the exchange . . . the mastery which defines excellence finds expression in the play made with time which transforms ritualized exchange into a confrontation of strategies.[7]

We see, therefore, that context-dependence does not mean just a more complex form of determinism. It means an open-ended, contingent relation between contexts and actions and interpretations. The rules of a ritual are not the ritual, a grammar is not a language, the rules for chess are not chess, and traditions are not actual social behavior. "The rules are no game," as Anthony Wilden concludes in his book on communication.[8]

It is the contradiction between scientific theories' necessary freedom from context and the actual context-dependence of people's expert decisions on what counts as relevant actions that causes predictions on the basis of "theories" about human activity to err at a specific moment; namely, at precisely the moment when an action which according to the theory belongs to a distinct category of actions, is no longer considered to belong to this category by the people within the group to which the theory applies. As Hubert Dreyfus observes, no corresponding problem exists for the natural sciences: the physicists' bubble chamber does not classify its own particle traces.

Economics as science of the second order

One attempt to get around this fundamental problem is to abandon the ambition to find first-order context-independent explanations in the study of society and instead remain content with what Bourdieu calls "second-degree" and Dreyfus "second-order" explanations. In Lévi-Strauss's case, for instance, a second-order element in an explanation might be the participants' evaluation of whether the object exchanged is classified as a gift. Such evaluations, which might be extracted from survey data or questionnaires, are treated afterwards as if they were context-independent characteristics, and are related to each other and to outcomes with the help of theory so as to explain and predict other evaluations and other information.

Economics – the social science which from a conventional epistemic point of view is often regarded as the most successful in its efforts to achieve genuine scientific status – attempts to present itself as such a second-order science.[9] What people consider to be money, property, economic behavior (for example, maximization of profits), etc., are taken as given. One thereafter seeks out laws, which relate these socially defined concepts to each other. And so long as there is a degree of constancy in the practices which define the objects and goals for a group of people or a society, economic laws can, in principle, predict just as well as physical laws. That they do not do so in practice is something else: the kind of economic theory which can reliably predict changes in exchange rates and stock market trends has yet to appear. Moreover, as stated, economic theories exist by virtue of the practices by which people define the concepts of money, property, economic behavior, etc., and these can change at any time and thereby undermine the theories' ability to predict.[10] We do not have, and probably never will have, a theory, which can predict the changes in these practices. "An economist," it has therefore been observed jokingly but acutely, "is an expert who will know tomorrow why the things he predicted yesterday did not happen today."[11]

Dreyfus says that on first sight, we might imagine that if a theory's limiting conditions were made explicit, we would at least be able to predict when the theory did not work. In biology, for example, ecological theories are valid as long as the earth's temperature is relatively constant. It is correct that if we could make the baseline conditions explicit for sciences such as economics, we could obtain a kind of closed theory by marking the boundaries within which the theory could predict. Anthony Giddens was once a spokesperson for this view of theories and laws in social studies: "Laws in the social sciences," Giddens stated, "are intrinsically 'historical' in character: they hold only given specific conditions of 'boundedness'."[12] Later on, in his explication of "structuration theory," Giddens softens his view. Remarking on the concept of "laws," he now states:

The task of constructing sets of stably established generalizations, which is (perhaps) the lynchpin of the endeavours of the natural sciences, is not an ambition of much relevance to social science . . . [I]t is preferable not to use the term [law] in social science.[13]

Giddens does not elaborate on why he has changed his view, but with a point of departure in Dreyfus and Bourdieu, we understand why there is good reason to do so. In general, an important difference between the social and the natural sciences is that the background conditions in the social world are not physical facts. Nor are they psychological facts about what individuals desire and what they believe to be rational. The background conditions are patterns of behavior, which are characterized by expert exercise of tacit skills.

The problem for social studies is that the background conditions change without the researcher being able to state in advance which aspects one should hold constant in order for predictions to continue to operate. As the background conditions are not facts – as is temperature for the ecological theories in biology – but context-dependent interpretations, even those social sciences which build upon second-order evaluations are incomplete and unstable. This is the case, not only when compared to ideal theoretical disciplines such as physics, but also when compared to disciplines such as ecology which also have background conditions that change. The background conditions in the two areas are fundamentally different.

Philosophers of science have differing views on what constitutes explanation. Yet there is one point on which there exists agreement: namely, that if all those factors which comprise a theory remain unchanged while the resulting activity, i.e., the activity to be explained by the factors, varies, then the theory has not provided a comprehensive explanation of the relevant behavior. This fact is in itself enough to make Dreyfus's and Bourdieu's argument devastating for second-order theories. For this is precisely what can happen – and in fact does happen – for second-order social-science theories such as economics. Bourdieu is unremittingly critical about this class of theories:

Our approach is thus radically opposed, on two essential points, to . . . [reducing] the constructions of social science to "constructs of the second degree, that is, constructs of the constructs made by the actors on the social scene," as Schutz does, or, like Garfinkel, to accounts of the accounts which agents produce and through which they produce the meaning of their world. One is entitled to undertake to give an "account of accounts," so long as one does not put forward one's contribution to the science of pre-scientific representation of the social world as if it were a science of the social world . . . Being the product of the same generative schemes as the practices they claim to account for, even the most fake and superficial of these "secondary explanations" only reinforce the structures by providing them with a particular form of "rationalization."[14]

Dreyfus and Bourdieu enable us to better understand the weakness of Foucault's argument described in the previous chapter. That which propels the social sciences – alas, without success – to objectivize their background practices is not only a specific historical configuration for these sciences, as Foucault asserts. It is the requirement that a truly explanatory and predictive science must operate independent of context together with the fact that context-independence seems impossible in the study of social affairs. Dreyfus therefore concludes:

The new structuralist and cognitivist sciences of human capacities have turned out to be as unstable and non-normal as were the old behaviorist sciences of man. All such theories must either refuse to make predictions or else confront repeated exceptions. Given the lack of any solid successes, other approaches inevitably arise in the discipline, which offer competing types of systematic accounts. Such competing types of account do not agree on method, evidence, or even on what are the problems. We then have neither normal science nor even revolutionary science, but just the sort of pre-paradigmatic instability characteristic of the social sciences from their inception to the present.[15]

Beyond theory

It is worth reiterating that Dreyfus's and Bourdieu's plea for the importance of context is not an ultimate proof that social science can *never* be explanatory and predictive. It only makes it *probable* that this is so. The core of their argument is that human activity cannot be reduced to a set of rules, and without rules there can be no theory. Dreyfus formulates it as follows:

In some cases our basic social skills may have been acquired by consciously following rules defined over elements but, like any skill which has reached a level of mastery, our ability to cope with everyday things and situations is no longer caused by and cannot be analyzed into the elements which went into its acquisition. Yet no one has found any other elements or is even trying to find them.[16]

That there is no one who has found such other elements which could make the study of human activity predictive does not rule out the possibility that these elements might exist. Nevertheless, we have no indication of what these would look like. And the mere possibility of the existence of such elements has no special value for the scientific development of the study of humans and society. It means only that one cannot *prove* that social science cannot become scientific in the sense of normal science. On the other hand, the fact that this cannot be proven does not make the social sciences' instability a historical coincidence, nor must we conclude that their lack of maturity is due to the complexity of their object of study.

The four arguments about the possibility and impossibility of social science theory outlined in this and the previous chapter can be summarized as follows:

1. *The pre-paradigmatic argument*, following the early Rorty, is correct insofar as there is, in principle, nothing to prevent social science from becoming normal science in the future. That is, it has not been demonstrated that it is *impossible* for social science to become normal science. Yet from here it is difficult, and perhaps misguided, to believe that this will actually come to pass. At present there exist no normal-science theories in the social sciences, and there is no reason to believe *a priori* in the existence of the abstract context-independent concepts which such theories would presuppose. Hence, the abstract normal-science possibility – which is but an unrealized possibility – is not especially useful in understanding the problems of the social sciences as science.

2. *The hermeneutic–phenomenological argument* of Anthony Giddens and Harold Garfinkel demonstrates that the study of human activity must be based on people's situational self-interpretation, and that such studies can only be as stable as these interpretations.

3. *The historical contingency argument* of Foucault in *The Order of Things* is that stable and cumulative sciences which study human behavior are not possible because humans both constitute these sciences and are at the same time their object. No science can objectivize the skills which make it possible. On this point Foucault is correct, but he errs in saying that the social sciences are plagued by these problems only during a given historical period. The problems are more general than Foucault depicts them.

4. *The "tacit skills" argument* of Dreyfus and Bourdieu is the most general and most rigorous of the four. It says that stable and cumulative social sciences presume a necessary but apparently impossible theory of human background skills. The theory is necessary in order to ensure predictability. It seems impossible because human skills are context-dependent and cannot be reduced to rules, whereas a theory must be free of context and have rules. The context cannot be excluded because, as Bourdieu shows, context defines the type of phenomenon which the theory encompasses. However, a theory must necessarily be context-free, otherwise it is not a general theory. This is the dilemma in which the social sciences find themselves, a dilemma which has existed since their inception, and which, it appears, will continue.[17] So far cognitivists and others have failed in their attempts to analyze context as just very complex sets of rules. Context-dependence appears to entail an open-ended, dependent

relation between contexts and actions and interpretations that cannot be brought under rule-based closure. For humans, "practice has a logic which is not that of logic," in the words of Bourdieu.[18]

In the conventional view of ideal science, it is precisely normal science that lies at the core of scientific identity. It is therefore not surprising that researchers tend to aspire to the normal-scientific ideal. That the ideal does not work in practice for social science and that there is nothing, which indicates that it ever will is another story. The goal is clear, even though it cannot be achieved. If the normal-scientific ideal were abandoned, we would be without both goals and results, where at present only the results are lacking. The two examples of the Science Wars mentioned in chapter one, that is, "Sokal's hoax" and the US National Opinion Research Center study of sexual practices illustrate the vigor with which the question of whether social science can achieve Kuhnian normality is discussed, and how strongly many social scientists hold on to the normal-science ideal, despite evidence that the ideal has not been and probably cannot be achieved.

Without faith in the possibility of theory and epistemology in social science, many scholars fear that the door would become open for scientific relativism and nihilism. In reality, the door is already wide open for relativistic and nihilistic tendencies, insofar as epistemically oriented social scientists ignore the fact that epistemic theory cannot serve as a bulwark against relativism and nihilism since such theory, as we have shown, does currently not exist and can probably never come to exist. (For more on relativism, see chapter nine.)

With these considerations, we have repealed the conventional normal-science ideal for social science. The question of what can be put in its place remains to be answered. Cognitivism, functionalism, structuralism, and neopositivism have so far failed to produce epistemic theory, as have other objectivist strands of social science. Hermeneutics by itself is inadequate. Critical Theory has long been preoccupied with Habermas's attempt to formulate a normative discourse theory and its consequences for politics and jurisprudence. What should researchers and students do in this situation? What are the consequences for our practical work? For the choice of problems we study? The choice of methodology? What are the consequences for social science aside from the obvious fact that context must have a more central position, and theory a less central one? It is in answering these questions that we can learn from Aristotle's considerations in the *Ethics* regarding what he calls the "intellectual virtues" of *episteme, techne,* and *phronesis.*

Before describing Aristotle's thought, I want to conclude this chapter by pointing out some of the pitfalls one encounters when attempting to address the above questions. The purpose of this and the previous chapter has been to deconstruct the conventional scientific ideal for the social sciences, with its emphasis on theory and context-independence. In a critique of deconstruction, the Danish linguist, Per Aage Brandt, has pointed out that making a philosophical principle out of difference is to invalidate our knowledge, and that understanding between humans represents the "victory of signs over difference."[19] In similar fashion, one might say that focusing on the particular, the non-rule-based, and on context is to dismiss scientific knowledge, and that scientific knowledge is precisely the victory of the general – of rules – over the particular.

In my judgment, this point of view, while containing an important insight, is still unproductive, for it sets against each other two equally invalid extremes: difference versus sign, the particular versus the rule-based. Dualisms like these may facilitate thinking and writing, but they inhibit understanding by implying a certain neatness that is rarely found in lived life. If not meaningless, it is counterproductive to meaning to speak of "the victory of signs over difference" or of rules over the particular. There are signs, and there is difference. There are rules, and there is the particular. This much can be observed phenomenologically, and it is this phenomenology which is our focus. To amputate one side in these pairs of phenomena into a dualistic "either–or" is to amputate our understanding. Rather than the "either–or," we should develop a non-dualistic and pluralistic "both–and." Hence, we should not criticize rules, logic, signs, and rationality in themselves. We should criticize only the dominance of these phenomena to the exclusion of others in modern society and in social science. Conversely, it would be equally problematic if rules, logic, signs, and rationality were marginalized by the concrete, by difference, and by the particular. This latter problem, however, is presently far less pressing than the former.

Part two

How social science can matter again

5   Values in social and political inquiry

[I]f you want a description of our age, here is one: the civilization of
means without ends.   *Richard Livingstone*

Value-rationality and instrumental rationality

Just as social science has not been able to contribute with Kuhnian
normal science and predictive theory to scientific development, so natural
science has had little to offer to the reflexive analysis of goals, values, and
interests that is a precondition for an enlightened development in any
society. However, where natural science is weak, social science is strong,
and vice versa. For Aristotle, the most important task of social and
political studies was to develop society's value-rationality *vis-à-vis* its
scientific and technical rationality. Aristotle did not doubt that the first
type of rationality was the most important and ought to influence the
second. Since Aristotle's time, however, this view has receded into the
background, especially after the Enlightenment and modernity installed
instrumental rationality in a dominant position in both science and
society. Social thinkers as diverse as Max Weber, Michel Foucault, and
Jürgen Habermas have pointed out that for more than two centuries
value-rationality (*Wertrationalität*) has increasingly given way to instrumental rationality (*Zweckrationalität*).[1] In the words of Richard Livingstone: "if you want a description of our age, here is one: the civilization of
means without ends."[2] Today the Aristotelian question of balancing
instrumental rationality with value-rationality is forcing its way back to
the foreground. Problems with both biosphere and sociosphere indicate
that social and political development based on instrumental rationality
alone is not sustainable.

   I have argued elsewhere that the Rationalist Turn – the narrowing of
modern society's notion of rationality to a predominantly instrumental
one – is constitutive of what has been called the "risk society."[3] Even
though we need not go further back than the heyday of logical positivism
in the 1950s and 1960s in order to see the rationalist ideal as dominant in

science and society, and even though this ideal also occupies a prominent position today in key scientific growth areas such as the new information sciences, cognitive science, linguistics, and computer science, many people now believe that alternatives to instrumental rationalism are needed. The precise content of such alternatives, however, remains vague. The Rationalist Turn has been so radical that possible alternatives, which might have existed previously, are beyond our current vision, just as centuries of rationalist socialization seems to have undermined the ability of individuals and society to even conceptualize a nonrationalist present and future.

One way of dealing with this situation is to study the era prior to the Rationalist Turn. We will not simply inquire about what it is we lost to rationalism. Nor will we ask how a less rationalistic past could be resurrected. Rather, we will probe the question of what we might learn about the present from the past, and how, in this light, our modern concept of rationality might be reformulated and extended. This strategy inevitably leads back to the Greek philosophers. Socrates, Plato, and Aristotle are often seen as forefathers of modern science and of present day rationalism. Aristotle, however, distinguished explicitly between several "intellectual virtues," of which epistemic science, with its emphasis on theories, analysis, and universals, was but one, and not even the most important. Aristotle added intellectual virtues dealing with context, practice, experience, common sense, intuition, and practical wisdom, especially the intellectual virtue named *phronesis*.

It is not my purpose to subject Aristotle or other Greek philosophers to a historical analysis in the traditional sense. Nor do I seek to analyze the society in which they worked, how their work was used, etc. I do not view Greek philosophy or classical Greek society as an ideal to be emulated today. Such an exercise would be sterile utopian idealism, and basically useless. I agree with Michel Foucault that "this idea that the Greek civilization is something like a model, which has been forgotten . . . doesn't make a lot of sense, since history is history. There is no way, no hope, no positive meaning in turning back on something."[4] Still, Foucault goes on to observe that in antiquity we have a unique example of an ethics that, unlike ours, was not related either to religion, or to civil law, or to science. "And I think," says Foucault, "that we are now at the point where we recognize that those three references for our ethics are not sufficient."[5] In the Greeks we have an example of a culture in which ethics have been very strong; the "philosophy of ethics" is one of the major achievements of this culture, and something we can learn from today. But, says Foucault, our solutions have to be very different from those of the Greeks.[6]

Foucault here talks about ethics in relation to "an aesthetics of existence," that is, the relationship you have to *yourself* when you act. Aristotle, in discussing *phronesis*, is mainly talking about ethics in relation to
social and political praxis, that is, the relationship you have to *society* when
you act.[7] In chapter eight we will return to the relationship between
Foucault and Aristotle. For now we will ask what we can learn about our
current situation from a contemporary reading of Aristotle and his considerations in the *Ethics* about the intellectual virtues of *episteme*, *techne*,
and *phronesis*. After having deconstructed the modern concepts of rationality and social science in chapters two to four, the purpose is now to
start reconstructing these concepts.

Aristotle is the classic philosopher of *phronesis* but he never elaborated
his conception of *phronesis* to include explicit considerations on power.
Similarly, Hans-Georg Gadamer's conception of *phronesis* also overlooks
issues of power. Yet as Richard Bernstein points out, "no practical
discussion is going to take place unless you understand the relevance of
phronesis. But no practical philosophy can be adequate for our time unless
it confronts the analysis of power."[8] This, then, is a methodological aim
of what follows: to develop the classic concept of *phronesis* to include
issues of power. In this chapter the classic concept of *phronesis* is ex-
plicated. In chapters seven and eight this concept is expanded to include
issues of power.

Aristotle on *episteme*, *techne*, and *phronesis*

The term "epistemic science" derives from the intellectual virtue that
Aristotle calls *episteme*, and which is generally translated as "science" or
"scientific knowledge."[9] Aristotle defines *episteme* in this manner:

What science [*episteme*] is . . . will be clear from the following argument. We all
assume that what we *know* cannot be otherwise than it is, whereas in the case of
things that may be otherwise, when they have passed out of our view we can no
longer tell whether they exist or not. Therefore, the object of scientific knowledge
is of necessity. Therefore it is eternal . . . Induction introduces us to first
principles and universals, while deduction starts from universals . . . Thus
scientific knowledge is a demonstrative state, (i.e., a state of mind capable of
demonstrating what it knows) . . . i.e., a person has scientific knowledge when his
belief is conditioned in a certain way, and the first principles are known to him;
because if they are not better known to him than the conclusion drawn from
them, he will have knowledge only incidentally. – This may serve as a description
of scientific knowledge.[10]

Episteme thus concerns universals and the production of knowledge which
is invariable in time and space, and which is achieved with the aid of

analytical rationality. *Episteme* corresponds to the modern scientific ideal as expressed in natural science. In Socrates and Plato, and subsequently in the Enlightenment tradition, this scientific ideal became dominant. The ideal has come close to being the only legitimate view of what constitutes genuine science, such that even intellectual activities like social science, which are not and probably never can be scientific in this sense, have found themselves compelled to strive for and legitimate themselves in terms of this Enlightenment ideal.

Whereas *episteme* resembles our ideal modern scientific project, *techne* and *phronesis* denote two contrasting roles of intellectual work. *Techne* can be translated into English as "art" in the sense of "craft"; a craftsman is also an *art*isan. For Aristotle, both *techne* and *phronesis* are connected with the concept of truth, as is *episteme*. Aristotle says the following regarding *techne*:

[S]ince (e.g.) building is an art [*techne*] and is essentially a reasoned productive state, and since there is no art that is not a state of this kind, and no state of this kind that is not an art, it follows that art is the same as a productive state that is truly reasoned. Every art is concerned with bringing something into being, and the practice of an art is the study of how to bring into being something that is capable either of being or of not being . . . For it is not with things that are or come to be *of necessity* that art is concerned [this is the domain of *episteme*] nor with natural objects (because these have their origin in themselves) . . . Art . . . operate[s] in the sphere of the variable.[11]

Techne is thus craft and art, and as an activity it is concrete, variable, and context-dependent. The objective of *techne* is application of technical knowledge and skills according to a pragmatic instrumental rationality, what Foucault calls "a practical rationality governed by a conscious goal."[12]

Whereas *episteme* concerns theoretical *know why* and *techne* denotes technical *know how*, *phronesis* emphasizes practical knowledge and practical ethics. *Phronesis* is often translated as "prudence" or "practical common sense." Let us again examine what Aristotle has to say:

We may grasp the nature of prudence [*phronesis*] if we consider what sort of people we call prudent. Well, it is thought to be the mark of a prudent man to be able to deliberate rightly about what is good and advantageous . . . But nobody deliberates about things that are invariable . . . So . . . prudence cannot be science or art; not science [*episteme*] because what can be done is a variable (it may be done in different ways, or not done at all), and not art [*techne*] because action and production are generically different. For production aims at an end other than itself; but this is impossible in the case of action, because the end is merely doing *well*. What remains, then, is that it is a true state, reasoned, and capable of action with regard to things that are good or bad for man . . . We consider that this quality belongs to those who understand the management of households or states.[13] [Italics in the original]

The person possessing practical wisdom (*phronimos*) has knowledge of how to behave in each particular circumstance that can never be equated with or reduced to knowledge of general truths. *Phronesis* is a sense of the ethically practical rather than a kind of science. Where rational humans for Plato are moved by the cosmic order, for Aristotle they are moved by a sense of the proper order among the ends we pursue. This sense cannot be articulated in terms of theoretical axioms, but rather, is grasped by *phronesis*.[14] Here, in Aristotle's original description of *phronesis*, one might get the impression that *phronesis* and the choices it involves in concrete circumstances are always good. Later, after we have introduced the concept of power into the discussion of *phronesis*, we will see that this is not necessarily the case. Choices must be deemed good (or bad) in relation to certain values and interests in order for good and bad to have meaning.

In sum, the three intellectual virtues *episteme, techne,* and *phronesis* can be characterized as follows:

> *Episteme* Scientific knowledge. Universal, invariable, context-independent. Based on general analytical rationality. The original concept is known today from the terms "epistemology" and "epistemic."
>
> *Techne* Craft/art. Pragmatic, variable, context-dependent. Oriented toward production. Based on practical instrumental rationality governed by a conscious goal. The original concept appears today in terms such as "technique," "technical," and "technology."
>
> *Phronesis* Ethics. Deliberation about values with reference to praxis. Pragmatic, variable, context-dependent. Oriented toward action. Based on practical value-rationality. The original concept has no analogous contemporary term.

The priority of the particular

Phronesis thus concerns the analysis of values – "things that are good or bad for man" – as a point of departure for action. *Phronesis* is that intellectual activity most relevant to praxis. It focuses on what is variable, on that which cannot be encapsulated by universal rules, on specific cases. *Phronesis* requires an interaction between the general and the concrete; it requires consideration, judgment, and choice.[15] More than anything else, *phronesis* requires *experience*. About the importance of specific experience Aristotle says:

[P]rudence [*phronesis*] is not concerned with universals only; it must also take cognizance of particulars, because it is concerned with conduct, and conduct has its sphere in particular circumstances. That is why some people who do not possess theoretical knowledge are more effective in action (especially if they are experienced) than others who do possess it. For example, suppose that someone knows that light flesh foods are digestible and wholesome, but does not know what kinds are light; he will be less likely to produce health than one who knows that chicken is wholesome. But prudence is practical, and therefore it must have both kinds of knowledge, or especially the latter.[16]

Some interpretations of Aristotle's intellectual virtues leave doubt as to whether *phronesis* and *techne* are distinct categories, or whether *phronesis* is just a higher form of *techne* or know-how.[17] Aristotle is clear on this point. Even if both of these intellectual virtues involve skill and judgment, one type of intellectual virtue cannot be reduced to the other; *phronesis* is about value judgment, not about producing things.

Similarly, in other parts of the literature one finds attempts at conflating *phronesis* and *episteme* in the sense of making *phronesis* epistemic. But insofar as *phronesis* operates via a practical rationality based on judgment and experience, it can only be made scientific in an epistemic sense through the development of a theory of judgment and experience. Alessandro Ferrara, in fact, has called for the "elaboration of a theory of judgment" as one of "the unaccomplished tasks of critical theory."[18] In line with Jürgen Habermas, Ferrara says that this is necessary in order to avoid contextualism, though he also notes that such a theory "unfortunately is not yet in sight."[19] What Ferrara apparently does not consider is that a theory of judgment and experience is not in sight because judgment and experience cannot be brought into a theoretical formula. Here, again, it is not possible to avoid context, even though this is the ambition of all epistemists and rationalists. Aristotle warns us directly against the type of reductionism that conflates *phronesis* and *episteme*.

With his thoughts on the intellectual virtues, Aristotle emphasizes properties of intellectual work, which in my judgment are central to the production of knowledge in the study of individuals and society. The particular and the situationally dependent are emphasized over the universal and over rules. The concrete and the practical are emphasized over the theoretical. It is what Martha Nussbaum calls the "priority of the particular" in Aristotle's thinking.[20] Aristotle practices what he preaches by providing a specific example of his argument, *viz.* light flesh foods versus chicken. He understands the "power of example." The example concerns human health and has as its point of departure something both concrete and fundamental concerning human functioning. Both aspects are typical of many Classical philosophers.

Later on we will return to these points. Here we may simply conclude that despite their importance, the concrete, the practical, and the ethical have been neglected by modern science. Today one would be open to ridicule if one sought to support an argument using examples like that of Aristotle's chicken. The sciences are supposed to concern themselves precisely with the explication of universals, and the conventional wisdom is that one cannot generalize from a particular case. Moreover, the ultimate goal of scientific activity is supposedly the production of theory. Aristotle is here clearly anti-Socratic and anti-Platonic. And if modern theoretical science is built upon any body of thought, it is that of Socrates and Plato. We are dealing with a profound disagreement here.

For those of us interested in power and political science it is worth noting that Aristotle links *phronesis* directly with political science:

Political science and prudence [*phronesis*] are the same state of mind [They are not identical, however. *Phronesis* is also found at the level of the household and the individual] . . . Prudence concerning the state has two aspects: one, which is controlling and directive, is legislative science; the other . . . deals with particular circumstances . . . [and] is practical and deliberative.[21]

Two things are worth noting in this context. The first is Aristotle's assertion that political science, as a consequence of the emphasis on the particular, on context, and on experience, cannot be practiced as *episteme*. To be a knowledgeable researcher in an epistemic sense is not enough when it concerns political science because "although [people] develop ability in geometry and mathematics and become wise in such matters, they are not thought to develop prudence [*phronesis*]."[22] Aristotle explains that a well-functioning political science based on *phronesis* is imperative for a well-functioning society, inasmuch as "it is impossible to secure one's own good independently of . . . political science."[23]

Secondly, Aristotle emphasizes in his concept of *phronesis* both the collective (the state) and the particular; control and circumstance; directives and deliberation; sovereign power and individual power. Since Aristotle, however, an unfortunate division has developed in philosophy and in the social and political sciences, of two separate traditions, each representing one of the two sides stressed by Aristotle. One tradition, the dominant one, has developed from Plato via Hobbes and Kant to Habermas and other rationalist thinkers, emphasizing the first of the two sides. The other, partly Aristotelian and partly sophist in origin, has developed via Machiavelli to Nietzsche, and to Foucault in some interpretations. Today the two traditions tend to live separate lives, apart from occasional, typically rhetorical attacks from thinkers within one tradition on thinkers within the other, the critique by Habermas of Foucault and Derrida, and vice versa, being cases in point. Aristotle insisted, however, that what is interesting, for understanding and for praxis, is what happens where the two now largely separate sides intersect, and that this point of intersection is the locus of appropriate phronetic activity.

In contemporary social science Pierre Bourdieu's "fieldwork in philosophy" and Robert Bellah's "social science as public philosophy" are examples of intellectual pursuits that involve elements of *phronesis*.[24] Bourdieu explicitly recognizes Aristotle as the originator of the habitus concept, which is so centrally placed in Bourdieu's work, and he sees the practical knowledge that habitus procures as analogous with Aristotle's *phronesis*.[25] In philosophy Richard Bernstein's and Stephen Toulmin's "practical philosophy" and Richard Rorty's philosophical pragmatism are also phronetic in their orientation, as are Foucault's genealogies (see chapters seven and eight).[26] As pointed out by Rorty, in this interpretation, "philosophy" is precisely what a culture becomes capable of when it ceases to define itself in terms of explicit rules, and becomes sufficiently leisured and civilized to rely on inarticulate know-how, to "substitute *phronesis* for codification."[27] Aristotle found that every well-functioning society was dependent on the effective functioning of all three intellectual virtues – *episteme*, *techne*, and *phronesis* – in, respectively, science, art/ crafts, and ethics. At the same time, however, Aristotle emphasized the crucial importance of *phronesis*, "for the possession of the single virtue of prudence [*phronesis*] will carry with it the possession of them all."[28]

Where natural science is weak and social science strong

Regardless of the lack of a term for *phronesis* in our modern vocabulary, the principal objective for social science with a phronetic approach is to carry out analyses and interpretations of the status of values and interests in society aimed at social commentary and social action, i.e. praxis. The point of departure for classical phronetic research can be summarized in the following three value-rational questions:

(1) Where are we going?
(2) Is this desirable?
(3) What should be done?

Later, when we have discussed the implications of power for *phronesis*, we will add a fourth question: Who gains and who loses; by which mechanisms of power? In asking and providing answers to these questions, we use social and political studies not just as a mirror for society but also as society's nose, eyes, and ears. And the questions are asked realizing there is no unified "we" in relation to which the questions can be given a final answer. Phronetic researchers can see no neutral ground, no "view from nowhere," for their work.

It should be stressed that no one is experienced enough and wise enough to give complete answers to the four questions, whatever such answers would be. Experience and wisdom of that kind should not be expected from social scientists, who are, on average, no more astute or ethical than anybody else. What should be expected, however, is attempts from phronetic social scientists to develop their partial answers to the questions; such answers would be input to the ongoing social dialogue about the problems and risks we face and how things may be done differently.

A first step toward achieving this kind of perspective in social science is for researchers to make explicit the different roles of science as *episteme*, *techne*, and *phronesis*, respectively. Today's researchers seldom make explicit which one of these three roles they are practicing. The whole enterprise is simply called "science," even though we are dealing with quite different activities. It is often the case that these activities are rationalized as *episteme* even though they are actually *techne* or *phronesis*. As demonstrated previously, it is not in their role as *episteme* that one can argue for the value of the social sciences. In the domain where the natural sciences have been strongest – production of theories that can explain and predict accurately – the social sciences have been weakest. Nevertheless, by emphasizing the three roles, and especially by reintroducing *phronesis*, we see there are other possibilities for the social sciences. The oft-seen image of impotent social sciences versus potent natural sciences derives from their being compared in terms of their epistemic qualities. Yet such a comparison is misleading, for the two types of science have their respective strengths and weaknesses along fundamentally different dimensions. In their role as *phronesis*, the social sciences are strongest where the natural sciences are weakest.

Max Weber was the first to carry out a comprehensive and systematic analysis of the consequences of a unidimensional development of instrumental rationality in modern society. Weber spoke of *occidental* rationalism: The "specific and peculiar rationalism" of the West.[29] Today, such occidental rationalism has become a global phenomenon, as have its consequences, even though there still exist cultures other than the rationalistic. Weber focused on rationalism's social and cultural consequences in the form of tendencies toward alienation and the erosion of traditional values, and in this connection spoke of the "disenchantment of the world."[30] Since Weber, in many analyses, including those of both Foucault and Habermas, the domain of instrumental rationality has continued to grow and has tended to marginalize value-rationality. To-day, the problems involved in this development relate not only to Weber's concerns with social and cultural affairs, but to the biosphere as well and to humankind's continued existence as a species. Balancing instrumental rationality with value-rationality, therefore, now seems all the more im-portant. And it is precisely here that social science as *phronesis* can make its most essential contribution.

Social science can also contribute to social development as *techne* in grappling with social, cultural, demographic, and administrative prob-lems. Here the social sciences can play an emancipatory role; or they may act as controlling, repressive, and legitimating. Which role they come to play is worth closer analysis and will depend on the specific interests and purposes they are made to serve in specific contexts. In any event, this role of social science will be linked to real problems with a material foundation that one can fight for or against, a far cry from the fictive role of social science as epistemic science.

It is also as *phronesis* and *techne* that the social sciences can provide a counterweight to tendencies toward relativism and nihilism. This, of course, makes attempts by social science to become a "real" theoretical science doubly unfortunate because such efforts draw attention and resources away from those areas where social science could make an impact and instead into areas where they do not have, never have had, and probably never will obtain any significance, that is, as genuinely normal and predictive sciences.

Finally, it is interesting to note that none of the giants in the study of individuals and society – Marx, Freud, Weber, for example – practiced their science as *episteme*, even though both the young Marx and young Freud had epistemic ambitions as we have seen. Marx's work especially has been depicted by both Marx himself and by many of his followers as "pure" science on a par with natural science. Today it seems clear that despite his many profound insights, Marx's "laws" are not laws in a natural-science sense, and that they have had profoundly problematic consequences where they have been used as such.

An example of phronetic social science

How ought we to live? How do we think about how to live? Who are we, as Americans? What is our character? These are questions we have asked our fellow citizens in many parts of the country.

Such read the very first lines of the Preface to *Habits of the Heart* by Robert Bellah, Richard Madsen, William Sullivan, Ann Swidler, and Steven Tipton, and the lines define the focus of what, in my interpretation, is an example of phronetic social science.[31] If we move from the Preface to the introductory chapter, the first paragraph reads like this:

Living well is a challenge. Brian Palmer, a successful businessman, lives in a comfortable San Jose suburb and works as a top-level manager in a large corporation. He is justifiably proud of his rapid rise in the corporation, but he is even prouder of the profound change he has made recently in his idea of success. "My value system," he says, "has changed a little bit as the result of a divorce and reexamining life values. Two years ago, confronted with the work load I have right now, I would stay in the office and work until midnight, come home, go to bed, get up at six, and go back in and work until midnight, until such time as it got done. Now I just kind of flip the bird and walk out. My family life is more important to me than that, and the work will wait, I have learned." A new marriage and a houseful of children have become the center of Brian's life. But such new values were won only after painful difficulties.[32]

With this opening, the scene is set for what has become a central work about the tensions between individualism and social commitment in the American way of life. Clearly, the opening questions of the Preface are a variation of the three value-rational questions that define the point of departure for classical phronetic inquiry and for praxis: Where are we going? Is it desirable? What should be done? In *Habits of the Heart* the questions are asked specifically of Americans about their life. And by combining these "big" questions with the immediacy of the life of Brian – and of Joe, Margaret, Wayne, and others – on the very first pages of the book, the authors emphasize that their study will be specific and general at the same time, just as Aristotle said we need to be in matters of *phronesis*.

Habits of the Heart has many of the characteristics that we will later identify for works of phronetic social science (see chapter nine): it focuses on values, the authors get close to the people and phenomena they study, they focus on the minutiae and practices that make up the basic concerns of life, they make extensive use of case studies in context, they use narrative as expository technique, and, finally, their work is dialogical, that is, it allows for other voices than those of the authors, both in relation to the people they study and in relation to society at large. The whole point of the study is to enter into a dialogue with individuals and society and to assist them – after they have assisted the researchers – in reflecting on their values. The aim is to make moral debate part of public life. This is the claim to social change made by the study. For an academic work, it has had substantial success in inducing such change.

The phronetic character of *Habits of the Heart* becomes clear, not only after careful study of several chapters of the book, nor after looking for guidelines in the book's methodological appendix. The authors demonstrate up front what they are up to; like Aristotle they understand the "power of example." The first few paragraphs of the book are a microcosmos of phronetic social science in operation, and the approach works through the simple but ingenious combination of the classical value-rational questions with the life of Brian Palmer.

The publisher classifies *Habits of the Heart* as sociology. This is too narrow, however, and the authors themselves, who are not all sociologists, expressly state that social science as they practice it defies easy categorization. *Habits of the Heart* may just as well be classified as political science or practical philosophy. In fact the authors open their methodological considerations in the book's appendix by invoking Alexis de Tocqueville in calling for a "new political science . . . for a world itself quite new."[33] Here the authors state that the type of social science they practice is different from conventional social science and conventional sociology. They call it "social science as public philosophy" and emphasize that they have attempted to develop a "new way to deal with new realities" by consciously trying to renew an older conception of social science, one in which the boundary between social science and philosophy is still open.[34] According to the authors, the aim of such a new, classical social science is to hold up a mirror to society thus encouraging and facilitating reflexivity, just as Aristotle wanted us to do in practicing *phronesis*. By probing the past as well as the present, by looking at values as much as at facts – or at values as facts – such a social science is able to make connections that are not obvious, and to ask difficult questions. In *Habits of the Heart* – by means of what the authors label the "active interview," which they see as a "primary method" for social science as public philosophy, and with the help of participant observation, historical analysis, and narrative – the authors uncover the nature of American individualism, its historical and philosophical roots as well as its present reality, and they ask the question whether individualism, as the dominant ideology of American life, is not undermining the conditions of its existence. This question is simultaneously sociological, political, and philosophical, and an answer to it requires not just an evaluation of arguments and evidence but ethical reflection, according to the authors.[35]

In relation to the aims of the present book, however, there is a problem with the approach employed in *Habits of the Heart*. Like classical Aristotelian *phronesis*, social science as public philosophy, as practiced by Bellah *et al.*, does not adequately incorporate issues of power. It is not that the question of power is completely ignored in *Habits of the Heart*. But the question stays at the margin, and the book's concept of power is an undeveloped one (see chapters seven and eight).[36] Below I will argue that the lack of an adequate concept of power is typical not just of *Habits of the Heart* but of much social and political science. Therefore, and given the many virtues of *Habits of the Heart*, it would be unfair to single out this study to carry the burden of what is a general deficiency. *Habits of the Heart* may still serve as an example to learn from for those of us who wish to practice social science as *phronesis*. In later chapters we will encounter examples of phronetic social science that deal differently and more effectively with the issue of power.

Before this, however, we will develop and strengthen Aristotle's concept of *phronesis* on three fronts. First, as a point of departure we will take Aristotle's insight that case knowledge is crucial to the practice of *phronesis* and we will analyze and clarify the status of case knowledge in contemporary social science (chapter six). Second, we will elaborate Aristotle's conception of *phronesis* to include explicit considerations on power (chapters seven and eight). Finally, and on this basis, we will develop a set of methodological guidelines for the practice of *phronesis* in contemporary social and political science (chapter nine).

6   The power of example

Learning to *see* – habituating the eye to repose, to patience, to letting things come to it; learning to defer judgement, to investigate and comprehend the individual case in all its aspects. This is the *first* preliminary schooling in spirituality.   *Friedrich Nietzsche*

In a standard reference book such as the *Dictionary of Sociology*, the full citation regarding the term "case study" reads as follows:

Case Study. The detailed examination of a single example of a class of phenomena, a case study cannot provide reliable information about the broader class, but it may be useful in the preliminary stages of an investigation since it provides hypotheses which may be tested systematically with a larger number of cases.[1]

This description is indicative of a general view of the case study, which, if not directly wrong, is so oversimplified as to be grossly misleading. It is correct that the case study is a "detailed examination of a single example," but it is not true that a case study "cannot provide reliable information about the broader class." While a case study *can* be used "in the preliminary stages of an investigation" to generate hypotheses, it is misleading to see the case study as a pilot method to be used only in preparing the real study's larger tests, systematic hypotheses testing, and theory building.

The problems of this view can be summarized in five misunderstandings or oversimplifications about the nature of the case study as a research method:

> *Misunderstanding 1.* General, theoretical (context-independent) knowledge is more valuable than concrete, practical (context-dependent) knowledge.
> *Misunderstanding 2.* One cannot generalize on the basis of an individual case; therefore, the case study cannot contribute to scientific development.
> *Misunderstanding 3.* The case study is most useful for generating hypotheses; that is, in the first stage of a total research process,

while other methods are more suitable for hypotheses testing and theory building.

Misunderstanding 4. The case study contains a bias toward verification, that is, a tendency to confirm the researcher's preconceived notions.

Misunderstanding 5. It is often difficult to develop general propositions and theories on the basis of specific case studies.

These five misunderstandings indicate that it is theory, reliability, and validity which are at issue; in other words, the very status of the case study as a scientific method.

This chapter will focus on these five misunderstandings and correct them one by one. In doing so, we will return to the Greek philosophers; to Aristotle, who emphasized the value of case knowledge, and to his predecessors, Socrates and Plato, who denigrated such knowledge.

Socrates, Plato, and cases

The single most important explanation for the persistence of the five misunderstandings about the case study is that the case method contradicts Plato's teachings and tradition, and that this tradition is at the core of modern social science. Plato's dialogues deal with Socrates' valiant yet unsuccessful search for universal truths. Socrates used much of his life discussing with Athenian craftsmen, teachers, students, wise men, poets, statesmen, and other citizens, questioning them about the universal aspects which lay beneath their respective domains of knowledge. Yet to his great frustration, when Socrates asked about general principles, the responses he received frequently took the form of concrete examples, that is, cases. Socrates' famous wit and sarcasm in these instances knew no bounds. He cast aspersion upon these responses, stubbornly insisting that there *had* to lie generally valid principles behind the multiplicity of cases.

In the *Meno* dialogue, for example, Socrates attempts to find a general definition of virtue and the universal rules for virtuous acts. But Meno continues to feed Socrates concrete examples; that is, cases illustrative of virtue. There is good reason to quote Socrates and Meno at some length here, inasmuch as the views expressed in this more than two-thousand-year-old dialogue continue to inform current opinions about the value of the case study and other social science methods:

SOCRATES: . . . By the gods, Meno, be generous and tell me what you say that virtue is . . .

MENO: There will be no difficulty, Socrates, in answering your question. Let us take first the virtue of man – he should know how to administer the state, and in the administration of it to benefit his friends and harm his enemies; and he must also be careful not to suffer harm himself . . . Every age, every condition of life, young or old, male or female, bond or free, has a different virtue: there are virtues numberless, and no lack of definitions of them; for virtue is relative to the actions and ages of each of us in all that we do. And the same may be said of vice, Socrates.

SOCRATES: How fortunate I am, Meno! When I ask you for one virtue, you present me with a swarm of them, which are in your keeping. Suppose that I carry on the figure of the swarm, and ask you, What is the nature of the bee? And you answer that there are many kinds of bees, and I reply: But do bees differ as bees because there are many and different kinds of them; or are they not rather to be distinguished by some other quality? . . . And so of the virtues, however many and different they may be, they have all a common nature which makes them virtues; and on this he who would answer the question "What is virtue?" would do well to have his eye fixed; do you understand? . . .

MENO: Will you have one definition of them all?

SOCRATES: That is what I am seeking.

MENO: If you want to have one definition of them all, I know not what to say, but that virtue is the power of governing mankind . . .

SOCRATES: . . . but do you not add "justly and not unjustly"?

MENO: Yes, Socrates; I agree there; for justice is virtue.

SOCRATES: Would you say "virtue," Meno, or "a virtue"?

MENO: What do you mean?

SOCRATES: I mean as I might say about anything; that a round, for example, is "a figure" and not simply "figure," and I should adopt this mode of speaking, because there are other figures.

MENO: Quite right; and that is just what I am saying about virtue – that there are other virtues as well as justice . . . Courage and temperance and wisdom and magnanimity are virtues; and there are many others.

SOCRATES: Yes, Meno; and again we are in the same case: in searching after one virtue we have found many . . . Do you not understand that I am looking for the *"simile in multis"* . . . fulfill your promise, and tell me what virtue is in the universal . . . [2]

In the *Euthyphro* dialogue, Socrates again attempts to find out what it means to be holy:

SOCRATES: . . . tell me, what do you say the holy is? And what is the unholy?

EUTHYPHRO: Well, I say the holy is just what I am doing now, prosecuting murder and temple theft and everything of the sort . . .

SOCRATES: Do you recall that I did not ask you to teach me about some one or two of the many things which are holy, but about that characteristic itself by which all holy things are holy . . . teach me what this same character is, so that I may look to it and use it as a standard, which, should those things which you or someone else may do be of that sort, I may affirm that they are holy, but should they not be of that sort, deny it. [3]

Like Meno, Euthyphro continues to provide Socrates with specific cases instead of the general definition and "standard," that is, rule that Socrates asks for. The result is that the dialogue becomes repetitious, and ultimately goes in circles. It ends with Euthyphro giving up and fleeing from Socrates:

SOCRATES: Let us begin again from the beginning, and ask what the holy is. For I shall not willingly give up until I learn. Please do not scorn me: bend every effort of your mind and now tell me the truth . . .
EUTHYPHRO: Some other time, Socrates. Right now I must hurry somewhere, and I am already late.
SOCRATES: What are you doing, my friend! You leave me and cast me down from my high hope . . . [4]

As a contemporary echo of Socrates, we can site Donald T. Campbell, whose early work criticizes the case study as unscientific. Campbell writes:

[S]uch studies have such a total absence of control as to be of almost no scientific value . . . Any appearance of absolute knowledge, or intrinsic knowledge about singular isolated objects, is found to be illusory upon analysis . . . It seems well-nigh unethical at the present time to allow, as theses or dissertations in education, case studies of this nature (i.e., involving a single group observed at one time only).[5]

Mattei Dogan and Dominique Pelassy, in comparative politics, similarly say that "one can validly explain a particular case only on the basis of general hypotheses. All the rest is uncontrollable, and so of no use."[6] Such views have been challenged by Harry Eckstein, Charles Ragin, and Howard Becker, among others.[7] The later Donald Campbell has even disputed his own earlier position. After evaluating and testing a number of case studies, Campbell made a 180-degree turn in his view of the method's value and is today considered one of the strongest proponents of case study methodology. We will return to Campbell and other contemporary case methodologists later. For the present, we conclude that Socrates encountered the same problem repeatedly during his wanderings in Athens: whenever he asked for universals he got cases. Inasmuch as he rejected the value of concrete practical knowledge, he concluded that nobody knew anything, including he himself, although he at least knew that he knew nothing.

Socrates was mistaken, of course. He knew a great deal, and this is why he remains part of the canon of Western philosophy and science. But Socrates, who had originally placed himself on the side of logic and universal rationality, ended up by questioning the value of this rationality. This is not how we remember Socrates, however. Another interpretation, Plato's, has become dominant.

Plato, who was Socrates' pupil, could not accept his teacher's conclusion that nobody knew anything. He continued Socrates' search for universals and became one of the authentic founders of Western philosophy and of theoretical science. Plato's ideal was mathematics, and he believed it possible to establish entire systems of theoretically objective principles, which like mathematical laws could be defended with rational argument and used to explain nature and human actions.

We have already seen that Aristotle, who was Plato's pupil, disagreed with Plato on this point. Aristotle, who may be seen as the founder of empirical science, asserted that in the study of human activity we cannot be satisfied with focusing on universals. The study of human activity, according to Aristotle, demands that one practice *phronesis*, that is, that one occupy oneself with values as a point of departure for praxis. And Aristotle considered that values and human behavior must be seen in relation to the particular. The passage from Aristotle which I have already quoted in chapter five, obtains new importance in this context. Unlike Socrates and Plato, Aristotle thus saw a decisive role for cases and context in the understanding of human behavior. "[*Phronesis*] is not concerned with universals only," Aristotle says, "it must also take cognizance of particulars, because it is concerned with conduct, and conduct has its sphere in particular circumstances."[8] We note that this way of seeing things resembles the perspectives that stand at the heart of the Dreyfus model and of Pierre Bourdieu's theory of practice as described in chapters two and four, respectively.[9]

Aristotle's thinking on this point was more or less forgotten, however, while Plato's teachings became the conventional scientific wisdom. This was especially the case after Galileo, who, two thousand years later, showed that Plato's ideas work well for the study of nature and set the natural sciences on their revolutionary trajectory.[10] A similar development has not taken place for the social sciences. As shown in chapters three and four, the social sciences have not made a breakthrough as epistemic sciences, and there is nothing which indicates that this will occur. Nevertheless, reinforced by the success of the natural sciences, Plato's thinking continues to thrive, as does the natural-science ideal in the study of humans and society. The systems of valuing great social science, from the Nobel Prize in economics on down, are largely aimed at reinforcing this ideal.

The case study is thus controversial because it stands opposed to Plato's tradition. Cases generate precisely that concrete, practical, and context-dependent knowledge which Socrates dismissed in his dialogues with Meno and Euthyphro. If we follow in the footsteps of Socrates and Plato and keep searching for the "*simile in multis*" which Socrates demanded in *Meno*, we arrive only at the hypothetico-deductive scientific model. Making deductions and discovering general principles across large samples become the key task. Going into depth with an individual case is seen as unproductive. The question, however, is where a singular focus on deduction and general principles leads. I will argue that in social science such a focus leads to a dead end.

Cases in human learning

In order to understand why Socrates' and Plato's views of the case study are problematic, we must return to the phenomenology of human learning described in chapter two, and the discussion of theory in chapters three and four. Two points can be made: first, the case study produces precisely the type of context-dependent knowledge which makes it possible to move from the lower to the higher levels in the learning process; second, in the study of human affairs, there exists only context-dependent knowledge, which thus presently rules out the possibility of epistemic theoretical construction. Let us examine these two points more closely. At the outset, however, we can assert that if they are correct, it will have radical consequences for the view of the case study in research and teaching.

The five steps in the human learning process described in chapter two emphasize the importance of gaining concrete experience as a precondition for the qualitative leap from the rule-governed analytical rationality of the first three levels to the intuitive, holistic, and synchronous performance of tacit skills of the last two levels. Dreyfus and Dreyfus's experts and Bourdieu's virtuosos operate on the basis of intimate knowledge of several thousand concrete cases in their areas of expertise. Context-dependent knowledge and experience is at the very heart of expert activity. Such knowledge and expertise also lies at the center of the case study as a research and teaching method; or to put it more generally, still: as a method of learning. The five-step process therefore emphasizes the importance of this and similar methods: it is only because of experience with cases that one can at all move from level three in the learning process to levels four and five. If people are exclusively trained in context-independent knowledge and rules, that is, the kind of knowledge which forms the basis of textbooks and computers, they will remain at the first levels of the learning process. This is the limitation of analytical rationality: it is inadequate for the best results in the exercise of a profession, as student, researcher, or practitioner.

Seeing the important association between the particular case and experience, Aristotle directly criticized Plato's favorite subjects, geometry and mathematics:

[A]lthough [people] develop ability in geometry and mathematics and become wise in such matters, they are not thought to develop prudence [*phronesis*]. The reason for this is that prudence also involves knowledge of particular facts, which become known from experience . . . We should therefore pay no less attention to the unproved assertions and opinions of experienced and older people (or of prudent people) than to demonstrations of fact; because they have an insight from their experience which enables them to see correctly.[11]

In a teaching situation, well-chosen case studies can help the student to achieve competence (level three in the learning process), while context-independent knowledge will bring the student only to the beginner's level (levels one and two). Beginner's knowledge should not be discounted: facts and rule-based knowledge are important in every area. But to make them the highest goal of learning is regressive. There is a need for both approaches. The highest levels in the learning process (four and five) are reached only via a person's own experiences as practitioner of the relevant skills. Therefore, beyond using the case method and other experiential methods for teaching, the best that teachers can do for students in professional programs is to help them achieve real practical experience; for example, via placement arrangements, internships, summer jobs, etc.

For researchers, the closeness of the case study to real-life situations and its multiple wealth of details are important in two respects. First, it is important for the development of a nuanced view of reality, including the view that human behavior cannot be meaningfully understood as simply the rule-governed acts found at the lowest levels of the learning process, and in much theory. Second, cases are important for researchers' own learning process in developing the skills needed to do good research. If researchers wish to develop their own skills to a high level, then concrete, context-dependent experience is just as central for them as to professionals learning any other specific skills. Concrete experiences can be achieved via continued proximity to the studied reality and via feedback from those under study. Great distance from the object of study and lack of feedback easily lead to a stultified learning process, which in research can lead to ritual academic blind alleys, where form becomes more important than the content. As a research method, the case study can be an effective remedy against this tendency.

The second main point in connection with the learning process is that there does not and probably cannot exist predictive theory in social science. As argued in chapter four, social science has in the final instance nothing else to offer than concrete, context-dependent knowledge, and the case study is especially well suited to produce this knowledge. In his later work, Donald Campbell arrives at a similar conclusion, explaining how his work has undergone "an extreme oscillation away from my earlier dogmatic disparagement of case studies," which was described above. In a logic that in many ways resembles that of Aristotle and the Dreyfus-model of human learning, Campbell now explains:

After all, man is, in his ordinary way, a very competent knower, and qualitative common-sense knowing is not replaced by quantitative knowing . . . This is not to say that such common-sense naturalistic observation is objective, dependable, or unbiased. But it is all that we have. It is the only route to knowledge – noisy, fallible, and biased though it be.[12]

Campbell is not the only example of a researcher who has altered his views about the value of the case study. Hans Eysenck, who originally did not regard the case study as anything other than a method of producing anecdotes, later realized that "sometimes we simply have to keep our eyes open and look carefully at individual cases – not in the hope of proving anything, but rather in the hope of learning something!"[13] Proof is hard to come by in social science because of the absence of "hard" theory, whereas learning is certainly possibly. More recently, similar views have been expressed by Charles Ragin, Howard Becker, and their colleagues in explorations of what the case study is and can be in social inquiry.[14]

As for predictive theory and universals, the study of human affairs thus stands where Euthyphro left Socrates more than two millennia ago: "Some other time, Socrates." In essence, we have only the specific cases which Meno and Euthyphro gave Socrates. The first of the five misunderstandings about the case study – that general theoretical (context-independent) knowledge is more valuable than concrete, practical (context-dependent) knowledge, can therefore be revised as follows:

Predictive theories and universals cannot be found in the study of human affairs. Concrete, context-dependent knowledge is therefore more valuable than the vain search for predictive theories and universals.

Cases as "black swans"

The view that one cannot generalize on the basis of a single case is usually considered to be devastating to the case study as a scientific method. This second misunderstanding about the case study is typical among proponents of the natural science ideal within the social sciences. Yet even researchers who are not normally associated with this ideal may be found to have this viewpoint. According to Anthony Giddens, for example,

Research which is geared primarily to hermeneutic problems may be of generalized importance in so far as it serves to elucidate the nature of agents' knowledge-ability, and thereby their reasons for action, across a wide range of action-contexts. Pieces of ethnographic research like . . . say, the traditional small-scale community research of fieldwork anthropology – are not in themselves generalizing studies. But they can easily become such if carried out in some numbers, so that judgements of their typicality can justifiably be made.[15]

It is correct that one can generalize in the ways Giddens mentions, and that often this is both appropriate and valuable. But it would be incorrect to assert that this is the only way to work, just as it is incorrect to conclude that one cannot generalize from a single case. It depends upon the case one is speaking of, and how it is chosen. This applies to the natural sciences as well as to the study of human affairs.[16]

For example, Galileo's rejection of Aristotle's law of gravity was not based upon observations "across a wide range," and the observations were not "carried out in some numbers." The rejection consisted primarily of a conceptual experiment and later on of a practical one. These experiments, with the benefit of hindsight, are self-evident. Nevertheless, Aristotle's view of gravity dominated scientific inquiry for nearly two thousand years before it was falsified.

In his experimental thinking, Galileo reasoned as follows: if two objects with the same weight are released from the same height at the same time, they will hit the ground simultaneously, having fallen at the same speed. If the two objects are then stuck together into one, this object will have double the weight and will according to the Aristotelian view therefore fall faster than the two individual objects. This conclusion operated in a counter-intuitive way for Galileo. The only way to avoid the contradiction was to eliminate weight as a determinant factor for acceleration in free fall. And that was what Galileo did.

Historians of science continue to discuss whether Galileo actually conducted the famous experiment from the leaning tower of Pisa, or whether it is simply a myth. In any event, Galileo's experimentalism did not involve a large random sample of trials of objects falling from a wide range of randomly selected heights under varying wind conditions, etc., as would be demanded by the thinking of the early Campbell and Giddens. Rather, it was a matter of a single experiment, that is, a case study, if any experiment was conducted at all.[17]

Galileo's view continued to be subjected to doubt, however, and the Aristotelian view was not finally rejected until half a century later, with the invention of the air pump. The air pump made it possible to conduct the ultimate experiment, known by every pupil, whereby a coin or a piece of lead inside a vacuum tube falls with the same speed as a feather. After this experiment, Aristotle's view could be maintained no longer. What is especially worth noting in our discussion, however, is that the matter was settled by an individual case due to the clever choice of the extremes of metal and feather. One might call it a *critical case*: for if Galileo's thesis held for these materials, it could be expected to be valid for all or a large range of materials. Random and large samples were at no time part of the picture. Most creative scientists simply do not work this way with this type of problem.

Carefully chosen experiments, cases, and experience were also critical to the development of the physics of Newton, Einstein, and Bohr. In correspondence with the Dreyfus model for human learning, Einstein thus comments upon the physical laws he had discovered, "to these elementary laws there leads no logical path, but only intuition, supported by being sympathetically in touch with experience."[18]

The case study also occupied a central place in the works of Darwin, Marx, and Freud. In social science, too, the strategic choice of case may greatly add to the generalizability of a case study. In their classic study of the "affluent worker," John Goldthorpe and his colleagues deliberately looked for a case that was as favorable as possible to the thesis that the working class, having reached middle-class status, was dissolving into a society without class identity and related conflict.[19] If the thesis could be proved false in the favorable case, then it would most likely be false for intermediate cases. Luton, a prosperous industrial center with companies known for high wages and social stability – fertile ground for middle-class identity – was selected as a case, and through intensive fieldwork the researchers discovered that even here an autonomous working-class culture prevailed, lending general credence to the thesis of the persistence of class identity. Below we will discuss more systematically this type of strategic sampling.

As regards the relationship between case studies, large samples, and discoveries, W. I. B. Beveridge observed immediately prior to the breakthrough of the quantitative revolution in the social sciences: "more discoveries have arisen from intense observation of very limited material than from statistics applied to large groups."[20] This does not mean that the case study is always appropriate or relevant as a research method, or that large random samples are without value. The choice of method should clearly depend on the problem under study and its circumstances.

Finally, it should be mentioned that formal generalization, be it on the basis of large samples or single cases, is considerably overrated as the main source of scientific progress. Economist Mark Blaug – a self-declared adherent to the hypothetico-deductive model of science – has demonstrated that while economists may pay lip service to the hypothetico-deductive model and to generalization, they rarely practice what they preach in actual research.[21] More generally, Thomas Kuhn has shown that the most important precondition for science is that researchers possess a wide range of practical skills for carrying out scientific work. Generalization is just one of these. In Germanic languages, the term "science" (German: *Wissenschaft*, Danish: *videnskab*) means literally "to create knowledge." And formal generalization is only one of many ways by which people create and accumulate knowledge. That knowledge cannot be formally generalized does not mean that it cannot enter into the collective process of knowledge accumulation in a given field or in a society. A purely descriptive, phenomenological case study without any attempt to generalize can certainly be of value in this process and has often helped cut a path toward scientific innovation. This is not to criticize attempts at formal generalization, for such attempts are essential and effective means of scientific development. It is only to emphasize the limitations which follow when formal generalization becomes the only legitimate method of scientific inquiry.

The balanced view of the role of the case study in attempting to generalize by testing hypotheses has been formulated by Harry Eckstein:

[C]omparative and case studies are alternative means to the end of testing theories, choices between which must be largely governed by arbitrary or practical, rather than logical, considerations . . . [I]t is impossible to take seriously the position that case study is suspect because problem-prone and comparative study deserving of benefit of doubt because problem-free.[22] (emphasis in original)

Eckstein here uses the term "theory" in its "hard" sense, that is, comprising explanation and prediction. This makes Eckstein's dismissal of the view that case studies cannot be used for testing theories or for generalization stronger than my own view, which is here restricted to the testing of "theory" in the "soft" sense, that is, testing propositions or hypotheses. Eckstein shows that if predictive theories exist in social and political science, then the case study could be used to test these theories just as well as other methods. More recently, John Walton has similarly observed that "case studies are likely to produce the best theory."[23] Eckstein observes, however, the striking lack of genuine theories within his own field, political science, but apparently fails to see why this is so:

Aiming at the disciplined application of theories to cases forces one to state theories more rigorously than might otherwise be done – provided that the application is truly "disciplined," i.e., designed to show that valid theory compels a particular case interpretation and rules out others. As already stated, this, unfortunately, is rare (if it occurs at all) in political study. One reason is the lack of compelling theories.[24]

Chapters three and four explain why there does not exist and probably never will appear "compelling theories" in political science and the other social sciences.

The case study is ideal for generalizing using the type of test which Karl Popper called "falsification." Falsification is one of the most rigorous tests to which a scientific proposition can be subjected: if just one observation does not fit with the proposition it is considered not valid generally and must therefore be either revised or rejected. Popper himself used the now famous example of "all swans are white," and proposed that just one observation of a single black swan would falsify this proposition and in this way have general significance and stimulate further investigations and theory-building. The case study is well suited to identifying "black" swans" because of its in-depth approach: what appears to be "white" often turns out on closer examination to be "black."

We will return to falsification below in discussing the fourth misunderstanding of case study research. For the present, however, we can correct the second misunderstanding – that one cannot generalize on the basis of a single case and that the case study cannot contribute to scientific development – so that it now reads:

One can often generalize on the basis of a single case, and the case study may be central to scientific development via generalization as supplement or alternative to other methods. But formal generalization is overvalued as a source of scientific development, whereas "the power of the good example" is underestimated.

The third misunderstanding about the case study is that the case method is claimed to be most useful for generating hypotheses in the first steps of a total research process, while hypothesis testing and theory building is best carried out by other methods later in the process. This misunderstanding derives from the previous misunderstanding that one cannot generalize on the basis of individual cases. And since this misunderstanding has been revised as above, we can correct our third misunderstanding as follows:

The case study is useful for both generating and testing of hypotheses but is not limited to these research activities alone.

Eckstein – contravening the conventional wisdom in this area – goes so far as to argue that case studies are better for testing hypotheses than for producing them. Case studies, Eckstein asserts, "are valuable at all stages of the theory-building process, but most valuable at that stage of theory-building where least value is generally attached to them: the stage at which candidate theories are tested."[25]

Cases and "casing"

The "generalizability" of case studies can be increased by strategic selection of *critical cases*. What constitutes a critical case? And how do we identify such cases?[26]

When the objective is to achieve the greatest possible amount of information on a given problem or phenomenon, a representative case or a random sample may not be the most appropriate strategy. This is because the typical or average case is often not the richest in information. Atypical or extreme cases often reveal more information because they activate more actors and more basic mechanisms in the situation studied. In addition, from both an understanding-oriented and an action-oriented perspective, it is often more important to clarify the deeper causes behind a given problem and its consequences than to describe the symptoms of the problem and how frequently they occur. Random samples emphasizing representativeness will seldom be able to produce this kind of insight; it is more appropriate to select a few cases chosen for their validity.[27]

Table 6.1 summarizes various forms of sampling. The *extreme cases* can be well suited for getting a point across in an especially dramatic way, which often occurs for well-known case studies such as Freud's "Wolf-Man" and Foucault's "Panopticon." In contrast, a *critical case* can be defined as having strategic importance in relation to the general problem. For example, an occupational medicine clinic wanted to investigate whether people working with organic solvents suffered brain damage. Instead of choosing a representative sample among all those enterprises in the clinic's area who used organic solvents, the clinic strategically located a single workplace where all safety regulations on cleanliness, air quality, etc., had been fulfilled. This model enterprise became a critical case: if brain damage related to organic solvents could be found at this particular facility, then it was likely that the same problem would exist at other enterprises which were less careful with safety regulations for organic solvents.[28] Via this type of strategic choice, one can save both time and money in researching a given problem.

Another example of critical case selection is the above-mentioned strategic selection of lead and feather for the test of whether different objects fall with equal velocity. The selection of materials provided the possibility of formulating a generalization characteristic of critical cases, a generalization of the sort "if it is valid for this case, it is valid for all (or many) cases." In its negative form, the generalization would be "if it is not valid for this case, then it is not valid for any (or only few) cases."

How does one identify critical cases? This question is more difficult to answer than the question of what constitutes a critical case. Locating a critical case requires experience, and no universal methodological principles exist by which one can with certainty identify a critical case. The only general advice that can be given is that when looking for critical cases, it is a good idea to look for either "most likely" or "least likely" cases, that is, cases which are likely either clearly to confirm or irrefutably to falsify propositions and hypotheses.

Table 6.1. *Strategies for the selection of samples and cases*

Type of selection	Purpose
A. Random selection	To avoid systematic biases in the sample. The sample's size is decisive for generalization.
1. Random sample	To achieve a representative sample which allows for generalization for the entire population.
2. Stratified sample	To generalize for specially selected subgroups within the population.
B. Information-oriented selection	To maximize the utility of information from small samples and single cases. Cases are selected on the basis of expectations about their information content.
1. Extreme/deviant cases	To obtain information on unusual cases, which can be especially problematic or especially good in a more closely defined sense.
2. Maximum variation cases	To obtain information about the significance of various circumstances for case process and outcome; e.g., three to four cases which are very different on one dimension: size, form of organization, location, budget, etc.
3. Critical cases	To achieve information which permits logical deductions of the type, "if this is (not) valid for this case, then it applies to all (no) cases."
4. Paradigmatic cases	To develop a metaphor or establish a school for the domain which the case concerns.

A classic example of a "least likely" case is Robert Michels's study of oligarchy in organizations.[29] By choosing a horizontally structured grassroots organization with strong democratic ideals – that is, a type of organization with an especially low probability of being oligarchical – Michels could test the universality of the oligarchy thesis; that is, "if this organization is oligarchic, so are most others." A corresponding classic example of a "most likely" case is W. F. Whyte's study of a Boston slum neighborhood, which according to existing theory should have exhibited social disorganization, but in fact showed quite the opposite.[30]

Cases of the "most likely" type are especially well suited to falsification of propositions, while "least likely" cases are most appropriate to tests of verification. It should be remarked that a most likely case for one proposition is the least likely for its negation. For example, Whyte's slum neighborhood could be seen as a least likely case for a hypothesis concerning the universality of social organization. Hence, the identification of a case as most or least likely is linked to the design of the study, as well as to the specific properties of the actual case.

A final strategy for the selection of cases is choice of the *paradigmatic case*. Thomas Kuhn has shown that the basic skills, or background practices, of natural scientists are organized in terms of "exemplars" the role of which can be studied by historians of science. Similarly, scholars like Clifford Geertz and Michel Foucault have often organized their research around specific cultural paradigms: a paradigm for Geertz lay, for instance, in the "deep play" of the Balinese cockfight, while for Foucault, European prisons and the "Panopticon" are examples. Both instances are examples of paradigmatic cases, that is, cases that highlight more general characteristics of the societies in question. Kuhn has shown that scientific paradigms cannot be expressed as rules or theories. There exists no predictive theory for how predictive theory comes about. A scientific activity is acknowledged or rejected as good science by how close it is to one or more exemplars; that is, practical prototypes of good scientific work. A paradigmatic case of how scientists do science is precisely such a prototype. It operates as a metaphor and may function as a focal point for the founding of schools of thought.

As with the critical case, we may ask, "How does one identify a paradigmatic case?" How does one determine whether a given case has metaphorical and prototypical value? These questions are even more difficult to answer than for the critical case, precisely because the paradigmatic case transcends any sort of rule-based criteria. No standard exists for the paradigmatic case because it sets the standard. Hubert and Stuart Dreyfus see paradigmatic cases and case studies as central to human learning.[31] In an interview with Hubert Dreyfus, I therefore asked what constitutes a paradigmatic case and how it can be identified. Dreyfus replied:

Heidegger says, you recognize a paradigm case because it shines, but I'm afraid that is not much help. You just have to be intuitive. We all can tell what is a better or worse case – of a Cézanne painting, for instance. But I can't think there could be any rules for deciding what makes Cézanne a paradigmatic modern painter . . . [I]t is a big problem in a democratic society where people are supposed to justify what their intuitions are. In fact, nobody really can justify what their intuition is. So you have to make up reasons, but it won't be the real reasons.[32]

That we have to "make up reasons" to justify intuitive choices is not necessarily a problem. Such justification need not be illegitimate rationalization since it can be the *ex-post* test of whether individual intuitive reasons are also generally valid and collectively acceptable. This is one reason why it is usually insufficient to justify an application for research funds by stating that one's intuition says that a particular piece of research should be carried out. A research council ideally operates as society's test of whether the researcher can provide collectively acceptable reasons for the researcher's intuitive choice, even though intuition may be the real reason why the researcher wants to execute the project.

It is not possible consistently, or even frequently, to determine in advance whether or not a given case is paradigmatic. Besides the strategic choice of case, the execution of the case study will certainly play a role, as will the reaction to the study by the research community, the group studied and, possibly, a broader public. The value of the case study will depend on the validity claims which researchers can place on their study, and the status these claims obtain in dialogue with other validity claims in the discourse to which the study is a contribution, both in the scientific discipline concerned and, possibly, in the public sphere. Like other good craftsmen, all that researchers can do is use their experience and intuition to assess whether they believe a given case is interesting in a paradigmatic context, and whether they can provide collectively acceptable reasons for the choice of case.

Finally, concerning considerations of strategy in the choice of cases, it should be mentioned that the various strategies of selection are not necessarily mutually exclusive. For example, a case can be simultaneously extreme, critical, and paradigmatic. The interpretation of such a case can provide a unique wealth of information, because one obtains various perspectives and conclusions on the case according to whether it is viewed and interpreted as one or another type of case.

Bias toward verification or falsification?

The fourth of the five misunderstandings about the case study is that the method maintains a bias toward verification, understood as a tendency to confirm the researcher's preconceived notions, so that the study therefore becomes of doubtful scientific value. Jared Diamond, for example, holds this view. He observes that the case study suffers from what he calls a "crippling drawback," because it does not apply "scientific methods," by which Diamond understands methods useful for "curbing one's tendencies to stamp one's pre-existing interpretations on data as they accumulate."[33]

Francis Bacon saw this bias toward verification, not simply as a phenomenon related to the case study in particular, but as a fundamental human characteristic:

The human understanding from its peculiar nature, easily supposes a greater degree of order and equality in things than it really finds. When any proposition has been laid down, the human understanding forces everything else to add fresh support and confirmation. It is the peculiar and perpetual error of the human understanding to be more moved and excited by affirmatives than negatives.[34]

Bacon certainly touches upon a fundamental problem here, a problem which all researchers must deal with in some way. Charles Darwin, in his autobiography, describes the method he developed in order to avoid the bias toward verification:

I had . . . during many years followed a golden rule, namely, that whenever a published fact, a new observation or thought came across me, which was opposed to my general results, to make a memorandum of it without fail and at once; for I had found by experience that such facts and thoughts were far more apt to escape from the memory than favorable ones. Owing to this habit, very few objections were raised against my views, which I had not at least noticed and attempted to answer.[35]

The bias toward verification is general, but the alleged deficiency of the case study and other qualitative methods is that they ostensibly allow more room for the researcher's subjective and arbitrary judgment than other methods: they are often seen as less rigorous than are quantitative, hypothetico-deductive methods. Even if such criticism is useful, because it sensitizes us to an important issue, experienced case researchers cannot help but see the critique as demonstrating a lack of knowledge of what is involved in case study research. Donald Campbell and others have shown that the critique is fallacious, because the case study has its own rigor, different to be sure, but no less strict than the rigor of quantitative methods. The advantage of the case study is that it can "close in" on real-life situations and test views directly in relation to phenomena as they unfold in practice. According to Campbell, Charles Ragin, Clifford Geertz, Michel Wieviorka, and others, researchers who have conducted intensive, in-depth case studies typically report that their preconceived views, assumptions, concepts and hypotheses were wrong and that the case material has forced them to revise their hypotheses on essential points. This is my own experience as well.[36] Ragin calls this a "special feature of small-N research," and goes on to explain that criticizing single-case studies for being inferior to multiple-case studies is misguided, since even single-case studies "are multiple in most research efforts because ideas and evidence may be linked in many different ways."[37]

Geertz says about the fieldwork involved in most in-depth case studies that "The Field" itself is a "powerful disciplinary force: assertive, demanding, even coercive." Like any such force, it can be underestimated, but it cannot be evaded. "It is too insistent for that," says Geertz.[38] That

we are speaking of a general phenomenon can be seen by simply examining case studies.[39] Campbell discusses the causes of this phenomenon in
the following passage:

> In a case study done by an alert social scientist who has thorough local acquaint-
> ance, the theory he uses to explain the focal difference also generates prediction or
> expectations on dozens of other aspects of the culture, and he does not retain the
> theory unless most of these are also confirmed . . . Experiences of social scientists
> confirm this. Even in a single qualitative case study, the conscientious social
> scientist often finds no explanation that seems satisfactory. Such an outcome
> would be impossible if the caricature of the single case study as presented . . . were
> correct – there would instead be a surfeit of subjectively compelling explana-
> tions.[40]

According to the experiences cited above, it is falsification and not
verification, which characterizes the case study. Moreover, the question
of subjectivism and bias toward verification applies to all methods, not
just to the case study and other qualitative methods. For example, the
element of arbitrary subjectivism will be significant in the choice of
categories and variables for a quantitative or structural investigation; e.g.,
a structured questionnaire to be used across a large sample of cases. And
the probability is high (1) that this subjectivism survives without being
thoroughly corrected during the study and (2) that it may affect the
results, quite simply because the quantitative/structural researcher does
not get as close to those under study as does the case study researcher.
According to Ragin:

> this feature explains why small-N qualitative research is most often at the fore-
> front of theoretical development. When N's are large, there are few opportunities
> for revising a casing [that is, the delimitation of a case]. At the start of the analysis,
> cases are decomposed into variables, and almost the entire dialogue of ideas and
> evidence occurs through variables. One implication of this discussion is that to the
> extent that large-N research can be sensitized to the diversity and potential
> heterogeneity of the cases included in an analysis, large-N research may play a
> more important part in the advancement of social science theory.[41]

Here, too, this difference between large samples and single cases can be
understood in terms of the model for human learning. If one thus assumes that the goal of the researcher's work is to understand and learn
about the phenomena being studied, then research is simply a form of
learning. If one assumes that research, like other learning processes, can
be described by the model for human learning, it then becomes clear that
the most advanced form of understanding is achieved when researchers
place themselves within the context being studied. Only in this way can
researchers understand the viewpoints and the behavior which characterize social actors. Relevant to this point, Anthony Giddens states that
valid descriptions of social activities presume that researchers possess

those skills necessary to participate in the activities described:

> I have accepted that it is right to say that the condition of generating descriptions of social activity is being able in principle to participate in it. It involves "mutual knowledge," shared by observer and participants whose action constitutes and reconstitutes the social world.[42]

From this point of view, the proximity to reality which the case study entails and the learning process which it generates for the researcher will often constitute a prerequisite for advanced understanding. In this context, one begins to understand Beveridge's conclusion that there are more discoveries stemming from the type of intense observation made possible by the case study than from statistics applied to large groups. With the point of departure in the learning process, we understand why the researcher who conducts a case study often ends up by casting off preconceived notions and theories. Such activity is quite simply a central element in learning and in the achievement of new insight. More simple forms of understanding must yield to more complex ones as one moves from novice to expert.

On this basis, the fourth misunderstanding – that the case study should contain a bias toward verification, understood as a tendency to confirm the researcher's preconceived ideas – is revised as follows:

> *The case study contains no greater bias toward verification of the researcher's preconceived notions than other methods of inquiry. On the contrary, experience indicates that the case study contains a greater bias toward falsification of preconceived notions than toward verification.*

The irreducible quality of good case narratives

Case studies often contain a substantial element of narrative. Good narratives typically approach the complexities and contradictions of real life. Accordingly, such narratives may be difficult or impossible to summarize in neat scientific formulae, general propositions, and theories.[43] This tends to be seen as a drawback by critics of the case study. To the researcher practicing *phronesis*, however, a particularly "thick" and hard-to-summarize narrative is not necessarily a problem. Rather, it may be a sign that the study has uncovered a particularly rich problematic. The question, therefore, is whether the summarizing and generalization, which the critics see as an ideal, is always desirable. Nietzsche is clear in his answer to this question. "Above all," he says about doing science, "one should not wish to divest existence of its *rich ambiguity*" (emphasis in original).[44]

Let us again examine the case study in relation to the model for human learning. Knowledge at the beginner's level consists precisely in the reduced formulas which characterize theories, while true expertise is based on intimate experience with thousands of individual cases and on the ability to discriminate between situations, with all their nuances of difference, without distilling them into formulas or standard cases. The problem is analogous to the inability of heuristic, computer-based expert systems to approach the level of virtuoso human experts, even when the systems are compared with the experts who have conceived the rules upon which these systems operate (see chapter two). This is because the experts do not use rules but operate on the basis of detailed case-experience. This is *real* expertise. The rules for expert systems are formulated only because the systems require it; rules are characteristic of expert *systems*, but not of real human *experts*.

In the same way, one might say that the rule formulation which takes place when researchers summarize their work into theories is characteristic of the culture of research, of researchers, and of theoretical activity, but such rules are not necessarily part of the studied reality constituted by what Bourdieu has called "virtuoso social actors."[45] Something essential may be lost by this summarizing – the possibility to understand virtuoso social acting, which, as Bourdieu has shown, cannot be distilled into theoretical formulae – and it is precisely their fear of losing this "something" which makes case researchers cautious about summarizing their studies. Case researchers thus tend to be skeptical about erasing phenomenological detail in favor of conceptual closure.

Ludwig Wittgenstein shared this skepticism in doing philosophy. He used the following metaphor in describing his use of the case study approach in philosophy:

In teaching you philosophy I'm like a guide showing you how to find your way round London. I have to take you through the city from north to south, from east to west, from Euston to the embankment and from Piccadilly to the Marble Arch. After I have taken you many journeys through the city, in all sorts of directions, we shall have passed through any given street a number of times – each time traversing the street as part of a different journey. At the end of this you will know London; you will be able to find your way about like a born Londoner. Of course, a good guide will take you through the more important streets more often than he takes you down side streets; a bad guide will do the opposite. In philosophy I'm a rather bad guide.[46]

This approach implies exploring phenomena firsthand instead of reading maps of them. Actual practices are studied before their rules, and one is not satisfied by learning only about those parts of practices that are open to public scrutiny; what Erving Goffman calls the "backstage" of social phenomena must be investigated, too, like the side streets which Wittgenstein talks about.[47] In order to stay close to the complexities and contradictions of existence, case researchers practicing *phronesis* demur from the role of omniscient narrator and summarizer in favor of gradually allowing the case narrative to unfold from the diverse, complex, and sometimes conflicting stories that people, documents, and other evidence tell them. This approach leaves ample scope for readers to make different interpretations and to draw diverse conclusions. Thus, in addition to the voice of case actors and case narrators, there is space for the voice of the reader in deciding the meaning of a given case and in answering that categorical question of any case study: "What is this case a case of?" Case researchers practicing *phronesis* encourage readers to occupy that space.

For readers who stick from beginning to end with the minutiae of a case narrative told in this manner the payback is likely to be an awareness of the issues under study that cannot be obtained from "maps," that is, summaries, concepts, or theoretical formulas. Achieving such awareness is central to developing judgment and expertise in social and political affairs, and in doing research into such affairs. With respect to intervention in social and political affairs, Andrew Abbott has rightly observed that a social science expressed in terms of typical case narratives would provide "far better access for policy intervention than the present social science of variables."[48] The sociolinguist William Labov writes that when a good narrative is over "it should be unthinkable for a bystander to say, 'So what?'"[49] Every good narrator is continually warding off this question. A narrative that lacks a moral that can be independently and briefly stated, is not necessarily pointless. And a narrative is not successful just because it allows a brief moral. A successful narrative does not allow the question to be raised at all. The narrative has already supplied the answer before the question is asked. The narrative itself is the answer.[50]

A reformulation of the fifth misunderstanding, which states that it is often difficult to summarize specific case studies in general propositions and theories, thus reads as follows:

It is correct that summarizing case studies is often difficult, especially as concerns process. It is less correct as regards outcomes. The problems in summarizing case studies, however, are due more often to the properties of the reality studied than to the case study as a research method. Often it is not desirable to summarize and generalize case studies. Good studies should be read in their entirety.

It must again be emphasized that despite the difficulty or undesirability in summarizing case studies, the case study method in general can certainly contribute to the cumulative development of knowledge; for example, in using the principles to test propositions described above under the second and third misunderstandings.

In summarizing this chapter, let me reiterate that the evaluation of the case study as a research method and the revision of the five misunder-standings described above should not be interpreted as a rejection of research which focuses on large random samples or entire populations; for example, questionnaire surveys. This type of research is essential for the development of social science; for example, in understanding the degree to which certain phenomena are present in a given group or how they vary across cases. The advantage of large samples is breadth, while their problem is one of depth. For the case study, the situation is the reverse. Both approaches are necessary for a sound development of social science.

This being said, it should nevertheless be added that the balance between case studies and large samples is currently biased in favor of the latter in social science, so biased that it puts case studies at a disadvantage within most disciplines. In this connection, it is worth repeating the insight that a discipline without a large number of thoroughly executed case studies is a discipline without systematic production of exemplars, and that a discipline without exemplars is an ineffective one. In social science, especially in those branches which find themselves to be weak, more good case studies could help remedy this situation.

7 The significance of conflict and power to social science

> The fundamental concept in social science is Power, in the same sense in which Energy is the fundamental concept in physics.
>
> *Bertrand Russell*

This chapter expands on Richard Bernstein's observation that no conception of *phronesis* can be adequate today unless it confronts the analysis of power. In addition it considers the question of why power is important to contemporary social science. The chapter achieves this by analyzing how Michel Foucault and Jürgen Habermas each deal with issues of power in their thinking. In the following chapter, we then tease out the implications of Foucault's power analytics for a *phronesis*–power approach to the study of social and political phenomena.

The works of Habermas and Foucault highlight an essential tension in thinking about power. This is the tension between consensus and conflict. With a point of departure in Kant, Habermas is the philosopher of *Moralität* (morality) based on consensus. Foucault, following Nietzsche, is the philosopher of *wirkliche Historie* (real history) told in terms of conflict and power. This chapter presents a comparative analysis of the central ideas of Habermas and Foucault as they pertain to the issue of power. We will ask whether solutions to problems of power are best understood in terms of consensus, or whether conflict is a more suitable frame of reference. To answer this question we need to understand the ideas behind the "discourse ethics" of Habermas and the "power analytics" and ethics of Foucault, contrasting the two and evaluating their merit for people interested in understanding power and its role in social and political change.

It should be emphasized at the outset that the juxtaposition of Habermas and Foucault is not an attempt to combine two intellectual traditions artificially. Habermas and Foucault are so profoundly different that it would be futile to envision any sort of theoretical or metatheoretical perspective within which these differences could be integrated into a common framework. Yet Habermas and Foucault are not simply opposites of each other; they are each other's shadows in their efforts to both understand and limit rationalization and the misuse of power. It is just such limitation, which both thinkers see as among the most important tasks of our time.

To be absolutely modern

"With Kant, the modern age is inaugurated," says Habermas, who cites the importance of Kant's attempt to develop a universal rational foundation for democratic institutions.[1] Habermas agrees with Kant as to the need to develop such a foundation for democracy and its institutions, but he points out that Kant failed to achieve his goal. According to Habermas, this was because Kant's thinking was based upon a subject-centered rationality.[2] Moreover, Habermas points out that the later philosophers, from Hegel and Marx to contemporary thinkers, have also been unable to develop the much sought-after rational and universal foundation for such social institutions. According to Habermas, this is because they have all worked within the tradition of "the philosophy of the subject."[3]

Most contemporary philosophers and social scientists have accepted the consequences of more than two millennia of failed attempts to establish a universal constitution of philosophy, social science, and social organization, having concluded that such a foundation does not seem feasible. Not Habermas, however, who thinks that his own work can provide this constitution, and that the consequences of abandoning it are unacceptable. Without a universally constituted philosophy, science, and democracy, says Habermas, the result would be contextualism, relativism, and nihilism; all of which Habermas sees as dangerous.

According to Habermas, the problem with Kant and with subsequent thinkers on modernity is not that they were mistaken in their goal of constituting society rationally, but that they had the wrong ideas of how to achieve the goal. For Habermas, the path toward a rational constitution and the establishment of a bulwark against power and relativism is a reorientation from earlier philosophers' focus on subjectivity, within which Habermas classifies both Hegel's "world spirit" and Marx's "working class," to a focus on intersubjectivity. And Habermas's own work, particularly his theory of communicative action and discourse ethics (*Diskursetik*), is located in the intersubjective approach to the problematic of modernity.[4]

The goal of Habermas's theory of communicative action is that of "clarifying the presuppositions of the rationality of processes of reaching understanding, which may be presumed to be universal because they are unavoidable."[5] In his *Philosophical Discourse of Modernity*, Habermas develops his intersubjective approach to power and modernity using the concept of "communicative rationality."[6]

This communicative rationality recalls older ideas of logos, inasmuch as it brings along with it the connotations of a noncoercively unifying, consensus-building force of a discourse in which the participants overcome their at first subjectively biased views in favor of a rationally motivated agreement.[7]

Although Habermas sees communicative rationality as being threatened by actual modern society, he nevertheless argues that the core of communicative rationality, "the unconstrained, unifying, consensus-bringing force of argumentative speech," is a "central experience" in the life of a human being.[8] According to Habermas, this central experience is inherent in human social life: "Communicative reason is directly implicated in social life processes insofar as acts of mutual understanding take on the role of a mechanism for coordinating action."[9] Habermas leaves no doubt that by "inherent" he means *universally* inherent. The universality derives from the fact that for Habermas human social life is based upon processes for establishing reciprocal understanding. These processes are assumed to be "universal because they are unavoidable."[10] In an earlier formulation, Habermas states this view even more clearly:

In action oriented to reaching understanding, validity claims are "always already" implicitly raised. These universal claims . . . are set in the general structures of possible communication. In these validity claims communication theory can locate a gentle, but obstinate, a never silent although seldom redeemed claim to reason, a claim that must be recognized de facto whenever and wherever there is to be consensual action.[11]

The consequence, for Habermas, is that human beings are defined as democratic beings, as *homo democraticus*.

As for the validity claims, Habermas explains that validity is defined as consensus without force: "a contested norm cannot meet with the consent of the participants in a practical discourse unless . . . all affected can *freely* [*zwanglos*] accept the consequences and the side effects that the *general* observance of a controversial norm can be expected to have for the satisfaction of the interests of *each individual*" (italics in original).[12] This principle of validity, Habermas calls "(U)," the "universalization principle" of discourse ethics.[13] Similarly, in a key passage on truth, Habermas states: "Argumentation insures that all concerned in principle take part, freely and equally, in a cooperative search for truth, where nothing coerces anyone except the force of the better argument."[14] The only form of power which is active in the ideal speech situation and in communicative rationality is thus this "force of the better argument," which consequently obtains a critical place in Habermas's work.

Validity and truth are ensured where the participants in a given discourse respect five key processual requirements of discourse ethics:

(1) no party affected by what is being discussed should be excluded from the discourse (the requirement of generality);
(2) all participants should have equal possibility to present and criticize validity claims in the process of discourse (autonomy);
(3) participants must be willing and able to empathize with each other's validity claims (ideal role taking);
(4) existing power differences between participants must be neutralized such that these differences have no effect on the creation of consensus (power neutrality); and
(5) participants must openly explain their goals and intentions and in this connection desist from strategic action (transparence).[15]

Finally, given the implications of the first five requirements, we could add a sixth: unlimited time.

In a society following this model, power and citizenship would be defined in terms of taking part in public debate. Participation is *discursive* participation. And participation is *detached* participation, inasmuch as communicative rationality requires ideal role taking, power neutrality, etc. Habermas's model, that is, discourse ethics, should not be confused with contingent types of bargaining or with models of strategically negotiated compromises among conflicting particular interests. What is missing in strategic pursuits and rational-choice models is the recourse to ultimate normative justification that Habermas claims to give us.[16] Empirically, Habermas sees the new social movements as agents of communicative rationality and of change in the public sphere.

Habermas's definitions of discourse ethics, communicative rationality, and power make it clear that we are talking about procedural as opposed to substantive rationality: "Discourse ethics does not set up substantive orientations. Instead it establishes a *procedure* based on presuppositions and designed to guarantee the impartiality of the process of judging."[17] Habermas is a universalistic, "top-down" moralist as concerns process: the rules for correct process are normatively given in advance, in the form of the requirements for the ideal speech situation. Conversely, as regards content, Habermas is a "bottom-up" situationalist: what is right and true in a given communicative process is determined solely by the participants in that process.

As a consequence, the study of processes for dealing with power by establishing consensus, and the validity claims on which the processes are built, stand at the center of Habermas's work. Habermas's view of power and democratic process is directly linked to judicial institutionalization.

"I wish to conceive of the democratic procedure as the legal institutional-ization of those forms of communication necessary for rational political will formation," Habermas says.[18] On the relationship between law and power in this process, Habermas states that "*authorization of power by law* and *the sanctioning of law by power* must both occur *uno acto*" (emphasis in original).[19] Habermas thus makes it clear that he operates within a per-spective of law and sovereignty in his understanding of power. As we will see below, this is a perspective, which contrasts with Foucault, who finds this conception of power "by no means adequate."[20] Foucault says about his own "analytics of power" that it "can be constituted only if it frees itself completely from [this] representation of power that I would term . . . 'juridico-discursive' . . . a certain image of power-law, of power-sover-eignty."[21] It is in this connection that Foucault made his famous argu-ment to "cut off the head of the king" in social and political analysis and replace it by a decentered understanding of power.[22] For Foucault, Habermas still has the head of the king very much on, in the sense that sovereignty is a prerequisite for the regulation of power by law.

Habermas is substantially more optimistic and uncritical about mo-dernity than both Max Weber and members of the Frankfurt School, such as Max Horkheimer and Theodor Adorno. Habermas's main "methods of progress," for instance for curbing power, are the writing of constitutions and institutional and legal development, which thereby become central elements in, and endpoints for, Habermas's project. It is hard to overemphasize the importance of this point. Habermas quite simply sees constitutions as the main device for uniting citizens and regulating power in a pluralist society:

What unites the citizens of a society shaped by social, cultural, and philosophical [*weltanschaulich*] pluralism are first of all the abstract principles of an artificial republican order, created through the medium of law.[23]

If Habermas is right about the importance of constitution writing and institutional reforms, the prospects look good indeed for regulating power and changing government in a more democratic direction by means of discourse ethics and the theory of communicative rationality. The prob-lem, however, as pointed out by Robert Putnam, is that "[t]wo centuries of constitution-writing around the world warn us . . . that designers of new institutions are often writing on water . . . That institutional reforms alter behavior is an hypothesis, not an axiom."[24] The problem with Habermas is that he has the axiom and the hypothesis reversed: he takes for granted that which should be subjected to empirical and historical test.

The basic weakness of Habermas's project is its lack of agreement between ideal and reality, between intentions and their implementation.

This incongruity pervades both the most general as well as the most concrete phenomena of modernity, and it is rooted in an insufficient conception of power. Habermas himself observes that discourse cannot by itself ensure that the conditions for discourse ethics and democracy are met.[25] But discourse about discourse ethics is all Habermas has to offer. This is the fundamental political dilemma in Habermas's thinking: he describes to us the utopia of communicative rationality but not how to get closer to it. Habermas himself mentions lack of "crucial institutions," lack of "crucial socialization" and "poverty, abuse, and degradation" as barriers to discursive decision-making.[26] But he has little to say about the relations of power that create these barriers and how power may be changed in order to begin the kinds of institutional and educational change, improvements in welfare, and enforcement of basic human rights that could help lower the barriers. In short, Habermas lacks the kind of concrete understanding of relations of power, which is needed for political change.

With his characteristically comprehensive approach, Habermas lets us know that his theory of communicative action opens him to criticism as an idealist: "It is not so simple to counter the suspicion that with the concept of action oriented to validity claims, the idealism of a pure, nonsituated reason slips in again."[27] I will argue here that not only is it difficult to counter this suspicion, it is impossible. And this impossibility constitutes a fundamental problem in Habermas's work.

"There is a point in every philosophy," writes Nietzsche, "when the philosopher's conviction appears on the stage."[28] For Habermas that point is the foundation of his ideal speech situation and universal validity claims upon a Kirkegaardian "leap of faith."[29] Habermas, as mentioned, states that consensus seeking and freedom from domination are universally inherent as forces in human conversation, and he emphasizes these particular aspects. Other important philosophers and social thinkers have tended to emphasize the exact opposite. Machiavelli, whom Bernard Crick and others have called a "most worthy humanist" and "distinctly modern," and whom, like Habermas, is concerned with "the business of good government,"[30] states: "One can make this generalization about men: they are ungrateful, fickle, liars, and deceivers."[31] Less radically, but still in contrast to Habermas, are statements by Nietzsche, Foucault, Derrida, and many others that communication is at all times already penetrated by power. "Power is always present," says Foucault.[32] It is therefore meaningless, according to these thinkers, to operate with a concept of communication in which power is absent. This holds for empirical studies, but also for normative ones, and no degree of Habermasian "reconstruction" is likely to change this state of affairs.

For students of power, communication is more typically characterized by rhetoric and maintenance of interests than by freedom from domination and consensus seeking. In rhetoric, "validity" is established via the mode of communication – for example, eloquence, hidden control, rationalization, charisma, and using dependency relations between participants – rather than through rational arguments concerning the matter at hand. Seen from this perspective Habermas seems overly naive and idealistic when he contrasts "successful" with "distorted" utterance in human conversation, because success in rhetoric is associated precisely with distortion.[33]

Whether the communicative or the rhetorical position is "correct" is not important here. What is decisive, rather, is that a nonidealistic point of departure must take account of the fact that both positions are possible, and even simultaneously possible. In an empirical–scientific context, which Habermas elsewhere says should be the touchstone of philosophy, the question of communicative rationality versus rhetoric must therefore remain open. The question must be settled by concrete examination of the case at hand. The researcher must ask how communication takes place, and how power operates. Is communication characterized by consensus seeking and absence of power? Or is communication the exercise of power and rhetoric? How do consensus seeking and rhetoric, freedom from domination and the exercise of power, eventually come together in individual acts of communication?

The basic question being raised here is whether one can meaningfully distinguish rationality and power from each other in communication, as does Habermas. To assume an answer to this question *a priori* is just as invalid as presuming that one can ultimately answer the biblical question of whether humans are basically good or basically evil.[34] And to assume either position *ex ante*, to universalize it, and build a theory upon it, as Habermas does, makes for problematic philosophy and speculative social science.[35] This is one reason we have to be cautious when using the theory of communicative rationality to understand and act in relation to power and democracy.

Constituting rationality and democracy on a leap of faith is hardly sustainable. Habermas here seems to forget his own axiom that philosophical questions ought to be subject to empirical verification. And it is precisely in this sense that Habermas must be seen as utopian. Richard Rorty does not use these exact words, but it is nevertheless the same issues which impel Rorty to criticize communicative rationality for having religious status in Habermas's thinking, and for being "a healing and unifying power which will do the work once done by God."[36] As Rorty says, "We no longer need [that]."[37]

There may be a substantial element of truth in the benefits of constitution writing à la Habermas. And Habermas's home country, Germany, clearly needed new constitutional principles after World War II, a fact that seems to have been formative for Habermas's thinking.[38] But Habermas relies on something as weak as *Verfassungspatriotismus* (constitutional patriotism) as the main means to have constitutional principles take root and gain practical importance in a society:

[C]onstitutional principles can only take root in the hearts of citizens once they have had good experiences with democratic institutions and have accustomed themselves to conditions of political freedom. In so doing, they also learn, within the prevailing national context, to comprehend the republic and its Constitution as an attainment. Without a historical, consciously formed vision of this kind, patriotic ties deriving from and relating to the Constitution cannot come about. For such ties are connected, for example, with pride in a successful civil rights movement.[39]

Studies of struggles over the actual writing, implementation, and modification of real constitutions in real societies prove this account – with its emphasis on conflict-free phenomena like "good experiences," "vision," and "pride" – to be far from sufficient.[40] Something infinitely more complex is at work in real-life situations, perhaps because humans are more complex than Habermas's *homo democraticus*. People know how to be, at the same time, tribal and democratic, dissidents and patriots, experts at judging how far a democratic constitution can be bent and used in nondemocratic ways for personal and group advantage.

Machiavelli is a more enlightened guide to social and political change than Habermas when it comes to constitution writing. In *The Discourses* Machiavelli recapitulates that "[a]ll writers on politics have pointed out . . . that in constituting and legislating for a commonwealth it must be taken for granted that all men are wicked and that they will always give vent to the malignity that is in their minds when opportunity offers."[41] If Machiavelli and other writers are right in this "worst-case" thinking, then we might clearly end up in trouble if we rely on Habermas's discourse ethics as a basis for regulating power and organizing our society, as Habermas advocates we do, since discourse ethics contains no checks and balances – other than an abstract appeal to reason – to control the wickedness which Machiavelli talks about. Such wickedness is assumed away by Habermas's leap of faith for the good. History teaches us, however, that assuming evil away may give free rein to evil. This is why Nietzsche emphatically says "perhaps there has never before been a more dangerous ideology . . . than this will to good."[42] Thus, the lesson to be learnt from Machiavelli and Nietzsche is not so much that all moralism is hypocrisy. The lesson is that the first step to becoming moral is realizing we are not. The next step is establishing checks and balances that adequately reflect this.

Furthermore, by determining validity, truth, justice, etc., as an outcome of "the better argument," Habermas simply moves the problems of determination from the former concepts to the latter. As Bernstein correctly points out, "the better argument," and with it communicative rationality, is an empirically empty concept: "Abstractly, there is something enormously attractive about Habermas's appeal to the 'force of the better argument' until we ask ourselves what this means and presupposes."[43] The problem here is that in nontrivial situations there are few clear criteria for determining what is considered an argument, how good it is, and how different arguments are to be evaluated against each other. This does not mean that we should not attempt to identify arguments and evaluate them. Yet as Bernstein says, any society must have some procedures for dealing with conflicts that cannot be resolved by argumentation, "even when all parties are committed to rational argumentation."[44] In real democracies – as opposed to Habermas's ideal types – it is precisely these kinds of conflicts, which are of interest, both empirically and normatively.

Agnes Heller, Albrecht Wellmer, Herman Lübbe, and Niklas Luhmann have expressed similar criticisms of discourse ethics. In commenting upon Habermas's universalization principle (U) mentioned earlier, Heller simply rejects the value of Habermas's approach: "Put bluntly, if we look to moral philosophy for guidance in our actions here and now, we cannot obtain any positive guidance from the Habermasian reformulation of the categorical imperative."[45] Wellmer is equally harsh when he writes that adhering to the universalization principle in moral judgment "would make justified moral judgment an impossibility [einem Ding der Unmöglichkeit]."[46] At the level of institutional analysis, Lübbe and Luhmann comment that upholding any concrete institutions to the demands of discourse ethics would paralyze institutional life to the point of breakdown.[47]

Even Habermas's most sympathetic interpreters, such as Seyla Benhabib and Alessandro Ferrara, have begun to criticize Habermas for his formalism, idealism, and insensitivity to context. They are trying to provide a corrective to Habermas's thinking on precisely these weak points and to introduce an element of phronesis into critical theory.[48] I would argue that critical theory and Habermas's work also need to bring in the element of power. In his Between Facts and Norms and other recent works Habermas has attempted to do just that, and he has, at the same time, developed a deeper analysis of democracy and civil society.[49] Despite these efforts, however, Habermas's approach remains as strongly procedural and normative as ever, paying scant attention to the preconditions of actual discourse, to substantive ethical values, and to the problem of how communicative rationality gets a foothold in society in the face of the massive noncommunicative forces whose existence Habermas duly recognizes. Habermas also continues to disregard the particular problems relating to identity and cultural divisions and the nondiscursive ways of safeguarding reason that have been developed by so-called minority groups and new social movements.

Habermas's universalization of the democracy problematic, besides being unsustainable, may also be unnecessary. For instance, the groups in civil society which worked for changing relations of power by the expansion of suffrage from property-owning men to include all adult men, did not necessarily have any ultimate democratic vision that voting rights should also include women. Nevertheless, their efforts unwittingly laid the groundwork for the subsequent enfranchisement of women. Similarly, those civil rights groups who worked for the right to vote for adult women did not necessarily envision a situation where suffrage would also include eighteen-year-olds, even though this later came to pass in many countries. The struggle was carried out from case to case and utilized the arguments and means which worked in the specific socio-historical context. This mode of action is also pertinent to today's social movements, where we still do not know what will be meant by democracy in the future; we only know that, as democrats, we would like to have more of it.

Rorty is correct in noting that the "cash value" of Habermas's notions of discourse ethics and communicative rationality consists of the familiar political freedoms of modern pluralist democracies.[50] But such notions are not "foundations" or "defenses" of free institutions; they *are* those institutions, says Rorty: "We did not learn about the importance of these institutions . . . by thinking through the nature of Reason or Man or Society; we learned about this the hard way, by watching what happened when those institutions were set aside."[51]

To be absolutely modern, writes Milan Kundera, means never to question the content of modernity.[52] It means to be forever hopeful about the grand ideas of modernity and to avoid looking at modernity as it is lived in actual detail, that is, the kind of detail where modern ideals meet the realities of power. Habermas seems absolutely modern in this sense. The vocabulary of Enlightenment rationalism, although it was essential to the beginning of liberal democracy, has become an impediment to the preservation and progress of democratic societies.[53] One reason for this is that Enlightenment rationalism has little to offer in understanding power and in understanding the related discrepancy between formal rationality and *Realrationalität* (real rationality) in modern democracies. In staying close to the Enlightenment vocabulary Habermas has developed little understanding of power and thus tends to become part of the problem he wishes to solve. Habermas's efforts to achieve more rationality and democracy, however laudable, draw attention away from critical relations of power. The neglect of power is unfortunate, because it is precisely by paying attention to power relations that we may achieve more democracy. If our goal is to move toward Habermas's ideal – freedom from domination, more democracy, a strong civil society – then our first task is not to understand the utopia of communicative rationality, but to understand the realities of power. Here we turn to the work of Michel Foucault, who has tried to develop such an understanding.

The Nietzschean democrat

Both Foucault and Habermas are political thinkers. Habermas's thinking is well developed as concerns political ideals, but weak in its understanding of actual political processes. Foucault's thinking, conversely, is weak with reference to generalized ideals – Foucault is a declared opponent of ideals, understood as definitive answers to Kant's question, "What ought I to do?" or Lenin's "What is to be done?" – but his work reflects a sophisticated understanding of *Realpolitik*. Both Foucault and Habermas agree that in politics one must "side with reason." Referring to Habermas and similar thinkers, however, Foucault warns that "to respect rationalism as an ideal should never constitute a blackmail to prevent the analysis of the rationalities really at work."[54] In the following comparison of Foucault and Habermas, emphasis will be placed on what Vincent Descombes has called the "American Foucault," the Foucault who saw liberal democracy as a promising social experiment, and who regarded himself as a citizen in a democratic society working on the project of human liberty.[55]

Foucault was familiar with the work of Habermas and the Frankfurt School, just as Habermas is familiar with the work of Foucault. Foucault occasionally even built upon the work of Habermas, which is a fact of some significance for someone who rarely made reference to contemporary philosophers. In an interview, Foucault said he was "completely in agreement" with Habermas regarding the importance of Kant. "If one abandons the work of Kant," explained Foucault, "one runs the risk of lapsing into irrationality."[56] And, like Habermas, Foucault was unequivocal in his evaluation of the significance of rationality as an object of study. Foucault suggests, however, that the work of Kant might have been too narrowly interpreted by Habermas and his followers. "[I]f the Kantian question was that of knowing what limits knowledge has to renounce transgressing," says Foucault, "it seems to me that the critical question today has to be turned back into a positive one . . . The point, in brief, is to transform the critique conducted in the form of necessary limitation into a practical critique that takes the form of a possible transgression."[57] This entails an obvious consequence, according to Foucault, namely that "criticism is no longer going to be practiced in the search for formal structures with universal value, but rather as a historical investigation."[58]

Habermas's main complaint about Foucault is what Habermas sees as Foucault's relativism. Thus Habermas has harshly dismissed Foucault's genealogical historiographies as *"relativistic, cryptonormative* illusory science"* (emphasis in original).[59] Such critique for relativism is correct, if by relativistic we mean unfounded in norms that can be rationally and universally grounded; and this is what Habermas means when he criticizes Foucault for not giving an "account of the normative foundations" for his thinking.[60] By this standard, however, Habermas's own work is also relativistic. As we have seen, Habermas has not, so far, been able to demonstrate that rational and universal grounding of his discourse ethics is possible, he has only postulated such grounding.[61] And Habermas is not alone with this problem. Despite more than two thousand years of attempts by rationalistic philosophers, no one has been able so far to live up to Plato's injunction that to avoid relativism our thinking must be rationally and universally grounded.

The reason may be that Plato was wrong. Perhaps the polarity relativism–foundationalism is just another artificial dualism that makes it easy to think but hard to understand. Such dualisms simplify things conceptually but with little reference to actual phenomena. Perhaps the horns of this dualism can be avoided by contextualism. This is the strategy of Foucault. As we will see, it is clearly wrong to criticize Foucault for being a relativist if we by relativistic mean "without norms" or "anything goes." "I do not conclude," says Foucault, "that one may say just anything within the order of theory."[62]

Foucault resolves the question of relativism versus foundationalism by following Nietzsche who says about "historians of morality" that

> [t]heir usual mistaken premise is that they affirm some consensus of the nations . . . concerning certain principles of morals, and then they infer from this that these principles must be unconditionally binding also for you and me; or conversely, they see the truth that among different nations moral valuations are *necessarily* different and then infer from this that *no* morality is at all binding. Both procedures are equally childish.[63] (Emphasis in original)

Employing this line of reasoning, Foucault rejects both relativism and foundationalism and replaces them by situational ethics, that is, by context; Foucault's norms are contextually grounded.

Paul Veyne has rightly observed about Foucault's contextualism, that anyone who equates contextualism with relativism's "anything goes" should imagine trying to ask the Romans to abolish slavery or to think about an international equilibrium.[64] The present effectively limits the possible preferences; humans cannot think or do just anything at any time.

With explicit reference to Kant and Habermas, Foucault says that unlike these two thinkers he "is not seeking to make possible a metaphysics that has finally become a science."[65] Distancing himself from foundationalism and metaphysics does not leave Foucault normless, however. His norms are expressed in a desire to challenge "every abuse of power, whoever the author, whoever the victims"[66] and in this way "to give new impetus, as far and wide as possible, to the undefined work of freedom."[67] Foucault here is the Nietzschean democrat, for whom any form of government – pluralist or totalitarian – must be subjected to analysis and critique based on a will not to be dominated, on voicing concerns in public, and on withholding consent about anything that appears to be unacceptable.[68] Foucault's norms are based on historical and personal context, and they are shared with many people around the world. The norms cannot be given a universal grounding independent of those people and that context, according to Foucault. Nor would such grounding be desirable, since it would entail an ethical uniformity with the kind of utopian–totalitarian implications that Foucault would warn against in any context, be it that of Marx, Rousseau, or Habermas: "The search for a form of morality acceptable by everyone in the sense that everyone would have to submit to it, seems catastrophic to me."[69] In a Foucauldian interpretation, such a morality would endanger democracy, not empower it. Instead, Foucault focuses on the analysis of evils and shows restraint in matters of commitment to ideas and systems of thought about what is good for man, given the historical experience that few things have produced more suffering among humans than strong commitments to implementing utopian visions of the good.

Foucault's view of the value of universals in philosophy and social science stands in diametrical opposition to that of Habermas. "Nothing is fundamental," says Foucault. "That is what is interesting in the analysis of society."[70] Compare this with Foucault's remark that "nothing in man – not even his body – is sufficiently stable to serve as the basis for self-recognition or for understanding other men."[71] Therefore, Foucault's analysis of the "rationalities really at work" begins with the assumption that because no one has yet demonstrated the existence of universals in philosophy and social science, we must operate as if the universals do not exist; that is, we should not waste our time searching in vain for universals. Where universals are said to exist, or where people tacitly assume they exist, universals must be questioned, according to Foucault. For Foucault, our history endows us with the possibility to become aware of those social arrangements which create problems, oppressive relations of power, for instance, and those which create satisfaction, strong democracy, for instance. It follows that we have the possibility either to oppose or to promote these arrangements. This, and not global moral norms, is Foucault's point of departure for social and political change.[72] We see that Foucault here builds his thinking directly upon the practical question of what is good and bad for humans, which is the core question of Aristotelian *phronesis*. (See also chapters five and eight).

The basis for understanding and acting is the attitude among those who understand and act, and this attitude is not based on idiosyncratic moral or personal preferences, but on a context-dependent common world view and interests among a reference group, well aware that different groups typically have different world views and different interests, and that there exists no general principle – including the "force of the better argument" – by which all differences can be resolved. For Foucault the socially and historically conditioned context, and not fictive universals, constitutes the most effective bulwark against relativism and nihilism, and the best basis for action. Our sociality and history, according to Foucault, is the only foundation we have, the only solid ground under our feet. And this socio-historical foundation is fully adequate.

According to Foucault, Habermas's "authorization of power by law" is inadequate.[73] "[The juridical system] is utterly incongruous with the new methods of power," says Foucault, "methods that are employed on all levels and in forms that go beyond the state and its apparatus . . . Our historical gradient carries us further and further away from a reign of law."[74] The law, institutions – or policies and plans – provide no guarantee of freedom, equality, or democracy. Not even entire institutional systems, according to Foucault, can ensure freedom, even where they are established with that purpose. Nor is freedom likely to be achieved by imposing abstract theoretical systems or "correct" thinking. On the contrary, history has demonstrated – says Foucault – horrifying examples that it is precisely those social systems which have turned freedom into theoretical formulas and treated practice as social engineering, that is, as an epistemically derived *techne,* that become most repressive. "[People] reproach me for not presenting an overall theory," says Foucault, "I am attempting, to the contrary, apart from any *totalization* – which would be at once *abstract* and *limiting* – to *open up* problems that are as *concrete* and *general* as possible" (emphasis in original).[75]

Given this background, theory-based writing of constitutions does not occupy a central place in Foucault's work as it does for Habermas, and constitution writing would not be seen as an effective way of empowering democracy in a Foucauldian interpretation. This is not because the writing of constitutions is without significance, but because Foucault views it as more important – both for understanding and for practice – to focus on the concrete struggle over a constitution in a specific society: how the constitution is interpreted, how it is practiced in actual institutions, and especially, how interpretations and practices may be changed. In other words, Foucault's thinking as concerns laws, constitutions, and democracy focuses more on how existing constitutions and their associated institutions can be utilized more democratically, whereas Habermas's project is to establish more democratic constitutions and institutions as such, where "democracy" is defined by Habermas's discourse ethics.

In this sense, what Foucault calls "the political task" is

> to criticize the working of institutions which appear to be both neutral and independent; to criticize them in such a manner that the political violence which has always exercised itself obscurely through them will be unmasked, so that one can fight them.[76]

This is what, in a Foucauldian interpretation, would be seen as an effective approach to institutional change and to power. With direct reference to Habermas, Foucault adds:

> The problem is not of trying to dissolve [relations of power] in the utopia of a perfectly transparent communication, but to give . . . the rules of law, the techniques of management, and also the ethics . . . which would allow these games of power to be played with a minimum of domination.[77]

Here Foucault overestimates his differences with Habermas, for Habermas also believes that the ideal speech situation cannot be established as a conventional reality in actual communication. Both thinkers see the regulation of actual relations of dominance as crucial, but whereas Habermas approaches regulation from a universalistic theory of discourse, Foucault seeks out a genealogical understanding of actual power relations in specific contexts. Foucault is oriented toward *phronesis*, whereas Habermas's orientation is toward *episteme*. For Foucault praxis and freedom are derived not from universals or theories. Freedom *is* a practice, and its ideal is not a utopian absence of power. Resistance, struggle, and conflict, in contrast to consensus, are for Foucault the most solid bases for the practice of freedom.

It is precisely on the issue of power and freedom that we find the most crucial difference between Foucault and Habermas, a difference reflected in Foucault's labeling of Habermas as "utopian," while Habermas responds in kind by terming Foucault a "cynic" and "relativist."[78] This kind of mudslinging is unproductive for concrete social and political studies, however, since nothing remains to be discovered if everything is power or if nothing is power, but instead ideal utopia.

Whereas Habermas emphasizes procedural macropolitics, Foucault stresses substantive micropolitics, though with the important shared feature that neither Foucault nor Habermas venture to define the actual content of political action. This is defined by the participants. Thus, both Habermas and Foucault are "bottom-up" thinkers as concerns the content of politics, but where Habermas thinks in a "top-down" moralist fashion as regards procedural rationality – having sketched out the procedures to be followed with his communicative rationality – Foucault is a "bottom-up" thinker as regards both process and content. In this interpretation, Habermas would want to tell individuals and groups in a society how to go about their affairs as regards procedure for discourse. He would not want, however, to say anything about the outcome of this procedure. Foucault would prescribe neither process nor outcome; he would only recommend a focus on conflict and on power relations as the most effective point of departure for the fight against domination. It is because of his double "bottom-up" thinking that Foucault has been described as nonaction oriented. Foucault says about such criticism:

It's true that certain people, such as those who work in the institutional setting of the prison . . . are not likely to find advice or instructions in my books to tell them "what is to be done." But my project is precisely to bring it about that they "no longer know what to do," so that the acts, gestures, discourses that up until then had seemed to go without saying become problematic, difficult, dangerous.[79]

The depiction of Foucault as nonaction-oriented is correct to the extent that Foucault hesitates to give directives for action, and he directly distances himself from the kinds of universal formulas which characterize procedure in Habermas's communicative rationality. Foucault believes that "solutions" of this type are themselves part of the problem.

Seeing Foucault as nonaction-oriented would be misleading, however, insofar as Foucault's genealogical studies are carried out in order to show how things can be done differently to "separate out, from the contingency that has made us what we are, the possibility of no longer being, doing, or thinking what we are, do, or think."[80] Thus Foucault was openly pleased when during a revolt in some of the French prisons the prisoners in their cells read his book *Discipline and Punish*. "They shouted the text to other prisoners," Foucault told an interviewer.[81] "I know it's pretentious to say," Foucault said, "but that's a proof of a truth – a political and actual truth – which started after the book was written." This is the type of situated action Foucault would endorse, and as a genealogist, Foucault saw himself as highly action oriented, as "a dealer in instruments, a recipe maker, an indicator of objectives, a cartographer, a sketcher of plans, a gunsmith."[82]

The establishment of a concrete genealogy opens possibilities for action by describing the genesis of a given situation and showing that this particular genesis is not connected to absolute historical necessity. Foucault's genealogical studies of prisons, hospitals, and sexuality demonstrate that social practices may always take an alternative form, even where there is no basis for voluntarism or idealism. Combined with Foucault's focus on domination, it is easy to understand why this insight has been embraced by feminists and so-called minority groups. Elaborating genealogies of, for instance, gender and race leads to an understanding of how relations of domination between women and men, and between different peoples, can be changed.[83] Given the interpretation above of Foucault as a practitioner of *phronesis*, it comes as no surprise that the appropriation of Foucault by feminists has recently been followed by a similar adoption of Aristotle – the philosopher of *phronesis* par excellence – despite the misogyny of some of Aristotle's thinking.[84] Finally, given the emphasis in *phronesis* on practical rationality and common-sense knowledge, it is also not unexpected that Habermas has distanced himself from *phronesis* and neo-Aristotelianism, both of which he rhetorically and unconvincingly has associated with neoconservatism.[85]

Foucault's emphasis on marginality and domination makes his thinking sensitive to difference, diversity, and the politics of identity, something which today is crucial for understanding power and affecting social and political change. Historically the very idea of democracy contains a gender bias. Feminists have found that overall Foucault is more helpful than Habermas in rooting out this bias, and progress has been slow in developing the theory of communicative rationality in ways that would be sensitive to gender. Even a sympathetic observer like Jean Cohen criticizes Habermas for his "peculiar blindness to gender issues."[86] Other feminists have been skeptical about Habermas's "confidence in abstract rationality" as the general cure to social and political ailments, and researchers working on race, ethnicity, and sexuality have received Habermas in a similar manner.[87] When Habermas was asked directly by Nancy Fraser in a conference on the occasion of the publication of the English translation of his *The Structural Transformation of the Public Sphere*, whether the "condition for the possibility of a public sphere," that is, the basic condition for communicative rationality, is not a utopian society with "economic equality – the end of class structure and the end of gender inequality,"[88] Habermas replied that he would "have to get over the shock to answer such a question," and then proceeded not to answer the question at all.[89] It is understandable that Habermas is reluctant to answer Fraser's critical question because it expresses a suspicion that Habermas's ideas on communicative rationality and democracy may be so abstract that we will never see them working in the affairs of real life. And Habermas's thinking contains little that may help counter such suspicion.

Habermas has acknowledged that his analysis does not include "gender, ethnicity, class, popular culture."[90] But Habermas insists, wrongly in my analysis, that "the critique of that which has been excluded from the public sphere," and from Habermas's analysis of it, can be carried out "*only* in the light of the declared standards and the manifest self-understanding of the proponents and participants of these very same public spheres." How could you "critically assess the inconspicuous repression of ethnic, cultural, national, gender, and identity differences," asks Habermas, "if not in the light of this *one* basic standard ['the force of more or less good reason'], however interpreted, of procedures that *all* parties presume will provide the most rational solution at hand, at a given time, in a given context?" (emphasis added).[91] Thus Habermas sees the struggle over access to the public sphere as a matter of rational discourse. But Habermas's analysis does not stand up to historical–empirical test. With the demarcations established by his use of the terms "only," "one," and "all" the analysis is too categorical.

For example, the critical assessment of the exclusion of certain groups from the public sphere Habermas talks about can be and has been carried out unilaterally by the very groups that have been excluded, and without regard to following the "declared standards" and "manifest self-understanding" of this sphere. As a matter of fact, such standards and self-understanding have often been seen as what was in need of change; they were the objects of critical assessment, not its basis.[92] Even where the standards and self-understanding were not seen as a problem, they may not have been viewed by excluded groups as the most efficient means for gaining access to the public sphere. Groups may therefore choose to use other, nondiscursive means to gain such access, the politics of activism or power politics, for instance. Feminist and environmental initiatives, today central to the structure and functioning of many societies, got their issues on the public agenda not primarily by rational consensus but through the power struggles and conflicts characteristic of activism and social change.[93] Moreover, as Geoff Eley and Mary Ryan have demonstrated, historically the very constitution of the public sphere took place, not solely from rational discourse and consensus, but "from a field of conflict, contested meanings, and exclusion."[94] In Eley's analysis, the claim to reason implied by the constitution of the public sphere was simultaneously a claim to power in Foucault's sense. Dankwart Rustow has similarly argued that democracy has generally come into existence not because people wanted this form of government or because they had achieved a wide consensus on "basic values," but because various groups had been fighting for so long they finally came to recognize their mutual inability to gain dominance and the need for some accommodation.[95]

In arguing that exclusion of ethnic, cultural, national, and gender groups from the public sphere needs to be assessed by the discursive standards of the public sphere, Habermas uses the conduct of court cases as a model for such assessment. "Court cases," says Habermas, "are meant to settle practical conflicts in terms of mutual understanding and intended agreement."[96] And agreement is arrived at, according to Habermas, by use of the "force of more or less good reason," that is, the force of the better argument, as "the *only* alternative to overt or covert violence" (emphasis added).[97] It is correct that courts are meant to settle conflicts and that arguments, rational or not, are used for this purpose. Yet such settlement is not dependent in the individual case on mutual understanding or agreement between the parties involved in the court case, as Habermas says it is. It is, instead, dependent on an understanding by the parties that once the arguments have been heard and the judge has ruled they will have to live by this ruling, whether they like it or not. If they choose not to respect the ruling, the judge is backed by an elaborate system of sanctions, and ultimately by police force and prisons. Thus court cases are typically settled by power, not by mutual understanding and agreement. Courts in pluralist democracies secure the type of conflict-resolution Richard Bernstein talked about above when he said that any society must have some procedures for dealing with conflicts that cannot be resolved by argumentation, even when all parties are committed to rational argumentation. If courts relied on Habermas's understanding of litigation, the court system would break down because many cases would never come to an end. While morally admirable and politically provocative, Habermas's thinking about rational argument here seems not only utopian but also sociologically naive both empirically and normatively.

If Habermas's discourse ethics were to be constituted as reality this would not signify an end to power, it would be a way to regulate power. And to the extent that actual implementation of discourse ethics would run counter to the interests of social and political actors – which is bound to be the case for societies and decisions of any complexity – discourse ethics will be opposed, whether such opposition can be rationally justified or not. The basic contradiction here is that coercion would be needed to arrive at Habermas's noncoercive (*zwanglos*) communication. Agreement would, in this sense, be forced. So even if one could imagine the existence of what Habermas calls a "political public sphere unsubverted by power,"[98] such a sphere could not be said to be free of power since it was established through a claim to power, just as German democracy was not implemented by public discourse but at the point of guns. The Nietzschean insight that historically morality has typically been established by immoral means would hold true for Habermas's morality, too. Power is needed to limit power. Even to understand how publicness can be established we need to think in terms of conflict and power. There is no way around it. It is a basic condition for understanding issues of exclusion and inclusion in a democracy.

Power as constitutive of social science

In sum, Foucault and Habermas agree that rationalization and the misuse of power are among the most important problems of our time. They disagree as to how one can best understand and act in relation to these problems. Habermas's approach is oriented toward universals, context-independence, and control via constitution writing and institutional development. Foucault focuses his efforts on the local and context-dependent and toward the analysis of strategies and tactics as a basis for power struggle.

The value of Habermas's approach is that it contains a clear picture of what Habermas understands by "democratic process," and what preconditions must be fulfilled for a decision to be termed "democratic." His scheme can be used as an abstract ideal for justification and application in relation to legislation, institutional development, and procedural planning. The problem, however, is that Habermas is idealistic. His work contains little understanding of how power functions or of those strategies and tactics which can ensure more of the sought after democracy. It is easy to point to constitution writing and institutional development as a solution; it is something else to implement specific constitutional and institutional changes. Aside from his general prescriptions regarding communicative rationality, Habermas provides us with little guidance as to how such implementation could take place.

The value of Foucault's approach is his emphasis on the dynamics of power. Understanding how power works is the first prerequisite for action, because action is the exercise of power. And such an understanding can best be achieved by focusing on the concrete. Foucault can help us with a materialist understanding of *Realpolitik* and *Realrationalität* (real rationality), and how these might be changed in a specific context. The problem with Foucault is that because understanding and action have their points of departure in the particular and the local, we may come to overlook more generalized conditions concerning, for example, institutions, constitutions, and structural issues.

From the perspective of the history of philosophy and social theory, the difference between Foucault and Habermas lies in the fact that Foucault works within a particularistic and contextualist tradition that focuses on conflict and has its roots with Aristotle via Machiavelli and Nietzsche.[99] Foucault is one of the more important twentieth-century exponents of this tradition. Habermas is the most prominent living exponent of a universalistic and theorizing tradition that focuses on consensus and derives via Kant from Plato. In power terms, we are speaking of "strategic" versus "constitution" thinking, about struggle versus control, conflict versus consensus.

Generally, conflicts have been viewed as dangerous, corrosive, and potentially destructive of social order and therefore in need of being contained and resolved. This view seems to cover Habermas's outlook on conflict, which is understandable given Germany's, and Habermas's, experience with Nazism, World War II, and their aftereffects. There is mounting evidence, however, that social conflicts themselves produce the valuable ties that hold modern democratic societies together and provide them with the strength and cohesion they need; that social conflicts are the true pillars of democratic society.[100] Governments and societies that suppress conflict do so at their own peril. A basic reason for the deterioration and loss of vitality of the Communist-dominated societies may be in their success in suppressing overt social conflict. In a Foucauldian interpretation, suppressing conflict is suppressing freedom, because the privilege to engage in conflict and power struggle is part of freedom.

If societies that suppress conflict are oppressive, perhaps social and political theories that ignore or marginalize conflict are potentially oppressive, too. And if conflict sustains society, there is good reason to caution against an idealism that ignores conflict and power. In real social and political life self-interest and conflict will not give way to some all-embracing communal ideal like Habermas's. Indeed, the more democratic a society, the more it allows groups to define their own specific ways of life and legitimates the inevitable conflicts of interest that arise between them. Political consensus cannot be expected to neutralize particular group obligations, commitments, and interests. To think that it can be, is to repeat the fallacy of Rousseau's belief in the General Will as distinct from the actual will of particular individuals and groups.[101] A more differentiated conception of political culture than Habermas's is needed, one that will be more tolerant of conflict and difference, and more compatible with the pluralization of interests.

As pointed out by Mary Ryan, because everyday politics inevitably falls short of the standards of communicative rationality, which was a chimera even in the heyday of the bourgeois public sphere, the goal of publicness might best be allowed to navigate through "wider and wilder territory."[102] Such territory is imbued with conflict. Public life is best cultivated, not in an ideal sphere that assumes away power, but in "many democratic spaces where obstinate differences in power, material status, and hence interest can find expression."[103] With the plurality that a contemporary concept for democracy must contain, conflict becomes an inevitable part of this concept. In strong democracies, distrust and criticism of authoritative action are omnipresent. Moral outrage is continuous, because actual authorities inevitably violate whatever ideal norms civil society has for justice. Democracy guarantees only the existence of a public, not public consensus.[104] A strong democracy guarantees the existence of conflict. A strong understanding of democracy must therefore be based on thought that places conflict and power at its center, as Foucault does and Habermas does not.

This is not to reject the importance of the public sphere as a bulwark of freedom. Nor is it to deny that Habermas's work has value, especially in a time when most philosophers have given up on the high ambitions for philosophy and social science that Habermas still pursues, for instance regarding universal grounding of our thoughts and actions. Even if such ambitions cannot be fulfilled, the history of philosophy and science shows that we have much to learn from attempts at doing so. It must be said, however, that forms of public life that are practical, committed, and ready for conflict provide a superior paradigm of democratic citizen virtue than do forms of public life that are discursive, detached, and consensus-dependent. For those who see things this way, in order to enable the public sphere to make a serious contribution to genuine democratic participation, one would have to tie it back to precisely what it cannot accept in Habermas's interpretation: Foucault's focus on conflict, power, and partisanship.[105]

8   Empowering Aristotle

> Not to call a thing good a day longer or a day earlier than it seems good
> to us is the only way to remain really happy.   *Friedrich Nietzsche*

In the previous chapter we saw that social and political thinking becomes
problematic if it does not contain a well-developed conception of power.
We also saw that for the public sphere to make a real contribution to
democracy, one would have to link it to conflict, power, and partisanship.
In forging this link, we will continue in the present chapter our focus on
Michel Foucault's analysis of power as a means of developing a more
adequate and contemporary conception of *phronesis*.

I wish to emphasize at the outset that the discussion of Foucault's work
that follows cannot be seen as a universal explication of Foucault's
method, but only as one pragmatic reading of it. I engage in Foucault's
work in order to better understand the special problems presented by a
specific area of research, that is, power in relation to *phronesis*; it is a
strategy which is entirely in the Foucauldian spirit. As Paul Rabinow has
observed, Foucault gave us tools to use not an agenda to follow.[1]

Aristotle, Nietzsche, and Foucault

"[P]hilosophy begins with Aristotle," Foucault says provocatively, not
with Socrates and Plato as the canon has it.[2] Foucault never speaks of any
relationship between his own work and Aristotelian *phronesis*, however. I
am aware of only one place where Foucault remarks on *phronesis* at all.
This is in his third lecture of 1984, where Foucault identifies *phronesis* as
practical reason, as is common, and he says that *phronesis* is what permits
one to chase away false opinions and make good decisions.[3] A decade and
a half earlier, when Foucault discussed Aristotle in his inaugural course at
the Collège de France, he focused on Aristotle's *Metaphysics* and epistemology and contrasted Aristotle with Nietzsche in *The Gay Science*.
Here Foucault saw Aristotle as representing the universal and naturalistic

pole. Had Foucault chosen to focus on Aristotle's *Ethics* with its considerations on *phronesis* rather than on his *Metaphysics*, Foucault would have
found an Aristotle much more concerned with the particular and the
contingent, that is, an Aristotle closer to Nietzsche and to Foucault
himself. Later, Foucault did re-examine his understanding of Aristotle
and Nietzsche and, as pointed out by Paul Rabinow, he came a good deal
closer to the Aristotle of the *Ethics* in the way he posed problems for
analysis, although Foucault did not adopt Aristotle's answers or his
metaphysics.[4] Thus, even if there are important differences between
Foucault and Aristotle, differences that deserve their own separate study,
I want here simply to indicate a basic convergence of focus that links their
work.

In terms of Aristotle's intellectual virtues *episteme, techne,* and *phronesis*
(see chapter five), Foucault significantly shifted his interests as his work
developed. As we have seen, when *The Order of Things* appeared, Foucault
was deeply involved with the question of whether the study of human
affairs could become scientific in the epistemic sense of the word. After
The Archaeology of Knowledge Foucault lost interest in this question and
reoriented his work from a focus on *episteme* to one on *techne*. Foucault
was now interested in the study of government, and he explicitly questioned the value of "constantly asking the question of whether government can be the object of an exact science."[5] "[W]hat interests me
more," Foucault continued, "is to focus on what the Greeks called the
techne, that is to say, a practical rationality governed by a conscious
goal."[6] Having discounted the possibility of epistemic social sciences,
Foucault now could not, and did not, study *techne* as applied *episteme*,
even if this is the conventional conception of the relationship between the
two, with *episteme* seen as pure science and *techne* as applied science.
Foucault studied *techne* without the superstructure of *episteme*. And by
linking *techne* to goals, Foucault now approached *techne* "from the other
side," that is from values – what is "good and bad for man," in Aristotle's
words – which is, in my interpretation, from *phronesis*.

Like Machiavelli and Nietzsche, the Foucault of *Discipline and Punish*
and the first volume of *The History of Sexuality* is best understood if one
starts with Aristotle. But with Foucault the influence from Aristotle, and
especially from Aristotle's *Ethics*, is indirect; it reaches to Foucault via
Nietzsche. Nietzsche's debt to Aristotle's *Ethics* is considerable, as Walter
Kaufmann has shown,[7] and Foucault, in turn, was thoroughly influenced
by Nietzsche.[8] Thus the Aristotelian disposition in Nietzsche's work is
refound with Foucault, even if it is often implicit. Central to this disposition is a focus in the study of humans and society, not on universals and
theory, but on deliberation about particular affairs aimed at praxis. In

chapter five, in defining *phronesis*, we saw that Aristotle emphasized deliberation about that which is variable in human affairs, and he added that "nobody deliberates about things that are invariable."[9] Foucault is the genealogist of the variable *par excellence*; his works are elaborate exercises in making that which appears invariable variable. "[I]t is fruitful," says Foucault, "to describe that which is, while making it appear as something that might not be, or that might not be as it is."[10] Why is this fruitful? Because it is the intellectual activity that most effectively opens up human affairs to deliberation and praxis. Human practice and human history are "made," Foucault the Aristotelian says, and since they are made, "they can be unmade, as long as we know how it was that they were made."[11] Foucault explicitly defines his ethics as the work involved in this type of "thinking differently"; and he defines the ethical subject as the person carrying out such work with a view to creating new social forms.[12] It would, perhaps, be an overstatement to say that Foucault's ethics *is phronesis*, but there is certainly more than a faint similarity between Aristotelian *phronesis* and Foucauldian ethics.

In the second and third volumes of *The History of Sexuality*, Foucault's thoughts on ethics reach their most explicit expression, especially in Foucault's discussions of the ethic of care for the self.[13] It would be a mistake, however, to think of these works and the time when they were written as Foucault's "ethical" period, as is sometimes the tendency, contrasting this period with an early and middle Foucault who supposedly avoided normative judgment. What Richard Rorty has described as a certain "cold-bloodedness" in Foucault's early and middle work cannot be seen as nihilistic cynicism. It is, instead, an integral part of the "will to truth" – the "will not [to] deceive, even myself" – which stands at the core of Foucault's ethics.[14] This ethics is firmly in place, if less visibly, also in Foucault's earlier work. As James Bernauer has pointed out, the collected works of Foucault have made it more difficult to think unhistorically, nonpolitically, and nonethically about praxis.[15] In my interpretation, this is what *phronesis* is about.

Real history, effective truth

Foucault never presented a thorough description of his research method, or methods. If we want to explicate Foucault's method, we are therefore compelled to extract it from a reading of his work, and from the various fragments of methodological comments which Foucault scattered in his books, his articles, and in several interviews. If one could say that Foucault's method is deconstructed, and deconstruction was Foucault's conscious strategy as regards method, the task in the following is to carry out the un-Foucauldian task of reconstructing his method. The focus here will be on Foucault's works concerning power.

As mentioned, Foucault was significantly inspired by Nietzsche, both methodologically and substantively, and he employed the Nietzschean concept of *genealogy* to designate one of the main activities of his method. In an interview given by Foucault a few weeks before his death, Foucault described himself as "simply Nietzschean."[16] Nietzsche biographer Ronald Hayman remarks, that given the strong influence of Nietzsche on Foucault, for instance regarding the genealogical method, the originality of Foucault is being overrated.[17] This view is partly correct but needs to be nuanced by looking at the division of work between Nietzsche and Foucault. Part of Nietzsche's originality lies in seeing that in order to understand society's morality we need in-depth genealogical studies of such phenomena as cruelty, punishment, and love. For instance, in *The Gay Science* under the heading "Something for the Industrious" (Foucault said of himself, "I worked like a dog all my life"[18]), Nietzsche spells out some of the "histories" that need to be written in the study of moral matters, explicitly mentioning areas Foucault would later cover. "So far, all that has given color to existence still lacks a history," Nietzsche says. "Where could you find a history of love, of avarice, of envy, of conscience, of pious respect for tradition, or of cruelty? Even a comparative history of law or at least of punishment is so far lacking completely."[19] It is one thing, however, to point out that such work needs to be done; it is quite another actually to carry it out. Whereas Nietzsche did go some of the way, but at a fairly general level, in doing this work, Foucault went much further in implementing Nietzsche's ideas, for instance, by extensively using the type of original archival material that Nietzsche recommended for doing genealogy but which he himself did not use. Herein lies the originality of Foucault, who, unlike Nietzsche, had the temper and skills of an experienced historian. Similarly, Nietzsche's considerations in his second essay in *On the Genealogy of Morals* on the development of "calculable" individuals through "the labor performed by man upon himself" was taken further by Foucault than by Nietzsche.[20]

The best description Foucault has provided of genealogy as he himself practiced it can be found in a short article, "Nietzsche, Genealogy, History," which is central to understanding Foucault's methodology and project.[21] In characteristic style, Foucault begins the article by noting that "genealogy is gray, meticulous, and patiently documentary. It operates on a field of entangled and confused parchments, on documents that have been scratched over and recopied many times."[22] Foucault's text closely follows Nietzsche's *On the Genealogy of Morals*. For example, it is

Nietzsche, not Foucault, who connects genealogy with the color gray, even though Foucault does not mention this in his text. "[I]t must be obvious which color is a hundred times more vital for a genealogist . . . than blue [the color of the idealist]," Nietzsche says, "namely *gray*, that is, what is documented, what can actually be confirmed and has actually existed" (emphasis in original).[23]

Like Aristotle when he speaks of *phronesis*, the genealogist emphasizes a focus on the particular, because the genealogical experience says that what is general is often empty and banal, whereas it is often in the deep, concrete detail that genuinely important interrelationships are expressed. In teaching a course on "general psychology," Foucault emphasized at the outset: "general psychology, like anything general, does not exist."[24] The genealogist seeks the large from within the small. Summarizing his method, Foucault again borrows from Nietzsche.

Genealogy, consequently, requires patience and a knowledge of details, and it depends on a vast accumulation of source material. Its "cyclopean monuments" are constructed from "discreet and apparently insignificant truths and according to a rigorous method" . . . it rejects the metahistorical deployment of ideal significations and indefinite teleologies. It opposes itself to the search for "origins."[25]

The genealogist writes what Nietzsche calls *wirkliche Historie*, "real history," and what Machiavelli calls *verita effettuale*, effective truth. Politics is studied as *Realpolitik* and rationality as *Realrationalität* (real rationality). Nietzsche explicitly mentions Machiavelli as a source of influence. "Thucydides, and . . . the *Principe* of Machiavelli, are related to me closely by their unconditional will not to deceive themselves and to see reason in *reality*," says Nietzsche. "Plato is a coward in the face of reality – consequently he flees into the ideal" (emphasis in original).[26] Machiavelli made clear that an understanding of politics requires distinguishing between formal politics and what later, with Ludwig von Rochau, would become known as *Realpolitik*. A similar distinction is rarely made in the study of rationality. The genealogist would argue, however, that distinguishing between formal rationality and *Realrationalität* is as important to the understanding of social and political affairs as the distinction between formal politics and *Realpolitik*.

For Nietzsche and Foucault, genealogy is fundamental to historiography. The phenomena under study are understood by means of a genealogical account of the way the phenomena can be seen as descendants – not as developments, manifestations, or appearances – of phenomena that came earlier.[27] Genealogy is not a new methodology for doing history with its own principles. It is, rather, an effort to take history seriously and to locate history where it has been least likely to be expected. Genealogy takes as its objects exactly those institutions and practices which, like rationality, are usually thought to be excluded from change. It tries to show the way in which they, too, undergo changes as a result of historical developments; and it also tries to demonstrate how such changes escape our notice, how it is often in the interest of those institutions and practices to mask their specific genealogy and historical character. Genealogy therefore has direct practical, often political, implications. By demonstrating the contingent character of those institutions and practices that traditional history exhibits as unchanging, genealogy creates the possibility of altering them.[28]

Writing *wirkliche Historie*, the researcher operates on the basis of the following premises:

(1) Researchers are both involved in, and partially produced by, the same cultural practices which they study; hence, researchers cannot stand completely outside of that which they study; researchers are not identical with that which they study, however.
(2) Practices – what "is done" – are more fundamental than discourses, including theory and theoretical discourses; practices are here understood as a "way of acting and thinking at once."[29]
(3) The meaning of discourses can be understood only as part of society's ongoing history.

Here it is worth noting that Foucault does not accept Jacques Derrida's and other deconstructivists' "textualisation" of practices, that is, the maxim that "there is nothing outside the text." Foucault, in a comment on Derrida, calls this a "little pedagogy" and dismisses it as a device that gives its practitioners "limitless sovereignty" by allowing them "to restate the text indefinitely."[30] For Foucault textual analysis needs to be disciplined by analysis of practices. Here, again, we see how Foucault's position is not relativism but contextualism. The context of practices disciplines interpretation.

As with *phronesis*, the main objective of genealogy is to produce input for ongoing social dialogue and social praxis rather than definitive, empirically verifiable knowledge, even though rigorous empirical study and verification of data are central to genealogy. Foucault said that he used "methods drawn from the classical repertoire: demonstration, proof of historical documentation, reference to texts, recourse to authorized commentaries, [interpretation of] relations between ideas and facts, proposition of explanatory schemes, etc."[31] Thus the results of genealogy may be confirmed, revised, or rejected according to the most rigorous standards of historiographic inquiry and such results are open for testing in relation to other interpretations. This does not mean that one interpretation can be just as good as the next, for each interpretation must be based on certain validity requirements. It does mean, however, that genealogical studies will be as prepared to defend such requirements as any other study.

The "how" of power

Power theory in social and political science comprises several traditions. First, there are the so-called "community power" theories as formulated by Robert Dahl, Floyd Hunter, G. William Domhoff, and others.[32] Second, there are the theories of "nondecisions" and "two faces of power" of Peter Bachrach and Morton Baratz, and the three-dimensional power concept of Steven Lukes.[33] Finally, there is Marxist power theory, as elaborated, for example, by Nicolas Poulantzas.[34] While these theories differ on many points, they all share a concern with power in terms of possession, sovereignty, and control – power as entity. Foucault, in contrast, understands power in terms of its concrete application in strategies and tactics – power as force relations. Let me illustrate the difference between these two approaches to the study of power by comparing Foucault with Steven Lukes, one of the most prominent exponents of the "power as entity" theories.[35]

In his book *Power*, Lukes poses the question, "What interests us when we are interested in power?"[36] Lukes responds that we are interested in the results of power and its localization: "those interested in power are interested in two questions," says Lukes. "Let us call the first an interest in the outcomes and the second an interest in the locus of power."[37] Lukes explains that one can advantageously study the two questions by focusing on a set of other questions, "various 'power questions' that people have in mind when they seek to locate and compare power."[38] Lukes lists these power questions as follows: Who can adversely affect whose interests? Who can control whom? Who can obtain what? Who can secure the achievement of collective resources? Who is responsible for the outcomes of power? Who benefits from the outcomes of power? Where are the sources of change localized? Where are the points at which alternative arrangements or events could have made a significant difference?

These types of questions are important in power studies and deserve a place in most analyses of power. Nevertheless, the questions posed and the perspective on power they express are insufficient for understanding certain central aspects of power, *viz.*, power as force relations. One of the values of Foucault's work lies in making this clear. In contrast to Lukes,

Foucault states that he is not primarily interested in the outcomes or localization of power, nor even in power in itself. Rather, his focus is the *relations* of power: "I hardly ever use the word 'power'," Foucault says, "and if I do sometimes, it is always a short cut to the expression I always use: the relationships of power."[39] Foucault argues against a view of power as something one possesses: "power is not something that is acquired, seized, or shared, something that one holds on to or allows to slip away."[40] Or as Foucault says elsewhere: "power is exercised rather than possessed."[41]

The question of who has power is therefore less prominent with Foucault than with other students of power. In accord with this view Foucault warns against power studies which try to identify the "headquarters" of power. "[L]et us not look for the headquarters that presides over [power's] rationality," Foucault says, "neither the caste which governs, nor the groups which control the state apparatus, nor those who make the most important economic decisions direct the entire network of power that functions in a society (and makes *it* function)."[42] Foucault states explicitly that power should not be sought in any kind of locus because "power is everywhere, not because it embraces everything, but because it comes from everywhere."[43] Foucault therefore explicates his concept of power like this: "power is not an institution, and not a structure; neither is it a certain strength we are endowed with; it is the name that one attributes to a complex strategical situation in a particular society."[44]

Here I should like to point out that contrary to what some critics have held, Foucault's decentralized power concept and his statement that power is not an institution or a structure do not imply that institutions cannot be significant objects for power studies.[45] Indeed, Foucault explicitly calls attention to the fact that it is both possible and legitimate to focus power studies on closely defined institutions. "[I do] not deny the importance of institutions on the establishment of power relations," says Foucault.[46] Institutions constitute privileged observation points according to Foucault. They are concentrated, ordered, and often effective. A focus for power studies on institutions, however, entails several pitfalls of which Foucault warns us. For example, since an important part of the mechanisms which operate in a given institution are designed to ensure the maintenance of that institution, studies of institutional power run the risk of unduly focusing on reproductive mechanisms, especially in the study of power relations among institutions. Foucault believes that institutional analyses also have had a tendency to explain the sources of power in terms of institutions, a kind of circular reasoning in which power is explained by power. "I wish to suggest that one must analyze institutions from the standpoint of power relations, rather than vice versa," says Foucault, "and that the fundamental point of anchorage of the relationships, even if they are embodied and crystallized in an institution, is to be found outside the institution."[47]

With his emphasis on strategy over sovereignty, Foucault's main focus in power studies is the Aristotelian and phronetic concern with "particular circumstances." Foucault's principal question, what he terms "the little question . . . flat and empirical," becomes a processual question. "How," asks Foucault, "is power exercised?"[48] The processual question supplements Steven Lukes's and other power theorists' focus on power as a static entity to be possessed, won, held, or lost. "How?" is thus added to "Who?" "What?" and "Where?" Foucault is emphatic about the importance of process over structure as a point of departure for power studies. He stresses that "to begin the analysis with a 'how' is . . . to suspect that an extremely complex configuration of realities is allowed to escape when one treads endlessly in the double question: What is power? and Where does power come from?"[49] It is precisely such a "complex configuration of realities" which escapes understanding when one studies power from the power-as-entity theories alone, and it is therefore the "little question" of "How?" with its emphasis on details and concrete practices which governs Foucault's genealogy and power analytics. Here, too, Foucault's approach is in agreement with the practice of *phronesis*.

Clifford Geertz similarly observes about power that politics is an extraordinarily difficult matter to assess "which is perhaps why we social scientists, who are not players but reasoners and onlookers, professional second-guessers, are so given to abstract representations of Power, the State, Domination, and Authority – the drum-roll words of spectator realism."[50] The problem with such an approach, says Geertz, is that it is less than helpful. To depict power as some sort of featureless, universal force producing an abstract, invariant relationship called "domination" is to block perception of both the texture of politics and its reach, according to Geertz. It leaves us "with hardly anything to say but that big fish eat little ones, the weak go to the wall, power tends to corrupt, uneasy lies the head, and master and man need one another to exist: the dim banalities of theory." Foucault's approach to the study of power is an effective remedy against the "banalities of theory" identified by Geertz.

In the following discussion of Foucault's considerations on power, we shall pay particular attention to the development of methodological guidelines for practical phronetic studies that attempt to answer the question "How is power exercised?" In concluding this section, it should be emphasized, however, that when Foucault focuses on the question of how, it is not because he believes that other questions – Steven Lukes's power questions, for instance – are unimportant in the study of power, but because he believes that the "How?" question has been neglected. "If . . . I grant a certain privileged position to the question of 'how' it is not because I would wish to eliminate the questions of 'what' and 'why'," says Foucault. "Rather it is that I wish to . . . know if it is legitimate to imagine a power which unites in itself a what, a why and a how."[51]

Just as Foucault never provided a comprehensive description of genealogy, he never fully described his method for studying power. The explicitly methodological considerations are again few and scattered, and one must refer to Foucault's empirical work as prototypes if one seeks to understand the method behind them.

One of the few places where Foucault in fact uses the term "method" and expends some pages explaining how he carries out his power studies is in the first volume of *The History of Sexuality*. Here Foucault explains that "the aim of the inquiries that will follow is to move less toward a 'theory' of power than toward an 'analytics' of power: that is toward a definition of the specific domain formed by relations of power, and toward a determination of the instruments that will make possible its analysis."[52] Here, too, we see a fundamental difference from the power-as-entity theories. The influence of the genealogical method is evident, in that Foucault explicitly distances himself from the traditional focus of power thinking on "theories" of power. Instead Foucault is interested in an "analytics of power." Foucault's critical stance regarding theory, which, as we have noted, is also a characteristic of Aristotelian *phronesis*, is elaborated in *Power/Knowledge*. "If one tries to erect a theory of power one will always be obliged to view it as emerging at a given place and time and hence deduce it, to reconstruct its genesis," Foucault says here. But if power is in reality an open, more-or-less coordinated cluster of relations, then the "only problem is to provide oneself with a grid of analysis which makes possible an analytic of relations of power," according to Foucault.[53]

Foucault uses various key words to characterize the conventional view of power: it is *negative*; limits and prohibitions are central to its logic. It is *rule-based*; rules determine what is permitted and forbidden, legal and illegal, acceptable and unacceptable, what constitutes legitimate and illicit activity. It requires a uniform and visible *apparatus* of power; power is exercised from above and downwards, uniformly and comprehensively; all are equal before power, differences are attributable only to differences in scale, not in the type of power to which one is exposed. The power apparatus is placed on the one side, the obedient subject on the other. "It is a power that only has the force of the negative on its side," says Foucault, "a power to say no; in no condition to produce, capable only of posting limits, it is basically anti-energy. This is the paradox of its effectiveness: it is incapable of doing anything, except to render what it dominates incapable of doing anything either, except for what this power allows it to do."[54] All the modes of domination, submission, and subjugation are ultimately reduced to an effect of obedience, according to Foucault.

What, then, does it mean for Foucault to ask questions such as, "What is power?" and "What is not power?" Taking the last question first, power is seen not simply as a set of institutions and mechanisms, which ensure servile citizens in a given state. Nor is power only a form of subordination, which instead of violence sets rules. Power is not only a general system of domination that one group exercises over another. Instead of assuming the existence of domination, sovereignty, law, etc., it is more fruitful to see these as forms which power may take, says Foucault. Hence, the existence of these forms of power must be made into an empirical question for further research instead of a precondition for power studies. The possibility of power and its conditions of existence must not only be sought in a center. Concepts such as "center of power" and "locus of power" are problematic, inasmuch as they derive from a concept of power based on law and sovereignty, Foucault says. The concepts assume too much, and leave too little open for empirical investigation.

Foucault's response to the question, "What is power?", takes the following form: Power must be understood as a multiplicity of force relations "immanent in the sphere in which they operate and which constitute their own organization."[55] Power is the process, which via struggles and confrontations transforms, supports, or reverses these force relations. Power is the support which the force relations find in each other via the creation of chains or systems, or conversely, via the separation and opposition which isolate them from each other. Power is the strategies in which the force relations obtain effects, whose general design or institutional crystallization can be found in the state apparatus, in the formation of the laws, and in various social hegemonies. Strategies and force relations are local and omnipresent, they are changeable and unstable. Power is dynamic and is everywhere, states Foucault, not because it is capable of uniting everything under its insurmountable unity, but because power is produced from one moment to the next in all points and all relations. The micropractices of power and of day-to-day activities – hour to hour and minute to minute sometimes – are what is significant. Power is productive, says Foucault, "We must cease once and for all to describe the effects of power in negative terms: it 'excludes,' it 'represses,' it 'censors,' it 'abstracts,' it 'masks,' it 'conceals'." In fact, continues Foucault, "power produces, it produces reality; it produces domains of objects and rituals of truth."[56]

More specifically, Foucault sets forth his concept of power in a number of propositions.[57]

Power relations do not stand in an external relationship to other forms of relations, for example, economic processes, relations of knowledge and rationality, or sexual relations. Power relations are inherent in these and are the immediate effect of the divisions, inequalities, and imbalances found in them, just as they, conversely, are preconditions for these differentiations. Power relations, as mentioned, also do not stand in a negative limiting relation to other relations, but play a directly positive and productive role in these.

Power comes from below. Power is not based upon a bipolar and comprehensive opposition between ruling and ruled, just as such an opposition cannot serve as a general framework for understanding power. There exists no general ordering principle for power. Foucault emphasizes that this does not mean that social classes and social domination do not exist. It means only that both the dominant and dominated enter into relations of power which none of them control in a simple, absolute way.

Power cannot be "acquired," "taken," or "shared," nor can it be "retained" or allowed to "slip away." Power is exercised, as said, from "innumerable points" in an interaction between unequal and mobile relations.[58] Inequalities in power relations must be traced back to their actual material functioning. Top-down dominance cannot be assumed as a point of departure, but must be made into an open empirical question. One must presume, says Foucault, that the varied power relations, which are created and are operative in production and business, in families, in other groups, and in institutions, are the basis for wide-ranging fragmentary effects, which permeate society. This fragmentation can in certain instances have a homogenizing, convergent, and consolidating effect on the relations of power, but an eventual consolidated dominance, for example, hegemony, is considered as an effect, not a point of departure.

Where there is power there is resistance. Foucault is clear on this point: "In the relations of power, there is necessarily the possibility of resistance, for if there were no possibility of resistance . . . there would be no relations of power."[59] And resistance never stands in an external relationship to power, resistance is a part of power. Nevertheless, according to Foucault, it would be a misunderstanding to say that one always subjects oneself to power, that one cannot escape domination, and hence lay oneself open to a cynical view of power, and to the kind of fatalism, determinism, and nihilism which may follow from such a view. This would be to misunderstand the relational character of power. Foucault is equally clear regarding the central significance of resistance to power studies:

I would like to suggest [a] way to go further towards a new economy of power relations, a way which is more empirical, more directly related to our present situation, and which implies more relations between theory and practice. It consists of taking the forms of resistance against different forms of power as a starting point. To use another metaphor, it consists of using this resistance as a chemical catalyst so as to bring to light power relations, locate their position, find out their point of application and the methods used. Rather than analyzing power from the point of view of its internal rationality, it consists of analyzing power relations through the antagonism of strategies.[60]

Relations of power are in their very existence dependent on a multiplicity of points of resistance, and they exist throughout any power network. Resistance, too, has no single center. According to Foucault there is no sole source of rebellion, no one law of revolutions. Instead there is a multiplicity of resistances, each of which is a special case for the study of power. This living multiplicity does not mean that there cannot occur radical breaks and profound bipolar fragmentation; for example, revolutions and massive struggles between classes. These certainly occur, but according to Foucault they neither typify nor dominate power relations. It is often a case of mobile and temporary points of resistance, which produce changeable fragmentations and regroupings: some groups disintegrate, others are created. The fragmentation may even penetrate individuals, dividing their points of reference and reconstituting their identities. Just as the network of power relations creates a tight web and system which penetrates apparatuses and institutions without actually being localized in these, the innumerable points of resistance crosscut social divisions. It is the strategic consolidation and ordering of points of resistance which make possible a rebellion or a revolution, in the same way as the state is dependent on institutional consolidation and ordering of stable power relations for its operations.

With Foucault's concept of power, a number of central tenets in power-as-entity theories – be they elitist, pluralist, or Marxist – become problematic. To seize the "centers of power," for example, might simply reproduce old patterns of government and domination instead of changing them: the class that succeeds in overthrowing the ruling class becomes the new ruling class. This, clearly, has been a problem for applied Marxism in socialist societies. Real change, according to Foucault, requires changing our selves, our bodies, our souls, and our ways of knowing – it requires "work of the self upon the self" – in addition to changing the economy and society.[61] The power-as-entity theories are insufficient.

Instead of the "Who?–What?–Where?" questions of power mentioned above, a Foucauldian, and phronetic, point of departure for particular case studies of power are the following questions: What are the most immediate and the most local power relations operating, and how do they operate? How has the active exercise of power in the relations being investigated affected the possibilities for the further exercise of power, with the resulting reinforcement of certain power relations and the attenuation of others? How are power relations linked together, according to what logic and strategy? How have these relations made certain rationalities possible and others impossible, and how do the rationalities support or oppose the power relations? How can the games of power be played differently?

Power, rationality, and truth

Foucault sees discourses not simply as surface projections of power mechanisms; via discourse and interpretation, rationality and power become interwoven. Here, too, Foucault follows a basic Nietzschean insight, namely that interpretation is not only commentary, as is often the view. "[I]nterpretation is itself a means of becoming master of something," says Nietzsche in *The Will to Power*,[62] and he adds elsewhere that "whatever exists, having somehow come into being, is again and again reinterpreted to new ends, taken over, transformed, and redirected by some power superior to it . . . all subduing and becoming master involves a fresh interpretation."[63] Discourses, therefore, must be viewed as a series of interrupted segments whose tactical function is neither uniform nor stable. One ought not to view the universe of discourses as divided into accepted and excluded discourses, into dominant and dominated discourses, or into successful and fallacious discourses. Rather, one should operate with a multiplicity of discursive elements, which can be put into operation in various strategies. According to Foucault, it is the distribution of this multiplicity of discursive elements which must be reconstructed in a concrete study of rationality and power.[64] This is done by describing that which is said and that which is hidden, the necessary articulations, and the forbidden ones, and relations between these. Variants and different effects of the discursive elements must be studied with reference to who speaks and from which position of power, in which institutional context, etc. Shifts and recycling of identical formulations with different purposes must also be identified. For example, one might well imagine that discursive elements, which are identical or immediately resemble each other when viewed out of context, could have diametrically opposing roles when seen in the context of different strategies. Thus, the same discursive act can legitimate widely differing ends.

Discourses, then, are not subordinated or set up against power once and for all. No discourse is unequivocally oppressive or always emancipatory. The researcher's methodology must take account of the complex and unstable process according to which discourses can be both an instrument of power and its effect, but also an obstacle, a point of resistance or a starting point for a counterposing strategy. Discourses thus transfer and produce power. They reinforce power, but they also subvert and conceal it, make it fragile and contribute to obstructing power. In the same way, secrecy and silence can mask power, but they can also weaken its grip and make possible the existence of obscure areas without public tolerance. It would be fallacious to assume the existence of a power discourse on the one hand and an opposing counterdiscourse on the other. Discourses are tactical elements, which operate in the field of force relations. Different and even opposing discourses may coexist within the same strategy. And according to Foucault one cannot expect that discourses disclose by themselves what strategy they are part of, or what moral divisions they follow, or what kind of ideology, be it dominant or dominated. Instead one must study discourses at two levels: (1) the level of their tactical productivity, where the key question is, "What reciprocal effects of power and knowledge [do] they ensure?" and (2) the level of strategic integration, where the question now becomes, What conjunction and what force relationship make it necessary to utilize discourses in a given episode of the various confrontations that occur?[65]

Foucault is unambiguous in his evaluation of the significance of rationality as an object of study:

I think that the central issue of philosophy and critical thought since the eighteenth century has always been, still is, and will, I hope, remain the question: *What is this Reason that we use? What are its historical effects? What are its limits, and what are its dangers? How can we exist as rational beings, fortunately committed to practicing a rationality that is unfortunately crisscrossed by intrinsic dangers?* One should remain as close to this question as possible, keeping in mind that it is both central and extremely difficult to resolve.[66]

In developing a more contemporary concept of *phronesis,* it is precisely one of the advantages of Foucault's view of power that it integrates rationality and power, knowledge and power, reason and power, truth and power. For Foucault, these phenomena do not stand in a bipolar external relationship to each other: power produces rationality and truth; rationality and truth produce power. The one side cannot be explained unilaterally in terms of the other or be reduced to the other. "Perhaps, too, we should abandon a whole tradition that allows us to imagine that knowledge can exist only where the power relations are suspended and that knowledge can develop only outside its injunctions, its demands and its interests," says Foucault.

> We should admit rather that power produces knowledge . . . that power and knowledge directly imply one another; that there is no power relation without the correlative constitution of a field of knowledge, nor any knowledge that does not presuppose and constitute at the same time power relations . . . [I]t is not the activity of the subject of knowledge that produces a corpus of knowledge, useful or resistant to power, but power-knowledge, the processes and struggles that traverse it and of which it is made up, that determines the forms and possible domains of knowledge.[67]

This view contrasts with any sort of separation of rationality and power and the associated view that the task of social and political science is to "speak truth to power," as C. Wright Mills and Aaron Wildavsky have put it.[68] The latter view, according to Foucault, is an oversimplification.

Foucault criticizes political philosophy and social science for practicing an unreflected "will to knowledge." Political philosophy and social science concern themselves with ideal social models for the functioning of society, with abstractions, basic principles, utopias, theories, and general criteria for the evaluation of existing conditions in society. According to Foucault it is precisely this unreflected will to knowledge which distracts us from the concrete operations of power and that makes power so poorly understood today. When we discuss research and politics, the task, according to Foucault, is to break with this mode of questioning in philosophy and social science and instead inquire how power actually functions.

In order to understand his considerations on the relation between truth and power, knowledge and power, and rationality and power, it is important to make clear what Foucault understands by "truth." "[B]y truth I do not mean 'the ensemble of truths which are to be discovered and accepted'," says Foucault, "but rather 'the ensemble of rules according to which the true and false are separated and specific effects of power attached to the true,' it being understood also that it's not a matter of a battle 'on behalf' of the truth, but of a battle about the status of truth and the economic and political role it plays."[69] According to Foucault, the concern for truth is "*the* question for the West" (emphasis in original),[70] and every society has its regimes of truth and its "politics of truth," understood as the types of discourse which society accepts and allows to operate as true; the mechanisms which make it possible to distinguish between true and false propositions; techniques and procedures regarded as valuable in the production of truth and for determining the status for those who concern themselves with determining what is true. Foucault asks us to consider whether the "problem of truth" is not the "most general of political problems," and he sees the task of speaking the truth as endless.[71] No power can avoid the obligation to respect this task in all its complexity, according to Foucault, "unless it imposes silence and servitude."[72] Herein lies the power of truth.

In sum, according to Foucault the political question is not one of mistake, illusion, false consciousness, or ideology, but truth itself: "truth is not by nature free – nor error servile," concludes Foucault. The production of truth "is thoroughly imbued with relations of power."[73]

Foucault's critical studies of rationality and power have led to speculations that Foucault sees himself and his work as somehow located above power relations. In fact, Foucault makes it clear in several places, that this is not the case. As with Aristotle and *phronesis*, Foucault does not see himself and his studies as located in an external relation to that which he analyzes. Such a location he sees as simply impossible. Foucault shares with Max Weber a concern with modern processes of rationalization. But where Weber set himself the goal of giving a rational and scientifically objective explanation for the rationalization problem, Foucault's genealogy is explicitly context-dependent. This means that Foucault avoids ending up in the same dilemma as Weber, that is, the dilemma of value-freedom. Weber saw rationalization as the modern era's great problem, but he was unable to scientifically argue for his suspicion that the costs of rationalization were greater than their potential advantages, and that rationalization ought to be resisted. As a scholar, he could not provide guidelines for relevant action even though he believed that there ought to be action. On the contrary, Weber looked negatively at his own theorization, seeing it as part of the development of which he disapproved. All Weber could do was to point out this paradox in his analysis.

Foucault's situation is fundamentally different because of the interpretative *engagement* of the genealogical analysis. As with *phronesis*, values, pragmatic considerations, and strategies for action are a prerequisite for, and part of, the method, and hence, do not stand in opposition to the understanding-oriented project. Foucault speaks of a "limit-attitude" which can be explicitly defined as positive and action-oriented. This contrasts with structuralism, which tends to analyze limits from without and sees them as constrictive for action. Foucault's perspective places itself neither beyond, nor within, but *on* the boundaries between the seemingly possible and impossible with the clear intention of shifting these boundaries. Here, again, Foucault attempts to move beyond some of the classical dualisms that tend to trouble social and political science: oppositions between the possible and the impossible, voluntarism and determinism, idealism and fatalism, agency and structure. There are grounds to quote Foucault at some length on this central point:

> This . . . ethos may be characterized as a *limit-attitude*. We are not talking about a gesture of rejection. We have to move beyond the outside–inside alternative; we have to be at the frontiers. Criticism indeed consists of analyzing and reflecting upon limits . . . [I]n what is given to us as universal, necessary, obligatory, what place is occupied by whatever is singular, contingent, and the product of arbitrary constraints? . . . [Criticism] will not deduce from the form of what we are what it is impossible for us to do and to know . . . it is seeking to give new impetus, as far and wide as possible, to the undefined work of freedom . . . I shall thus characterize [the ethos] as a historico-practical test of the limits that we may go beyond, and thus as work carried out by ourselves upon ourselves as free beings.[74]

For Foucault "[t]hought is freedom in relation to what one does."[75] Thought is not what inhabits a certain conduct and gives it meaning. Thought is, rather, what allows one to step back from this conduct and to "question it as to its meaning, its conditions, and its goals." Thus thought is the motion by which one detaches oneself from what one does and "reflects on it as a problem." Thought is the ability to think differently in order to act differently.[76] Thought defined in this manner – as reflexive thought aimed at action – stands at the core of Foucault's ethics, which, then, is an ethics antithetical to any type of "thought-police." Reflexive thought is therefore the most important "intellectual virtue" for Foucault, just as for Aristotle it is *phronesis* (see chapter five). In fact, when analyzed conceptually, as opposed to historically, the similarities are striking between Foucauldian thought, defined as above, and Aristotelian *phronesis*.

According to Foucault, freedom is not ensured by the institutions and the legislation established with the presumed intention of guaranteeing freedom. An originally emancipatory institutional system may turn into its own opposition and become repressive, precisely because it is a system and is thereby totalizing. Individual institutions and legislation can in most cases be turned against their original goals in the same ways as truth and rationality. Not only because they are open for interpretation, but according to Foucault because they must be practiced in order to have an impact in the project of freedom and justice and in the relations of power of which they are a part. This is why any type of blueprint social engineering (*techne*) based on science (*episteme*) is as unacceptable to Foucault as it was to Aristotle. These two thinkers give priority to public deliberation, that is *phronesis*, over science in social matters, including concerns about institutions and laws.

According to Foucault, freedom is ensured even less by philosophy and theory than by institutions and laws. Philosophy and theory, too, can be reversed and transformed according to pragmatic, opportunistic objectives. During a meeting in 1983 between Habermas and Foucault, Habermas mentioned how upset he had been one day when he came across some texts of one of his former teachers, a well-known Kantian. The texts, from 1934, were thoroughly Nazi in their orientation. Foucault relates that he reflected upon Habermas's experience, especially after Foucault himself was later subjected to a similar experience. Foucault stumbled upon a text by the stoic Max Pohlenz, also from 1934, about the *Führer* ideal in stoicism and about true humanism in *das Volk* under the *Führer's* inspiration.[77] Foucault points out that philosophical and theoretical positions can be used and abused, and that one cannot expect that potentially emancipatory theoretical positions, or their authors, will automatically operate in an emancipatory fashion in practice: "certain great themes such as 'humanism' can be used to any end whatever – for example to show with what gratitude Pohlenz would have greeted Hitler."[78]

For Foucault, the association between political philosophy and social theory on the one hand and political practice on the other thus tends to be a weak one. From this perspective, Foucault states that attempts to solve the problems of our time by developing potentially emancipatory philosophical and theoretical positions become problematic. The struggles against rationalization and repression, which both Foucault, Weber, and Habermas see as one of our era's most important tasks, cannot – Foucault says – be effectively conducted at the theoretical level. Rather, they must be carried out in relation to specific instances of rationalization and repression in their particular contexts. Precisely on this point lies one of the most decisive differences between Habermas and Foucault as we saw in chapter seven.

Foucault's position does not mean that "anything goes" in a theoretical context. Nor does it imply that theory is not important.[79] Rather, it means that theories, and conceptualization in general, must be constantly confronted with praxis, including the praxis of the individual scholar. Here, again, Foucault shows himself to be closer to Aristotle and *phronesis* than to Plato and epistemology. "If I have insisted on all this 'practice',' says Foucault, "it has not been in order to 'apply' ideas, but in order to put them to the test and modify them."[80] Practice and freedom, according to Foucault, and to Aristotle, are not derived epistemologically or by theoretical work. Freedom *is* a practice, not a result or a state of affairs. And *phronesis* is the intellectual virtue most relevant to the project of freedom.

9   Methodological guidelines for a reformed social science

[T]he way to re-enchant the world . . . is to stick to the concrete.

Richard Rorty

After having explored in the previous two chapters the importance of power to a contemporary interpretation of *phronesis* and to social science, let us now begin to sum up the argument of the book by bringing together more explicitly what it might mean today to practice social science as *phronesis*. We will do this, firstly, by developing a set of methodological guidelines for phronetic social science in this chapter, and, secondly, by giving illustrations and examples of phronetic research in chapter ten.

I would like to stress immediately that the methodological guidelines summarized below should not be seen as methodological imperatives; at most they are cautionary indicators of direction. Let me also mention that undoubtedly, there are ways of practicing phronetic social science other than those outlined here. The most important issue is not the individual methodology involved, even if methodological questions may have some significance. It is more important to get the result right, that is, arriving at a social science which effectively deals with public deliberation and praxis, rather than being stranded with a social science that vainly attempts to emulate natural science.

As mentioned earlier, few researchers seem to have reflected explicitly on the strengths and weaknesses of social science practiced as *episteme*, *techne*, and *phronesis*, respectively. Even fewer are carrying out actual research on the basis of such reflection, and fewer still have set out the methodological considerations and guidelines for a *phronesis*-based social science. In fact, it seems that researchers doing *phronesis*-like work have a sound instinct for getting on with their research and not getting involved in methodology, a case in point being the sparseness of methodological considerations and guidelines in Michel Foucault's work already remarked upon. Nonetheless, given the interpretation of the actual and potential role of the social sciences as laid out in this book, it is essential for the development of these sciences that such guidelines are elaborated.

The main point of departure for explicating methodological guidelines for phronetic social science is our reading of Aristotle and Foucault in the previous chapters. We will supplement this reading, however, with a reading of other thinkers – Pierre Bourdieu, Clifford Geertz, Alasdair MacIntyre, Richard Rorty, and others – who emphasize practical before epistemic knowledge in the study of humans and society, despite important differences in other domains.[1]

Focusing on values

By definition, phronetic researchers focus on values; for example, by taking their point of departure in the classic value-rational questions: Where are we going? Is it desirable? What should be done? As described in chapter five, in the discussion of value-rationality and *phronesis*, the objective is to balance instrumental rationality with value-rationality by increasing the capacity of individuals, organizations, and society to think and act in value-rational terms. Focusing on values, the phronetic researcher is forced to face the question of foundationalism versus relativism, that is, the view that central values exist that can be rationally and universally grounded, versus the view that one set of values is just as good as another.

Phronetic researchers reject both of these "isms" and replace them by contextualism, that is, by situational ethics. Distancing themselves from foundationalism does not leave phronetic researchers normless, however. They take their point of departure in their attitude to the situation in the society being studied. They seek to ensure that such an attitude is not based on idiosyncratic morality or personal preferences, but instead on a common view among a specific reference group to which the researchers refer. For phronetic researchers, the socially and historically conditioned context – and not the rational and universal grounding which is desired by certain philosophers, but which is not yet achieved – constitutes the most effective bulwark against relativism and nihilism. Phronetic researchers realize that our sociality and history is the only foundation we have, the only solid ground under our feet. And that this socio-historical foundation is fully adequate for our work as social scientists.

As regards validity, phronetic research is based on interpretation and is open for testing in relation to other interpretations and other research. But one interpretation is not just as good as another, which would be the case for relativism. Every interpretation must be built upon claims of validity, and the procedures ensuring validity are as demanding for phronetic research as for any other activity in the social and political sciences. Phronetic researchers also oppose the view that any one among a number of interpretations lacks value because it is "merely" an interpretation. As emphasized by Alexander Nehamas, the key point is the establishment of a *better* alternative, where "better" is defined according to sets of validity claims.[2] If a better interpretation demonstrates the previous interpretation to be "merely" interpretation, this new interpretation remains valid until another, still better interpretation is produced which can reduce the previous interpretation to "merely" interpretation. This is the procedure which a community of social scientists would follow in working together to put certain interpretations of social and political life ahead of others (see also the section on "dialogue" pp. 139–40 below). The procedure describes not an interpretive or relativistic approach. Rather, it sets forth the basic ground rules for any social or political inquiry, inasmuch as social science and philosophy have not yet identified criteria by which an ultimate interpretation and a final grounding of values and facts can be made.

Placing power at the core of analysis

Besides focusing on the three value-rational questions mentioned above, which are the classical Aristotelian questions, a contemporary reading of *phronesis* also poses questions about power and outcomes: Who gains, and who loses? Through what kinds of power relations? What possibilities are available to change existing power relations? And is it desirable to do so? Of what kinds of power relations are those asking these questions themselves a part? Phronetic research poses these questions with the intention of avoiding the voluntarism and idealism typical of so much ethical thinking. The main question is not only the Weberian: "Who governs?" posed by Robert Dahl and most other students of power. It is also the Nietzschean question: What "governmental rationalities" are at work when those who govern govern? With these questions and with the focus on value-rationality, phronetic researchers relate explicitly to a primary context of values and power. Combining the best of a Nietzschean–Foucauldian interpretation of power with the best of a Weberian–Dahlian one, the analysis of power would be guided by a conception of power that can be characterized by six features:

(1) Power is seen as productive and positive and not only as restrictive and negative.
(2) Power is viewed as a dense net of omnipresent relations and not only as localized in "centers" and institutions, or as an entity one can "possess."
(3) The concept of power is seen as ultradynamic; power is not only

something one appropriates, but also something one reappropriates and exercises in a constant back-and-forth movement in relations of strength, tactics, and strategies.

(4) Knowledge and power, truth and power, rationality and power are analytically inseparable from each other; power produces knowledge, and knowledge produces power.

(5) The central question is how power is exercised, and not only who has power, and why they have it; the focus is on process in addition to structure.

(6) Power is studied with a point of departure in small questions, "flat and empirical," not only, nor primarily, with a point of departure in "big questions."[3]

Analyses of power following this format cannot be equated with a general analytics of every possible power relation. Other approaches and other interpretations are possible. They can, however, serve as a possible and productive point of departure for dealing with questions of power in doing *phronesis*.

Getting close to reality

Donald Campbell, Charles Lindblom, and others have noted that the development of social research is inhibited by the fact that researchers tend to work with problems in which the answer to the question "If you are wrong about this, who will notice?" is "Nobody."[4] Mary Timney Bailey calls the outcome of this type of research "'so what' results."[5] Phronetic researchers seek to transcend this problem of relevance by anchoring their research in the context studied and thereby ensuring a hermeneutic "fusion of horizons." This applies both to contemporary and historical studies. For contemporary studies one gets close to the phenomenon or group whom one studies during data collection, and remains close during the phases of data analysis, feedback, and publication of results. Combined with the above-mentioned focus on relations of values and power, this strategy typically creates interest by outside parties, and even outside stakeholders, in the research. These parties will test and evaluate the research in various ways. The researchers will consciously expose themselves to reactions from their surroundings – both positive and negative – and may derive benefit from the learning effect, which is built into this strategy. In this way, the phronetic researcher becomes a part of the phenomenon studied, without necessarily "going native" or the project becoming simple action research.[6]

Phronetic researchers doing historical studies carry out much of their work in those locales where the relevant historical materials are placed, and they also typically probe deeply into archives, annals, and individual documents. Foucault, for instance, spent a large part of his typical Paris working day in the archives of the Bibliothèque Nationale or the Bibliothèque du Saulchoir. Here he found a knowledge whose visible body "is neither theoretical or scientific discourse nor literature, but a regular, daily practice."[7] In historical studies, as in contemporary ones, the objective is to get close to reality. *Wirkliche Historie* (real history), says Foucault, "shortens its vision to those things nearest to it."[8] C. Roland Christensen of Harvard University, arguably one of the fathers of the case method, expresses a similar attitude about his research by invoking Henry Miller to describe the approach taken by case researchers: "My whole work has come to resemble a terrain of which I have made a thorough, geodetic survey, not from a desk with pen and ruler, but by touch, by getting down on all fours, on my stomach, and crawling over the ground inch by inch, and this over an endless period of time in all conditions of weather."[9]

Emphasizing little things

Phronetic researchers begin their work by phenomenologically asking "little questions" and focusing on what Clifford Geertz, with a term borrowed from Gilbert Ryle, calls "thick description."[10] This procedure may often seem tedious and trivial. Nietzsche and Foucault emphasize that it requires "patience and a knowledge of details," and it depends on a "vast accumulation of source material."[11] Geertz explicates the dilemma involved in skipping minutiae. The problem with an approach, which extracts the general from the particular and then sets the particular aside as detail, illustration, background, or qualification, is that "it leaves us helpless in the face of the very difference we need to explore," Geertz says. "[It] does indeed simplify matters. It is less certain that it clarifies them."[12] Nietzsche, who advocates "patience and seriousness in the smallest things,"[13] expresses a similar, though more radical, point regarding the importance of detail when he says that "[a]ll the problems of politics, of social organization, and of education have been falsified through and through . . . because one learned to despise 'little' things, which means the basic concerns of life itself."[14]

The focus on minutiae, which directly opposes much conventional wisdom about the need to focus on "important problems," has its background in a fundamental phenomenological experience, that small questions often lead to big answers. In this sense, phronetic research is decentered in its approach, taking its point of departure in local micropractices, searching for the Great within the Small and vice versa. "God is in the detail," the proverb says. "So is the Devil," the phronetic researcher would add, doing work that is at the same time as detailed and as general as possible.

Looking at practice before discourse

Through words and concepts we are continually tempted to think of things as being simpler than they are, says Nietzsche, "there is a philosophical mythology concealed in *language*" (emphasis in original).[15] Michel Serres puts the matter even more succinctly. "Language has a disgust for things," he says. Phronetic research attempts to get beyond this problem. Thus, practice is seen as more fundamental than either discourse or theory. Goethe's phrase from *Faust*, "Am Anfang war die Tat" (in the beginning was the deed), could be the motto for phronetic research. It is echoed by Foucault who says, "discourse is not life," regular, daily practice is.[16] As pointed out in the previous chapter, phronetic research does not accept the maxim that there is nothing outside the text, or outside discourse. Discourse analysis must be disciplined by the analysis of practices.

Phronetic research focuses on practical activity and practical knowledge in everyday situations. It *may* mean, but is certainly not limited to, a focus on known sociological, ethnographic, and historical phenomena such as "everyday life" and "everyday people." What it *always* means, however, is a focus on the actual daily practices which constitute a given field of interest, regardless of whether these practices take place on the floor of a stock exchange, a grassroots organization, a hospital, or a local school board.

At the outset, practices are recorded and described simply as events. "The question which I ask," says Foucault, "is not about codes but about events . . . I try to answer this question without referring to the consciousness . . . the will . . . intention."[17] The researcher records what happened "on such a day, in such a place, in such circumstances."[18] In *The Will to Power*, in describing his "principles of a new evaluation," Nietzsche similarly says that when evaluating human action one should "take doing *something*, the 'aim,' the 'intention,' the 'purpose,' back into the deed after having artificially removed all this and thus emptied the deed" (emphasis in original).[19] Data, events, and phenomena are presented together with their connections with other data, events, and phenomena. Discontinuities and changes in the meaning of concepts and discourses are documented. The hermeneutic horizon is isolated and its arbitrariness elaborated. Initially, the researcher takes no position regarding the truth-value and significance ascribed by participants to the practices studied. No practice is seen as more valuable than another. The horizon of meaning is that of the individual practice. The researcher then attempts to understand the roles played by the practices studied in the total system of relations. If it is established, for example, that a certain practice is rational according to its self-understanding, but not when viewed in the context of other horizons of meaning, the researcher then asks what role this "dubious" rationality plays in a further context, historically and politically, and what consequences this might have.[20]

In addition to the Nietzschean removal of the doer from the deed, the focus on practices as events also involves a self-removal on the part of the researcher to allow him or her to disinterestedly inspect the *wirkliche Historie* of human action. This distancing enables the researcher to master a subject matter even where it is hideous, and there may be a "brutality of fact" involved in the approach. This, in turn, may offend people who mistake the researcher's willingness to uncover and face the morally unacceptable for immorality. There may also be intensity and optimism, however, in facing even the pessimistic and depressing sides of power and human action. The description of practices as events endures and gains its strength from detecting the forces that make life work. And a reality that is ugly or even terrifying when judged by the moral standards which we like to think apply in modern society, may also be deeply human and may have to be faced squarely by researchers, readers, and the general public if this reality is to be changed. Nietzsche acutely named this approach to research "The Gay [*fröhliche*] Science," and he called those practicing the approach "free spirits" and described them as "curious to a vice, investigators to the point of cruelty, with uninhibited fingers for the unfathomable, with teeth and stomachs for the most indigestible . . . collectors from morning till late, misers of our riches and our crammed drawers."[21]

Studying cases and contexts

We have seen that Aristotle explicitly identifies knowledge of "particular circumstances" as a main ingredient of *phronesis*.[22] Foucault similarly worked according to the dictum "never lose sight of reference to a concrete example."[23] Phronetic research thus benefits from focusing on case studies, precedents, and exemplars. *Phronesis* functions on the basis of practical rationality and judgment. As I have argued elsewhere, practical rationality and judgment evolve and operate primarily by virtue of deep-going case experiences.[24] Practical rationality, therefore, is best understood through cases – experienced or narrated – just as judgment is best cultivated and communicated via the exposition of cases. The significance of this point can hardly be overstated, which is why Richard Rorty, in responding to Max Weber's thesis regarding the modern "disenchantment of the world," invokes John Dewey to say: "the way to re-enchant the world . . . is to stick to the concrete."[25] A focus on concrete cases does not exclude the attempts at empirical generalizations typical of much social and political science. Such generalizations are perfectly compatible with cases and with narrative.[26]

Cases exist in context. What has been called the "primacy of context" follows from the empirical fact that in the history of science, human action has shown itself to be irreducible to predefined elements and rules unconnected to interpretation.[27] Therefore, it has been impossible to derive praxis from first principles and theory. Praxis has always been contingent on context-dependent judgment, on situational ethics. It would require a major transformation of current philosophy and science if this view were to change, and such a transformation does not seem on the horizon. What Pierre Bourdieu calls the "feel for the game" is central to all human action of any complexity, and it enables an infinite number of "moves" to be made, adapted to the infinite number of possible situations which no rule, however complex, can foresee.[28] Therefore, the judgment, which is central to *phronesis* and praxis, is always context-dependent. The minutiae, practices, and concrete cases which lie at the heart of phronetic research are seen in their proper contexts; both the small, local context, which gives phenomena their immediate meaning, and the larger, international and global context in which phenomena can be appreciated for their general and conceptual significance.[29] Given the role of context in phronetic research, insofar as such research is practiced as applied ethics, it is situational ethics. The focus is on *Sittlichkeit* (ethics) rather than *Moralität* (morality).

Asking "How?" Doing narrative

Phronetic research focuses on the dynamic question, "How?" in addition to the more structural "Why?". It is concerned with both *verstehen* (understanding) and *erklären* (explanation). Effects of social phenomena are investigated and interpreted in relation to process. In the study of relationships of power, we saw how Foucault emphasized the how-question, "the little question . . . flat and empirical," as particularly important. Foucault stressed that our understanding will suffer if we do not start our analyses with a "How?"

Asking "How?" and doing narrative analysis are closely interlinked activities. Earlier we saw that a central question for *phronesis* is: What should we do? To this Alasdair MacIntyre answers: "I can only answer the question 'What am I to do?' if I can answer the prior question 'Of what story or stories do I find myself a part?'"[30] This is why Nietzsche and Foucault see history as fundamental to social science and philosophy and criticize social scientists and philosophers for their lack of "historical sense."[31] It is also why history is central to phronetic research in both senses of the word; that is, *both* as narrative containing specific actors and events, in what Clifford Geertz calls a story with a scientific plot; *and* as the recording of a historical development.[32] Narratology, understood as the question of "how best to get an honest story honestly told," is more important than epistemology and ontology.[33]

Several observers have noted that narrative is an ancient method and perhaps our most fundamental form for making sense of experience.[34] To MacIntyre, the human being is a "story-telling animal," and the notion of a history is as fundamental a notion as the notion of an action.[35] In a similar vein, Cheryl Mattingly points out that narratives not only give meaningful form to experiences we have already lived through. They also provide us a forward glance, helping us to anticipate situations even before we encounter them, allowing us to envision alternative futures.[36] Narrative inquiries do not – indeed, cannot – start from explicit theoretical assumptions. Instead, they begin with an interest in a particular phenomenon that is best understood narratively. Narrative inquiries then develop descriptions and interpretations of the phenomenon from the perspective of participants, researchers, and others. In the historical analysis, both event and conjuncture are crucial, just as practices are studied in the context of several centuries, akin to what Fernand Braudel calls "*longue durée.*" The century-long view is employed in order to allow for the influence on current practices of traditions with long historical roots.

Joining agency and structure

Phronetic research focuses on both the actor level and the structural level, as well as on the relation between the two in an attempt to transcend the dualisms of actor/structure, hermeneutics/structuralism, and voluntarism/determinism.[37] Actors and their practices are analyzed in relation to structures and structures in terms of agency, not so that the two stand in an external relation to each other, but so that structures are found as part of actors and actors as part of structures. Understanding from "within" and from "without" are both accorded emphasis. This is what Pierre Bourdieu, in adapting the Aristotelian and Thomist concept of "habitus," calls "the internalization of externality and the externalization of internality."[38] Elsewhere Bourdieu explicitly states that the use of the notion of habitus can be understood as a way of escaping from the choice between "a structuralism without a subject and the philosophy of the subject."[39]

As anyone who has tried it can testify, it is a demanding task to account simultaneously for the structural influences that shape the development of a given phenomenon and still craft a clear, penetrating narrative or microanalysis of that phenomenon.[40] Diane Vaughan has pointed out that theorizing on actors and structures remains bifurcated.[41] Social scientists tend to generate either macrolevel or microlevel explanations, ignoring the critical connections. Empirical work follows the same pattern. Instead of research that attempts to link macrolevel factors and actors' choices in a specific social or political phenomenon, scholars dichotomize. Structural analyses and studies of actors each get their share of attention, but in separate projects, by separate researchers. Those who join structure and actor in empirical work most often do so by theoretical inference: data at one level of analysis are coupled with theoretical speculation about the other. While issues of actor and structure come together with particular emphasis in institutions, social-science research methodology is less developed for studying institutions than for studying individuals and aggregate patterns.[42] On this background, many social scientists may not be convinced that there is a way out of the duality of structural and individual analysis, no middle ground; the very recalcitrance of the problem seems to attest to its intractableness.

There is mounting evidence, however, that the actor/structure connection is not an insurmountable problem. In fact, it may not be a problem at all, says Vaughan, but simply an artifact of data availability and graduate training.[43] And we now have excellent examples showing us how to integrate actors and structures. Clifford Geertz's classic description of the Balinese cockfight progressively incorporates practices, institutions, and symbols from the larger Balinese social and cultural world in order to understand the seemingly localized event of the cockfight.[44] Robert Putnam and his associates similarly combine individual and structural analysis – as well as contemporary history and the history of the *longue durée* – in their attempt at explaining the performance of modern, democratic institutions in Italy.[45] And Stella Tillyard works from the basis of personal histories and family dynamics to incorporate the larger socioeconomic and political scene of the entire Hanoverian Age.[46] Phronetic researchers deliberately seek out information for answering questions about what structural factors influence individual actions, how those actions are constructed, and their structural consequences.[47]

Dialoguing with a polyphony of voices

Phronetic research is dialogical in the sense that it includes, and, if successful, is itself included in, a polyphony of voices, with no one voice, including that of the researcher, claiming final authority. Thus, the goal of phronetic research is to produce input to the ongoing social dialogue and praxis in a society, rather than to generate ultimate, unequivocally verified knowledge. This accords with Aristotle's maxim that in questions of social and political action, one ought to trust more in the public sphere than in science.[48] In *Habits of the Heart*, Robert Bellah and his coauthors expressed their hope that "the reader will test what we say against his or her own experience, will argue with us when what we say does not fit, and, best of all, will join the public discussion by offering interpretations superior to ours that can then receive further discussion."[49] This is as fine an expression of the phronetic dialogical attitude as we will find.

Thus, phronetic research explicitly sees itself as not having a privileged position from which the final truth can be told and further discussion stopped. We cannot think of an "eye turned in no particular direction," as Nietzsche says. "There is *only* a perspective seeing, *only* a perspective 'knowing;' and the *more* affects we allow to speak about one thing, the *more* eyes, different eyes, we can use to observe one thing, the more complete will our 'concept' of this thing, our 'objectivity,' be" (emphasis in original).[50] Hence, "objectivity" in phronetic research is not "contemplation without interest" but employment of "a *variety* of perspectives and affective interpretations in the service of knowledge" (emphasis in original).[51]

The significance of any given interpretation in a dialogue will depend on the extent to which the interpretation's validity claims are accepted, and this acceptance typically occurs in competition with other validity claims and other interpretations. The discourses in which results of phronetic research are used have, in this sense, no special status, but are subordinated to the same conditions as any other dialogical discourse. Some may fear that this dialogue, instead of becoming the desired polyphony of voices, will all too easily become a shouting match, a cacophony of voices, in which the loudest carries the day. In phronetic research, the means to prevent this from happening is no different from in other research: only to the extent that the validity claims of phronetic research are accepted will the results of such research be accepted in the dialogue. Phronetic research thus recognizes a human privilege and a basic condition: meaningful dialogue in context. "Dialogue" comes from the Greek *dialogos*, where *dia* means "between" and *logos* "reason." In contrast to the analytical and instrumental rationality which lie at the cores of both *episteme* and *techne*, the practical rationality of *phronesis* is based on a socially conditioned, intersubjective "between-reason."

Phronetic social science

The result of phronetic research is a pragmatically governed interpretation of the studied practices. The interpretation does not require the researcher to agree with the actors' everyday understanding nor to discover some deep, inner meaning of the practices. Phronetic research is in this way interpretive, but it is neither everyday nor deep hermeneutics. Phronetic research is also not about, nor does it try to develop, theory or universal method. Thus, phronetic research is an analytical project, but not a theoretical or methodological one.

For this kind of research, practiced according to these heuristical guidelines, I suggest the term "phronetic social science." One task of research practiced on the basis of the heuristics presented above would be to provide concrete examples and detailed narratives of how power works and with what consequences, and to suggest how power might be changed and work with other consequences. Richard Rorty observes about this that, "[i]n so far as political situations become clear, they get clarified by detailed stories about who's doing what to whom."[52] Such clarification is a principal concern for phronetic social science and provides the main link to praxis. Phronetic social science explores historic circumstances and current practices to find avenues to praxis. The task of phronetic social science is to clarify and deliberate about the problems and risks we face and to outline how things may be done differently, in full knowledge that we cannot find ultimate answers to these questions or even a single version of what the questions are.

In the following chapter, I will illustrate how phronetic social science may be carried out in practice.

10   Examples and illustrations: narratives of value and power

Long years must pass before the truths we have made for ourselves become our very flesh.

Paul Valéry

Something happened

One summer, something happened that would prove consequential to my professional trajectory in life. I was employed as a student intern with the newly established Regional Planning Authority with Ribe County Council in Denmark. Parliament had just passed the first law on nationwide regional planning and the counties were in the process of preparing the first generation of regional plans. The atmosphere was one of novelty and aspiration. As a planner-to-be, I felt I was in the right place at the right time.

The central question of the regional planning exercise was the classic one of whether future development should be encouraged chiefly in the main urban centers or whether development should be decentralized and take place in smaller towns. My job was to carry out a survey of social, educational, and health services with the purpose of finding arguments for and against centralization and decentralization in these three sectors. One of the arguments I found was in a British study showing how young children's performance in school decreases with increasing distance between home and school. The study was presented in a well-known textbook with an instructive figure documenting the negative correlation between distance and learning. "Thus it would appear," the authors concluded, "that there are good psychological as well as economic reasons for minimizing the school journeys of young children."[1] This was a clear-cut argument for decentralized schools, that is, many schools close to where the children live, as opposed to fewer schools with longer distances to travel between home and school. I included this knowledge and the figure in my draft report together with many other results that might count as pros and cons in the County Council's decision regarding whether to centralize or decentralize urban development.

141

After approval from my boss, my report was sent for comment to the administrative heads of the county's social, educational, and health services, respectively. When they returned the report, there was plenty of red ink on its pages. The text and figure about young children's performance in school was crossed out, among other things. A note in the margin, in finicky handwriting, read, "Cancel, may not apply in Denmark," followed by the initials of the county director of schools. Going through the director's corrections, it became clear that knowledge which could be taken as arguments for a geographically decentralized school structure had to go. On the other hand, knowledge that supported a decision to centralize the schools could stay in the report. The school administration had already unofficially decided on centralization and the Regional Planning Authority was not allowed to interfere with knowledge that might question the wisdom of the decision. Our report had to show that centralization was desirable.

From the way the matter was handled – with a certain tension in the air; things that could not be said had to be done – it was immediately clear to me that something important was going on. Later, I experienced a similar episode as an intern with the Ministry of Environment in Copenhagen. We had not learned about this in school. Our education was based on the Baconian dictum that "knowledge is power," knowledge is important. The university itself was built on that assumption. As students we were not exposed to knowledge that addressed the question of whether it is true that knowledge is always important, or what decides whether knowledge gets to count as knowledge or not. Such questions were not asked.

Today we would say that our education lacked reflexivity on this point. Yet, in my practical work I had seen, on the one hand, that knowledge can be so important that people in powerful positions find it worth their while to repress it. On the other hand, I had also seen examples of knowledge being so weak that this repression actually succeeded. I had seen knowledge being marginalized by power, and power producing the knowledge that served its purposes best. I concluded that knowledge about the phenomena which decide whether economic, social, geographic, or other knowledge gets to count as important is at least as important as that knowledge itself. If you are not knowledgeable about the former, you cannot be effective with the latter. Even if it would take me more than a decade before I could formulate my experiences in scholarly formulas, I had, in fact, already found my professional interest: the relationship between rationality and power, truth and politics.

Modernity's blind spot

Later, as a university lecturer, I found that modernity and democracy have a "blind spot" in their reflexivity regarding the real relationship between rationality and power. Ideals seem to block the view to reality. Modern democratic constitutions typically prescribe a separation of rationality and power, much like the untenable separation of fact and value in conventional social and political thinking. The ideal prescribes that first we must know about a problem, then we can decide about it. For example, first the civil servants in the administration investigate a policy problem, then they inform their minister, who informs parliament, who decides on the problem. Power is brought to bear on the problem only after we have made ourselves knowledgeable about it.

In reality, however, power often ignores or designs knowledge at its convenience. A consequence of the blind spot is that the real relationship between rationality and power gets little attention both in conventional constitution writing and in the research literature. There is a large gray area between rationality and power, which is underinvestigated. This is the area where the sort of thing takes place which happened with the schools in Ribe County. The literature contains many studies of rationality and many of power, but much fewer of the relationship between the two.

I decided that as a scholar I would study this gray area. Accepting the ideal that democratic decisions should be rational and informed – an ideal to which I, like other democrats, subscribe – should clearly not keep us from trying to understand how rationality and power really relate in real decisions in real democracies. Firstly, I wanted to study the phenomenon that modern ideals of how rationality and power ought to relate are often a far cry from the realities of how rationality and power actually relate, with only weak guiding power and impact from ideals to reality. Secondly, I wanted to focus on what can be done about this problem. I decided to study these issues not only in theory, but also in practice. I figured that a focus on concrete cases in particular contexts would help better understand practice. And I reckoned that such an understanding is necessary for changing practice in a direction that would leave less scope for the kind of undemocratic power–knowledge relations I had witnessed in Ribe and elsewhere. Eventually, I decided to study how rationality and power shape politics, administration, and planning in the town where I live and work, Aalborg, Denmark.

Aalborg and Florence

Aalborg is the main urban administrative and commercial center for northern Jutland, a region of a half-million people, idyllically adjoined by the North Sea to the west and the Baltic Sea to the east. A typical medium-sized European city, Aalborg has a high-density historical center several centuries old. When I moved to Aalborg to start teaching in the university there, a major urban renewal project was being implemented in the city center. Aalborg, like many other European cities, was overrun by cars, and the city government had decided to do something about it. The project they were implementing was aimed at preserving the character of the historical downtown area; radically improving public transportation; enhancing environmental protection; developing an integrated network of bike paths, pedestrian malls, and green spaces; and developing housing stock. Specifically, automobile traffic was to be reduced by a third in the downtown area. With these measures, city government was a good decade ahead of their time in trying to cut a path to what would later be known as "sustainable development." The planning exercise they had just started would become known as the award-winning "Aalborg Project;" it would become one of the town's most sensitive and enduring political and planning issues for a decade and a half; and it would be recommended by the Organization for Economic Cooperation and Development (OECD) as a model for international adoption, on how to integrate environmental and social concerns into city politics and planning, including how to deal with the car in the city.

I had heard about the plans for the Aalborg Project previously, but I only began to consider the project as a potential candidate for my own research when, as a newcomer, I mused over the many changes happening to the urban landscape. Some of these were hard to explain rationally; for instance how certain regulations aimed at reducing car traffic were repeatedly being reorganized. If there was logic to the reorganizations, it escaped me, and I got curious. I did a pilot study of the Aalborg Project and then an actual study, covering almost fifteen years in the life of the project. The results of the research are described in my book *Rationality and Power: Democracy in Practice*.[2] I refer the reader who is interested in seeing an example of phronetic social science at work in an actual study, to this book. The methodology I developed for doing the Aalborg study is that described in the previous chapters. In what follows, I will not focus on the results of the study as such. Instead, I will illustrate what makes this study a study in phronetic social science. I will give examples of how, in carrying out the study, I employed key elements of the methodological guidelines described in chapter nine. I want to stress immediately, however, that the examples are necessarily brief and selective. The promise of this methodology is better understood through examining cases of its employment in their entirety, or, even better, by employing the methodology oneself in an actual study.

I wanted Aalborg to be to my study what Florence was to Machiavelli – no other comparison intended. I wanted to write what Machiavelli calls the *verita effettuale*, effective truth, of democracy in Aalborg. In so doing, I hoped to contribute to the discussion of democracy, in Aalborg and elsewhere. Aalborg would be a laboratory for understanding the real workings of power and what they mean for our more general concerns of social and political organization. In carrying out the study, I employed Wittgensteinian narratology, as described in chapters six and nine. The case story, accordingly, can neither be briefly recounted nor summarized in a few main results. The story is itself the result. It is a "virtual reality," so to speak, of politics, administration, and planning at work. For the reader willing to enter this reality and explore the life and death of the Aalborg Project from beginning to end, the payback is meant to be a sensitivity to issues of democracy, rationality, and power that cannot be obtained from theory. Students can safely be let loose in this kind of reality, which provides a useful training ground with insights into practice that academic teaching often does not provide.

Where are we going?

Returning to chapter nine's methodological guidelines for phronetic social science, in studying Aalborg I took my point of departure in the four value-rational questions, following Aristotle on the first, third, and fourth questions, and adding the second one in order to ensure that the study would adequately deal with issues of power:

1. Where are we going with democracy in Aalborg?
2. Who gains, and who loses, by which mechanisms of power?
3. Is it desirable?
4. What should be done?

The main sources for answering the questions were archival data, interviews, participant observation, and informants. For a while I had my own desk and coffee mug with the municipal administration, just as I was a frequent visitor with the other actors in the Aalborg Project. Empirically, I wanted the study to be particularly deep and detailed because I wanted to test the thesis that the most interesting phenomena, and those of most general import, would be found in the most minute and most concrete of details. Or to put the matter differently, I wanted to see whether the dualism general/concrete would vanish if I went into sufficiently deep detail. In chapter nine we saw how Nietzsche advocates a focus on "little things" if we are to understand the problems of politics and social organization, and how Rorty says that such a focus is the way to re-enchant the world. Both Nietzsche and Rorty seem right to me. And, for reasons I will touch upon below, I definitely wanted to re-enchant my world. I saw the Aalborg case as being made up of the type of little things that Nietzsche talks about. Indeed, I saw the case itself as such a thing, as what we have seen Nietzsche call a discreet and apparently insignificant truth, which, when closely examined, would reveal itself to be pregnant with paradigms, metaphors, and general significance, what Nietzsche calls "cyclopean monuments."[3] Let us now see what these terms might mean in practical research.

One day in the municipal archives, I was searching for material on the genealogy of the Aalborg Project. I was "meticulously and patiently" poring over some of the tens of thousands of pages of "entangled and confused" documents, which made up the archival side of the case, and which often were "scratched over and recopied many times," as Nietzsche and Foucault said I should be doing when doing genealogy.[4] At one point, a particular document attracted my attention. It was the minutes from a meeting about the planning of a major new thoroughfare in Aalborg's city center. I was trying to understand the context of the Aalborg Project and was studying urban policy and planning in Aalborg in the years immediately prior to the launching of the project. At first, I did not know exactly why this particular set of minutes drew my attention more than the many other pages I was perusing that day in the archives. In particular, five lines of text, buried within the minutes under the fifth of six items on the meeting-agenda, kept alerting me. Here is how the five lines read in full:

Before November 13, the City Center Group must organize a meeting plan for orientation of the following groups:

a. The [City Council] Technical Committee.
b. The Chamber of Industry and Commerce.
c. The Police.

The City Center Group is a group of officials responsible for planning and policy in downtown Aalborg, and the three groups listed for orientation – no more and no less – are the external parties that the City Center Group decides to inform about what the Group has in mind for the new thoroughfare. Since I could not come to grips with what it was about this text that kept exciting my attention I moved on to other documents. Later in the day, I returned to the five lines and asked myself "a, b, and c, yes, but the ABC of what?" I did not get any further, however. This went on for several days. I kept returning to the text, but to no avail. I felt like you sometimes do when you look at a certain gestalt-type figure with a hidden image. You know the image is there, but you cannot see it; it will not become a gestalt. And the harder you try the more difficult the task seems to be.

Then one day, when I returned to the document one more time, in a flash I finally saw the image: here is a private interest group, the Chamber of Industry and Commerce, sandwiched between two constitutionally determined powers. On one side, there is the *political power* of the democratically elected City Council Technical Committee, representing the political parties of the Council in matters of planning and environment. On the other side, there is the *executive power* of the police. What is a private interest group doing in the middle of such company? Does its inclusion here not constitute a deeply problematic deviation from democratic standards? And, finally, the question with monumental potential of Nietzsche's cyclopean kind: could the abc-list be indicative of the ABC of power in Aalborg? Did I have here, in fact, an image of the tripartition and separation of powers à la Aalborg?

The five lines of text and the questions they sparked would prove invaluable for understanding the Aalborg Project and for answering the four basic value-rational questions above. Following this approach, and documenting case after case of special treatment of the Chamber of Industry and Commerce by elected and administrative city officials, I eventually established that the Chamber was the most important player in city politics and planning in Aalborg. Only by factoring in the hidden power relations between the Chamber and the city government could I begin to understand the curious changes to the urban landscape that had first made me interested in the Aalborg Project. In relation to the central traffic and environment component of the project, the rationality of the Chamber could be summarized in the following three propositions: (1) What is good for business is good for Aalborg; (2) People driving automobiles are good for business; ergo, (3) What is good for people driving automobiles is good for Aalborg, whereas, conversely, what is bad for auto drivers is bad for Aalborg. In short, "the car is king" was the rationality of the Chamber.

In contrast, the rationality of the Aalborg Project was built on the basic premise that the viability of downtown Aalborg as the historic, commercial, and cultural center of the city and of northern Denmark could be secured if, and only if, automobile traffic was significantly reduced in the city center. The fate of the Aalborg Project would be decided by these two rationalities fighting it out, and the group who could place the most power behind their interpretation of what was rational and what was not would win. Below we will see how. Here I will note only, that in this fight over rationality and power, the Chamber of Industry and Commerce – through century-old and well-maintained relations of power – was able to position itself as a clandestine advisory board to top officials in the municipal administration. "You know, we had the possibility to change the proposals [the planners] came up with" a former chairperson of the Chamber explained to me in a startlingly frank interview.[5] The Chamber secretly reviewed and negotiated changes to the Aalborg Project before proposals for the project were presented to the politicians on the City Council Technical Committee and to the Council itself. This happened despite the fact that by law and constitution it was the politicians who were supposed to make the decisions that the Chamber were now making with administrative officials. The Chamber preferred things this way, needless to say, "[f]or it has turned out that if [the proposals] first reach the Technical Committee, and are presented there and are to be discussed in the City Council, then it is almost impossible to get them changed," as the ex-chairperson clarified for me.[6]

The power relations I uncovered through interviews, in the archives, and with the help of my informants are too complex to be accounted for here. Enough to say that they were of a premodern kind that could not be defended publicly vis-à-vis standards of modern democracy. In a sense, there was both too much and too little democracy in Aalborg. When I evaluated the city government against conventional standards of representative democracy, I found there was too much democracy, because the Chamber of Industry and Commerce were participating where they should not be in the role of what they themselves were eager to stress was not a "supreme city council," which is exactly what it was. Their participation was distorting the outcomes of representative democracy and transforming the rationality of the Aalborg Project. When, on the other hand, I evaluated the city government against more recent ideas of stakeholder and citizen participation approaches to democracy, I found too little democracy, because involving only one stakeholder is clearly not enough when others are affected.

For these and for other reasons given in *Rationality and Power*, my answer to the first of the four value-rational questions, "Where are we going with democracy in Aalborg?" was a clear "Astray."

Who gains, and who loses, by which mechanisms of power?

In answering the second question "Who gains, and who loses, by which mechanisms of power?", I was particularly interested in the interplay between rationality and power in defining winners and losers. Let me give just one example, though at some length, of how I addressed this question.[7]

Above I mentioned the "car is king" rationality of the Chamber of Industry and Commerce. The city planners were aware of the barriers this rationality might create for the Aalborg Project. Therefore, at one stage in the project they decided to try and shoot down the Chamber's rationality by agreeing to do a shopping survey of where customers in downtown Aalborg came from and which means of transportation they used. The Chamber of Industry and Commerce had been claiming over and over, like a mantra, that 50 to 60 percent of gross revenues, if not more, in the city center's shops came from customers driving cars and that policies and planning which were hostile to drivers would thereby lead to a reduction in retail earnings. When the survey was done it showed, in stark contrast to the Chamber's claim, that each of the three groups – (1) motorists, (2) pedestrians, bicyclists, and moped drivers, and (3) users of public transportation – accounts for equal shares of gross revenues.

Aalborg Stiftstidende, the local newspaper interviewing the chairperson of the Chamber's City Center Committee, tells its readers that the chairperson "acknowledges being astonished as to how many customers use public transportation."[8] At the same time, however, the chairperson points out that one should not look at total gross revenues alone but should examine the share of specialty goods as compared to the share of sales of staples, etc. According to the chairman, who owns a specialty shop himself, this is because (1) it is the specialty shops which distinguish a center more than the sales of groceries, and (2) specialty goods generate the largest share of earnings. Specialty goods are thus more important for the retailers and for the downtown economy than are other types of goods.

The chairperson also cites these factors in my interview with him, in which he comments on my interpretation of the survey results as rendered above:

CHAIRPERSON: Well, it shows that you, too, have not understood [the results of the survey]. Because what counts for the city's retailers is not the giant sales which lie in the supermarkets' food sections. If you subtract them, you will obtain other percentages. And the purchases made by those driving their cars have a *much, much* higher average. It is the specialty goods which create the gross earnings, the profits. It is the specialty goods which create a center at all. If the specialty goods are not found in a center, then you get an American-style situation. Slums. Food products make up a very large part of sales. Try and subtract them and then analyze where the earnings come from.

INTERVIEWER: Has the Chamber tried to do that?

CHAIRPERSON: Oh yes, yes. We also presented it to the municipality. I think that we reach a figure where those driving cars make up far more than 50 percent of the specialty goods trade. Now specialty goods also include clothes, etc. It is hardly so marked for clothes. But as soon as you go over to genuine specialty goods [i.e., excluding clothes and other textiles], then the proportion of drivers gets very, very large . . .

INTERVIEWER: Are everyday goods not so important for a center?

CHAIRPERSON: No, because it is only a question of supplying the local residents, right? It certainly has nothing to do with creating an atmosphere in a town. This is not what makes a town fun and nice to be in and interesting to walk around in.

But even if we allow for the revamped categories, which the chairperson of the Chamber's City Center Committee proposes, he still overestimates the significance of automobile drivers. Their share of purchases in downtown Aalborg is not, "much, much higher" or "far more than 50 percent." Subtracting both conventional goods and clothes and textiles from gross revenues and then examining the remaining sector of pure specialty goods, as the chairperson proposes, it appears that motorists account for 45 percent of the revenues in this group of goods. Since pure specialty goods constitute 33 percent of total earnings, the share of specialty goods purchased by drivers thus comprises but 15 percent of gross revenues (i.e., 45 percent of 33 percent). Were we to accept the chairperson's argument, it would mean that city policy makers ought to accord highest priority to the specific activities (specialty shopping) of a specific customer group (drivers) who contribute only 15 percent of the total sales in downtown Aalborg. Even when seen from a narrow sales point of view, such a policy would seem problematic. However, through a complicated web of influences and rationalizations that cannot be accounted for here this is precisely what the actual policy becomes in Aalborg.

In contrast to the Chamber of Industry and Commerce, the planners view the results of the shoppers' survey as unavoidable evidence against the Chamber's views and in favor of their own strategy: the bicyclists, those on mopeds, pedestrians, and those using public transportation must be accorded higher priorities in downtown Aalborg, say the planners; the interests of those driving private cars must be downgraded. It therefore seems strongly misleading and unusually provocative to the planners when the *Aalborg Stiftstidende* chooses to report on the shopping survey with the following four-column headline: "Aalborg's Best Customers Come Driving in Cars."[9] The headline is misleading, inasmuch as drivers are shown to be much less significant as a customer group than originally thought. After all, the text of the article makes clear that two-thirds of total sales are made to people who do *not* come by car. Headline and text thus convey two opposing messages, as if two different people wrote them – which is probably the case, the text by a reporter and the headline by an editor.

For the planners, this misleading headline is the straw that breaks the camel's back. It is captions like these, together with a number of very critical editorials about the Aalborg Project, which force the head of the Aalborg Project, a conservative alderman, to uncharacteristically complain about lack of fairness in the paper's coverage of the project.[10] The alderman explains in an interview:

I think that I, not I but everyone here in the house [the City's headquarters for planning and environment], hardly received a totally fair treatment [in the press]. I think that a line was already in place, coming from *Aalborg Stiftstidende* among others, that this [project] was garbage.

The chief of city planning now wants to strike back at both the *Aalborg Stiftstidende* and the Chamber of Industry and Commerce. He is fed up with both of them. The chief asks permission from the alderman to submit a reply to the paper. At first the alderman says no, but the chief asks again and finally the alderman gives in, on the condition that the reply is printed as the chief's personal opinion.

One cannot . . . talk about, for example, the purchases of drivers being dominant in relation to those of other road users, bus passengers, or pedestrians . . . It is just as important to plan for bus passengers, bicyclists, and pedestrians, who taken together make up 65 percent of the purchases . . . The City Council has resolved that major new roads and extensions of existing roads in the dense part of the city must be avoided, which accords well with many other tendencies in society, including the interest in maintaining the urban environment, improving traffic safety, and converting from private to public transportation.

The instruments of planning, as previously mentioned, therefore consist of regulating traffic within the possibilities accorded by the existing street area; that is, removing the unwanted through-traffic and other measures which can lead extraneous vehicles out to the main traffic arteries as directly as possible.

When the Chamber of Industry and Commerce, in its alternative to the city center project, calls attention to the fact that private cars should be able to drive unhindered through the downtown area, that parking conditions be improved, that public transportation be expanded, that bicycles and motorbikes have unhindered access everywhere (outside the pedestrian streets), that the conditions for "non-vehicular" road users be improved, that retail deliveries can operate without problems, that better conditions be created for pedestrians – all this together with the establishment of more green areas, expansion of housing, maintenance of downtown functions, more jobs, and better public services, then it is a list of wishes which everyone could put their name to. The problem lies in fulfilling, within the existing framework, the often contradictory goals. Priorities must be set, and it must be accepted that it will entail restrictions on freedom within one domain to achieve important advantages in others . . . In my opinion, the report on shopping in the city center does not produce any need to propose changes in the planning objectives. On the contrary, I think that [these objectives] have been confirmed on many points.[11]

The chief of city planning never publishes his article, however. He explains why:

CHIEF OF CITY PLANNING: It was a kind of self-criticism, you know. It didn't promote the case, and now we had just received a certain amount of goodwill from the Chamber of Industry and Commerce. So there was no reason to dig [trenches] . . .

INTERVIEWER: But was it you yourself who decided that the article would not appear?

CHIEF OF CITY PLANNING: Yes!

The goodwill from the Chamber of Industry and Commerce which the chief talks about is explained by the fact that the shopping survey has opened the Chamber's eyes to the fact that there are groups of customers other than those driving private cars. And these other groups put significant amounts of cash into the shopkeepers' cash registers. However, the chief of city planning and his staff are mistaken in their evaluation of the Chamber's good will. The Chamber in fact draws a fundamentally different conclusion from the shoppers' survey than the planners, a conclusion, which they do not understand until it is too late. The Chamber's leadership realize that there are indeed other important customers than those who drive cars. And this causes the Chamber to reduce or withdraw their previous criticism of those subprojects aimed at improving conditions for bicyclists, public transportation, etc., such as the network of bicycle paths and a large bus terminal. After the publication of the shopping survey, the previous harsh criticism of these subprojects simply ceases.

Nevertheless, the Chamber's view of reality is not structured by the same analytical rationality as that of the chief of city planning and his staff. The Chamber therefore do not draw the same conclusions about trade-offs and priorities as the planning chief. The Chamber want "to have their cake and eat it too," as the alderman would later put it.

In other words, there exists a single survey and two interpretations. The planners interpret the survey as solid, analytical documentation for the Aalborg Project's downgrading of automobile traffic and its upgrading of public transportation and nonautomotive forms of transport in order to achieve environmental improvements and improved traffic safety. For the Chamber, however, the survey documents the possibility to increase earnings for the city's shops by improving conditions for nonautomotive and public transportation. It is a classically clear example of an evaluation which is dependent on the eyes of the beholder.

Empirically speaking, the survey results are not interesting in themselves. They may or may not reveal a single reality, but that is not important. Rather, the interpretations of the survey results are important.

And the decisive aspect in relation to the fate of the Aalborg Project is not whether the one or the other interpretation is "correct" or "rational" or "true," but which party can put the greatest power behind its interpretation. The interpretation, which has the stronger power base, becomes Aalborg's truth, understood as the actually realized physical, economic, ecological, and social reality. The stronger power base turns out to be that of the Chamber who, by means of a multiplicity of clever strategies and tactics, successfully blocks most of the city's measures for reducing auto traffic while, as said, allowing measures that facilitate walking, biking, and the use of public transportation.

The Chamber here confirms a basic Nietzschean insight which we came across in chapter eight, namely that interpretation is not only commentary, "interpretation is itself a means of becoming master of something" and "all subduing and becoming master involves a fresh interpretation."[12] With the help of the very survey that the planners carried out to disprove the Chamber of Industry and Commerce, the Chamber came up with a fresh interpretation of the Aalborg Project – and became master of the project.

In this manner power defined a reality in which the winners were the business community in downtown Aalborg. Via their strategy of opposing measures to restrict cars, combined with acceptance of improvements for public transportation, pedestrians, and bicyclists, they have seen an increase in retail sales in downtown Aalborg following the implementation of the Aalborg Project, while sales figures declined at the national level during the same period.

With roughly a 50 percent increase in bicycle and public transportation in downtown Aalborg during the first decade of the Aalborg Project, and without the projected 35 percent decline in automobile traffic, but an increase instead, the actual situation stood in sharp contrast to what was envisioned. Without the downgrading of automobiles, the pressure on downtown road space has produced harmful effects on environment, traffic safety, and traffic flow. It was this very situation which the Aalborg Project was supposed to prevent, but which it has instead exacerbated.

Thus the losers in the struggle over the Aalborg Project were those citizens who live, work, walk, ride their bicycles, drive their cars, and use public transportation in downtown Aalborg, that is, virtually all of the city's and the region's half-million inhabitants plus many visitors. Every single day residents, commuters, and visitors in downtown Aalborg were exposed to increased risks of traffic accidents substantially higher than the national average and the planners' projections. They were also exposed to higher levels of noise and air pollution, and a deteriorating physical and social environment. The taxpayers were also losers, because the considerable funds and human resources used in the Aalborg Project have largely been wasted.

The rationality and interests of one group, the Chamber of Industry and Commerce, was allowed to penetrate and transform the project. The main viewpoints of the Chamber have overlapped with the views of the Aalborg Police Department and the *Aalborg Stiftstidende*. As the *Stiftstidende* has a near monopoly on the printed press in Aalborg, and as the police hold a powerful position in questions of traffic policy, this three-fold overlapping of interests has endowed the Chamber's viewpoints with a special impact.

The *Realpolitik* for the Aalborg Project was shaped by these interests in classic Machiavellian style, while the *formal* politics in democratically elected bodies like the City Council have had only minor impact on the project. Rational, deliberative democracy gave way to premodern rule-by-the-strongest. Distorted relations of power produced a distorted project. Power thus defined a reality in which the *real* Aalborg Project, that which has become reality, deviates from, and on principal objectives directly counteracts the *formal* Aalborg Project, which was ratified by the City Council with a 25–1 vote, but which exists only on paper.

Briefly summarized, my untangling of the web of rationality–power relations in the Aalborg Project showed that while power produces rationality and rationality produces power, their relationship is asymmetrical. Power has a clear tendency to dominate rationality in the dynamic and overlapping relationship between the two. Paraphrasing Pascal, one could say that power has a rationality that rationality does not know. Rationality, on the other hand, does not have a power that power does not know. The result is an unequal relationship between the two. Illegitimate rationalization and not rationality came to dominate the fate of the Aalborg Project.[13]

Is it desirable?

After this example of what I found when probing the mechanism of power that produced winners and losers in the Aalborg Project, let us move on to the third value-rational question. This question asks whether the situation depicted in answering the first two questions is desirable. My answer to this was No!

I did not need ideals of strong democracy or strong ecology to support this conclusion. Most, if not all, informed persons who subscribe to the ground rules of democracy and who agree with the 25–1 majority on the City Council, which ratified the environmental objectives of the Aalborg

Project, would also have to agree with my analysis that the development which I had uncovered was neither desirable nor justifiable. Thus, my analysis could not be easily rejected on grounds of being idiosyncratic. This was strategically important, because as I moved on to answering the fourth question – What should be done? – I wanted as broad popular support as possible for my conclusions and suggestions for action.

I have already mentioned Francis Bacon's dictum that knowledge is power. This dictum expresses the essence of Enlightenment thinking. "Enlightenment is power," and the more enlightenment – the more rationality – the better. The Aalborg study shows that Bacon is right, knowledge *is* power. But the study also shows that the inverse relation between power and knowledge holds and that it is more important: "Power is knowledge." In this sense, the study stands Bacon on his head. It shows how power defines what gets to count as knowledge. It shows, furthermore, how power defines not only a certain conception of reality. It is not just the social construction of rationality which is at issue here, it is also the fact that power defines physical, economic, social, and environmental reality itself.

Modernity relies on rationality as the main means for making democracy work. But if the interrelations between rationality and power are even remotely close to the asymmetrical relationship depicted in the Aalborg case – which the tradition from Thucydides, Machiavelli, and Nietzsche tells us they are – then rationality is such a weak form of power that democracy built on rationality will be weak, too. The asymmetry between rationality and power makes for a fundamental weakness of modernity and of modern democracy. The normative emphasis on rationality leaves the modern project as ignorant of how power works as the guardians of the Aalborg Project and therefore as open to being dominated by power. Relying solely on rationality, therefore, risks exacerbating the very problems modernity attempts to solve. Modernity and power must be reconciled.

We need to assess the weakness of modernity and democracy in light of the context-dependent nature of rationality, taking a point of departure in thinkers like Machiavelli, Nietzsche, and Foucault. Constitution writing and institutional reform based on discursive rationality à la Jürgen Habermas are shown in the Aalborg study to be inadequate. As I argued in chapter seven, to enable democratic thinking and the public sphere to make a real contribution to democratic action, we have to tie them back to what they cannot accept in much of modern democratic theory: power, conflict, and partisanship. This, then, was the next step in my work with the Aalborg Project: to become a partisan, to face conflict, and to exercise power.

What should be done?

In deciding on my praxis in relation to the Aalborg Project, I reasoned that if the arrangements and outcomes of city politics and planning in Aalborg were not publicly justifiable, as my studies showed they were not, then, perhaps, I could help change things for the better, even if only modestly, by calling public attention to my results.[14] In this way, my studies would become part of the power relations they had uncovered.

I already mentioned that I chose to study the relationship between rationality and power because this particular area of research was relatively unexplored, and because I hoped to help improve democracy's reflexivity on this point. By the time I began the Aalborg study, however, another, more personal, motive had come along. I had now been a social scientist long enough to be only too familiar with the problem of the "so what results" mentioned in chapter nine, research results that nobody cares about. At one point I considered leaving the university altogether because of this problem. Social science, without natural science's link to technological development, and with only sporadic political relevance and support, seemed to me too isolated from what is important in life to be worth the effort of a lifetime's work. I chose to stay, however, and tried to solve my problem, in part by gradually developing and practicing the methodology described in this book. Phronetic social science would be an antidote to the "so what" problem.

Instead of natural science's relevance to technological development, I would conduct my research in ways that would make it relevant to practical politics, administration, and planning. I tried to secure such relevance by adopting two basic criteria. First, I would choose to work with problems that are considered problems, not only in the academy, but also in the rest of society. Second, I would deliberately and actively feed the results of my research back into the political, administrative, and social processes that I studied. For reasons I will return to below, at one stage I called this way of working "research on the body."

Employing this approach in the Aalborg study has been a tall order and has worked much better than I had reason to expect when I first began to develop it. One day, for example, I found myself in a studio of the Danish Radio (DR), participating in a direct, national broadcast about preliminary results from my study. In order to get my feet wet and to gain step-by-step experience with my new methodology, I had published partial results of my research as I went along. "Trial balloons," I called them. This was the second time I sent up a balloon, and one of the results that drew public attention, nationally and locally, was the fact that whereas the Aalborg City Council had decided with the Aalborg Project that higher than average traffic accidents for bicyclists in the city center was cause for special concern and must be reduced by 30–40 percent, now – several years into the implementation of the project – I documented that instead of the planned reduction there was a steep increase in accidents. Moreover, the increase had happened without politicians and officials noticing. They, quite simply, were not monitoring the project on which they had spent millions for planning and implementation. I also showed how the increase in accidents was caused by city officials allowing the rationality of the Chamber of Industry and Commerce to slowly, surely, and one-sidedly, influence and undermine the rationality of the Aalborg Project as explained above. Also participating in the radio broadcast were the alderman for planning and environment, the chairman for the local chapter of the Danish Cyclist's Federation – a force to be reckoned with in a bicycle nation like Denmark – and two interviewing journalists. When the journalists asked the alderman what he thought about the results of my study, he pulled from his briefcase a sheet of statistics, waved it, and said to the nation that here he held proof that my numbers were wrong.

This, of course, is as bad as it gets for a scholar. We are paid to be that group in society which is best equipped to produce data, knowledge, and interpretations of the highest validity and reliability. This is a main basis of our credibility and existence. Consequently, if someone questions that credibility our existence is at issue.

The journalists immediately turned to me and asked for my reaction to the alderman's attack. The green light on my microphone went on, I crossed my fingers for luck under the table, and answered that if there were any errors in my numbers, they must originate with the police, who do the registration of traffic accidents on location, or with the Danish Highway Administration, who maintain the national database for traffic accidents. When the broadcast was over, I went to my office and prepared a large package for the alderman containing the raw computer printouts of my data and other details of my analyses plus a cover letter asking the alderman to please identify the errors he said I had made. Three weeks later the material was returned to me with a message stating that the alderman's staff had been able to identify no errors. The same day I wrote a short press release stating the facts of the matter in order to clear myself of the accusations of poor scholarship. That evening on television, I watched with pleasure the alderman retract his accusations. The next day the printed media carried the story, and I was in the clear again.

There were other incidents like this, and I mention them here to emphasize four things. Firstly, and most importantly, this way of working helps effectively to begin the dialogue with groups outside of academia, which is at the heart of phronetic social science. Some groups and individuals, like the alderman above, may not be interested in beginning a dialogue; they would rather do without the extra attention and transparency it entails. In the Aalborg case, they would have preferred to turn a blind eye to the traffic accidents and environmental problems, and not be held accountable. But the very *raison d'être* of phronetic social science is to help society see and reflect, and transparency is a key prerequisite for this and for democractic accountability. Where there is resistance to seeing and hearing, the dialogue may need to be jumpstarted as was the case in Aalborg. Nevertheless, after some initial difficulties, a real dialogue was established which went on for several years and covered many aspects of politics, administration, and planning in Aalborg.

Secondly, the dialogical approach to research is also effective in ensuring that research results reach the relevant target groups. This is a question of effective communication. The highly specialized media of scholarly journals and monographs are well suited for reaching academic audiences. But they are sorely lacking when it comes to the target groups that are relevant in the practical world of politics, administration, and planning. Here public dialogue, including communication via everyday media, is necessary.

Thirdly, the dialogical approach generates the type of outside stakeholders in the research that we need in order to get beyond the stigma of "so what results."[15] The stakeholders care about the research, for good and for bad, some as supporters, and some as antagonists.

Fourthly and finally, your senses are definitely sharpened when you carry out your research with the knowledge that people with an interest in the results might do what they can to find errors in your work, like the alderman and his staff did with my analyses of the Aalborg Project. For me, the consequence is a state of heightened awareness in data collection and processing that helps take the drudgery and dullness out of these activities. External scrutiny is also an excellent motivation for achieving the highest possible levels of validity and reliability: facts and data have to be handled with excruciating accuracy, and interpretations have to be clear and balanced. Otherwise the work will be self-defeating and not allowed to count as a voice in the phronetic dialogue that it is aimed at.

Because of the stakes involved and because of the engagement with other actors, I experience an almost bodily responsibility for and involvement in the research. This engagement seems to me to enhance the learning process, which is in the best of the traditions of experiential learning and very different from didactics and theory. Learning becomes embodied. I understand from colleagues in the field of education that recent research corroborates the experience that human learning is generally more effective with this type of engagement and with an excited sensory system; that learning is more effective when the proprioceptors are firing, so to speak. This is why I called my methodology "research on the body," here understood not as research with the body as an object of study, but as research that is embodied and where researchers experience, on their own bodies, society's reactions to their research.

As a consequence of my trial balloons and the debates they generated, when later I published the Aalborg study in earnest – in the two-volume, 640 pages Danish edition of *Rationalitet og Magt* – the alderman and other actors with stakes in the Aalborg Project knew that they would not get away with postulating another reality for my research than that which could be documented. That type of tactics may work in politics, but it rarely does in research. Therefore the debate about the Aalborg Project, though still spirited, now became much less polemical and confrontational and more dialogical. For instance, the alderman and I would give back-to-back talks about the project, each presenting our views, followed by discussion, in and out of Aalborg. Our "road show," we would eventually call it. The alderman and his staff began to listen to the research instead of fighting it; they realized the research was influencing public opinion about their work together with expectations of accountability. Soon they were ready to make changes in the Aalborg Project.

Reaching the dialogical mode of communication seems crucial to me for practicing *phronesis* in a democratic society. Polemics typically does not facilitate democracy but is more closely related to the tactics of rhetoric and antagonistic power play. Dialogue, on the other hand – not necessarily detached and without combat, but with respect for other parties and a willingness to listen – is a prerequisite for informed democratic decision-making. And dialogue is the vehicle by means of which research can best hope to inform the democratic process, whereas polemics has only limited use for research in achieving its goals. Thus, in order to be effective, phronetic researchers avoid polemics and look for dialogue. They also look for how they themselves may contribute to establishing the conditions for dialogue where such conditions are not already present.

The debate about the Aalborg Project, which again was both local and national, and this time also spilled over into Sweden and Norway, now placed so much attention on the Aalborg Project that it became hard for the city government to continue to defend the project and refuse to be held accountable for what was going wrong with it. At the practical level, this was the situation I had hoped to bring about by publishing the Aalborg study. As we saw in chapter seven, the aim of exposing dubious social and political practices through phronetic research is, in Michel

Foucault's words, precisely to bring it about that practitioners no longer know what to do, "so that the acts, gestures, discourses that up until then had seemed to go without saying become problematic, difficult, danger-ous."[16] For the Aalborg Project, my study led to transparency, transpar-ency led to public attention, and public attention led to accountability. And after accountability, no more Aalborg Project. Or, to put it more accurately: after accountability, another Aalborg Project, since the prob-lems in downtown Aalborg had not by any means disappeared. Quite the opposite; they had been exacerbated and needed to be taken care of more than ever.

The alderman put it like this in an interview:

> I simply took the consequence of Flyvbjerg's study, and I could see that the process we had been through then [with the Aalborg Project] could in any case not be allowed to happen again. I let myself be much inspired by [the idea that] now we must have a broad popular element [in city planning] so that it did not proceed on those power positions [which had dominated the Aalborg Project].[17]

As mentioned in chapter seven, Foucault said about his work that practi-tioners are not likely to find constructive advice or instructions in it; they would find only the kind of problematizations mentioned above.[18] Such problematizations are useful and may lead to action and change in them-selves. But unlike Foucault, based on my problematizations of the Aal-borg Project, I reconstructed a set of policy and planning measures for how city governments may significantly reduce their risk of ending up with the type of counterproductive and undemocratic policies seen in Aalborg.[19]

One of seven key measures I proposed was the use of "planning councils" in the decision-making process, not as detached Habermasian or Cartesian fora devoid of power, but as devices that acknowledge and account for the working of power and for the passionate engagement of stakeholders who care deeply about the issues at hand.[20] I developed the idea from a set of semi-institutionalized, semi-secret, and often intense meetings that were already being held on a regular basis between city officials and the Aalborg Chamber of Industry and Commerce. The problem with these meetings was that only a single stakeholder was invited to participate; this was one reason why decisions became unbal-anced. But from the meeting minutes and from my interviews with participants I could see that such meetings were not necessarily a bad idea in themselves. The interactions they involved resulted in additional infor-mation and in ideas that proved useful in the decision-making process. And the collaboration between project owner and stakeholder led to external support for aspects of the project that might not have gained support without stakeholder participation. Finally, real negotiations and real decisions with real commitments took place in the meetings. In my version of a planning council, however, it would be open to not only one stakeholder but to all stakeholders in addition to all other interested and affected parties. Moreover, as the composition of such councils, and decisions about who should count as stakeholders, are clearly political acts, I suggested that city government take an active role in identifying participants and in facilitating their involvement with councils with the purpose of ensuring that discussions and decisions would be as democratic and have as wide support as possible. I suggested that planning councils should be active in the decision-making process from beginning to end, from policy idea to design to ratification to implementation.

When the alderman and his staff decided to end the Aalborg Project and to build something new on its ruins, they looked to the measures I had proposed. Eventually they launched a new round of planning under the name "Aalborg Better Town" (*Aalborg Bedre By*), including the use of planning councils, now called "planning panels." City officials took an active part in identifying external parties to participate on the panels instead of staying locked with the ideas and initiatives of the Chamber of Industry and Commerce.

In the process of starting up the panels, officials also contacted me and encouraged me to become a panel member. In this way, I could use my knowledge about Aalborg to improve the new planning. I was tempted but felt I had to choose between roles. Also, at this time I was moving into another area of research, namely that of mega project decision-making, and I was keen to see what the phronetic research methodology honed on the Aalborg Project might do in this field, which I had chosen, in many respects, as a contrast to Aalborg. I wanted to move from local issues to national and international ones, and from small projects to very big and very expensive ones.[21] Right or wrong, I decided not to participate in the planning panels. Nevertheless, when a few years later, the European Union in Brussels awarded Aalborg its "European Planning Prize" for the new planning, I could not help but feel – however impudent this might seem to others and to myself – that in a small way perhaps I had a share in what had transpired. Triumphing over 300 nominees from all over the European Union, Aalborg received the prize for having developed what the jury viewed as an innovative and democratic urban policy and planning with particular emphasis on the involvement of citizens and interest groups.[22]

Other examples of social science that take values and power seriously

What identifies a work in social science as a work of phronetic social science is the fact that for a particular area of concern, it focuses social analysis on praxis in answering the four value-rational questions to which we have returned repeatedly in this book: (1) Where are we going? (2) Who gains, and who loses, by which mechanisms of power? (3) Is it desirable? (4) What should be done? The questions can be answered in many different ways for a given area of concern. Thus, there exists neither one fixed methodology for doing phronetic social science nor only one type of examples of such work. In chapter nine, I described the methodological guidelines which I developed for my own work in this field. In the current chapter I have given an example of how I used those guidelines in a particular case. By way of concluding the chapter, I would like to mention briefly a few other examples of phronetic social science and of *phronesis*-like research. I have given most room to my own work, not because I consider it more important or more interesting than other work – far from it – but simply because this is what I know about and can explain best. The list of examples below is by no means exhaustive; it is selective, perhaps even idiosyncratic in places. It is no more than a briefly annotated shortlist of further readings, supplementing the theoretical and methodological literature mentioned in the previous chapters. The emphasis is on literature that takes values and power seriously and adopts a relational understanding of power.

In the field of philosophy and the history of ideas, I have already mentioned Michel Foucault as a main exponent of phronetic social science, especially as regards innovative ways of understanding power relations in phronetic work. The Foucault of *Discipline and Punish* and the first volume of *The History of Sexuality* are particularly interesting in this respect, though there is much to learn from Foucault's entire œuvre, including books, articles, lectures, interviews, and his work as an activist.[23] In addition to Foucault's own work there is also the work of Foucauldian scholars such as Mitchell Dean, Jacques Donzelot, Jan Goldstein, Agnes Horváth, Giovanna Procacci, Nikolas Rose, and Arpád Szakolczai, who have all done work that, though more narrowly academic in scope, is more or less in the spirit of Foucault and contains elements of *phronesis*.[24] Finally, I would like to mention the work of Ian Hacking and Joseph Rouse, especially Hacking's *Rewriting the Soul* which in many ways exemplifies Foucauldian genealogy better than Foucault's own work.[25]

In sociology, the work of Pierre Bourdieu, a self-declared Aristotelian, stands out. If Foucault was the heir of Jean Paul Sartre as Paris's "master thinker" who continued the tradition of combining critical thought with progressive praxis, then Bourdieu may be seen as the successor to Foucault. And if it was less apparent before, then after the publication of *Acts of Resistance* and *On Television*, the political Bourdieu has shown that public dialogue and social action are not coincidental side effects of his work; they are placed at its very heart.[26] In developing the concept of phronetic social science described in the previous chapters, I have made use of Bourdieu's *The Logic of Practice* and *Outline of a Theory of Practice*, the latter still his most important methodological work, in my judgment.[27] Bruno Latour is another important figure in sociology. In relation to my own line of work, I have found particularly useful his *Aramis, or the Love of Technology* and *Science in Action*.[28] Finally, I have already mentioned in chapter five, *Habits of the Heart* by Robert Bellah and his associates, although this particular work is less developed regarding issues of power than the other works mentioned above.

Political science does not have quite the conspicuous figures doing *phronesis*-like research that we find in philosophy and sociology. Even though the thinkers of prudence par excellence, Aristotle and Machiavelli, are central to the intellectual history of political science, today their influence is limited in the discipline. For reasons that must remain unexplored here, the mainstream in contemporary political science does not place at its core the questioning of values and power that was central to classical political science and is central to phronetic social science. Outside the mainstream, however, work is being carried out that shares many of the characteristics of phronetic social science, just as certain works inside the mainstream have phronetic qualities. In the first category, we find Wendy Brown's *States of Injury*, Barbara Cruikshank's *The Will to Empower*, Éric Darier's *Discourses of the Environment*, and François Ewald's, *L'Etat providence*.[29] Barry Hindess's work in *Discourses of Power* and *Governing Australia* also comes to mind.[30] In the second category a study like Robert Putnam's (with Robert Leonardi and Raffaella Nanetti) *Making Democracy Work*, which is presented by the authors as a fairly conventional although exceptionally rigorous work of hypothetico-deductive political science, has turned out to have important phronetic effects regarding our understanding of where we are going with civil society and what to do about it.[31] This again underscores the point made earlier, that phronetic social science can be practiced in different ways, so long as the value-rational questions at its core are addressed in one way or another, and the public has use for the answers in their deliberations about praxis.

We saw in chapter seven, how feminists and minority groups have been particularly successful in making use of Foucauldian genealogy and power studies in combining critical thought and progressive praxis. Those who have elaborated genealogies of gender, sexuality, and race have developed an understanding of how relations of domination between women and men, and between minority groups and others, can be changed. In gay studies Martin Duberman's *Stonewall* stands out.[32] From the large literature in women's studies, let me mention Sandra Bartky's *Femininity and Domination*, Judith Butler's *Gender Trouble*, and Nancy Fraser's *Unruly Practices*.[33] On the less academic, though still scholarly informed, side of things Naomi Wolf's *Promiscuities* deserves notice.[34] This study is a historical and personal genealogy of female adolescence and I recommend it to anyone who parents girls and has an interest in understanding how, as a society and as parents, we may assist our daughters better than we currently do in making their passage from girlhood to womanhood. In parenthesis – and as advice from one reader/parent to another – let me hasten to say that Wolf's book has more value for praxis if you read it, not only before your daughters, but before they reach puberty.

In anthropology, Paul Rabinow's *French DNA* and *Making PCR* are examples of phronetic works inspired by Foucault and genealogy.[35] In management and accounting there is the work of Peter Miller.[36] The field of urban studies and planning still lacks central monographs and a coherent body of work in this area, but contributions are being made by Jonathan Crush, Raphaël Fischler, Margo Huxley, Ole Jensen, Tim Richardson, and Oren Yiftachel.[37] In geography, there is the work of Ed Soja, and, finally, in the field of development studies, that of James Ferguson.[38]

In development studies, I have had the opportunity to work over an extended period in the Kilimanjaro region in Africa with a group of local colleagues employing both phronetic social science and more conventional approaches to development research. We found one aspect of phronetic research to be particularly attractive in this context: this approach turned out to be less Eurocentric than conventional methods. The reason for this lies with the central place of narrative in phronetic social science.[39] Most, perhaps all, cultures have a tradition for doing narrative, and we may tap into this tradition when doing phronetic studies. Not all cultures have traditions for doing theory or surveys or other highly structured methods developed in the North. We found, therefore, that it is possible to be less obtrusive, to violate fewer local norms, and to gain more information when practicing phronetic social science. In our African studies, my local colleagues, who were born and raised in the area where we did our work, asked local residents to tell their stories about the research issues at hand. The issues were struggles over land and water, that is, struggles over the basic preconditions of life in that area. On this basis, we developed our own narratives, embedded in the local context and with a large element of *vox populi*. These narratives eventually became the main results of the research, including recommendations for how to improve the current situation practically, which was deeply problematic with people literally killing for access to land and water. Part of our study and its recommendations was later used by forces within the Government of Tanzania in ongoing efforts to change the national land-use planning system from a centralized, top-down system, with roots in colonial times and postcolonial socialism, and with little capacity for conflict resolution, to a more contemporary decentralized, bottom-up approach taking its point of departure in local conflicts and local participation.[40] When my colleagues went into the field to record the stories that would be at the core of the research, I was asked to stay behind. As an outsider my presence would bias the results, they said. For someone who loves to be in the field this was hard to accept. But my colleagues were right and, what is worse, they used my own arguments to make their point. When we were preparing to do the research, I had argued – as I have in this book – that social science is inextricably bound up with context and that phronetic social science must be carried out with a high sensitivity to that context. In a development setting such sensitivity includes awareness of issues of ethnocentrism as they pertain to social science methodology, and to social scientists themselves. When my colleagues left me in my monk-cell-like room at the Lutheran Uhuru Hostel at the foot of Kilimanjaro, I would have ample time to ponder these issues, and to write about them as I have done here.

11   Social science that matters

Indeed he knows not how to know who knows not also how to un-know.
                                                            Richard Francis Burton

If we want to re-enchant and empower social science, and if we want to recover social science from its current role as loser in the Science Wars, then we need to do three things. First, we must drop the fruitless efforts to emulate natural science's success in producing cumulative and predictive theory; this approach simply does not work in social science. Second, we must take up problems that matter to the local, national, and global communities in which we live, and we must do it in ways that matter; we must focus on issues of values and power like great social scientists have advocated from Aristotle and Machiavelli to Max Weber and Pierre Bourdieu. Finally, we must effectively communicate the results of our research to fellow citizens. If we do this, we may successfully transform social science from what is fast becoming a sterile academic activity, which is undertaken mostly for its own sake and in increasing isolation from a society on which it has little effect and from which it gets little appreciation. We may transform social science to an activity done in public for the public, sometimes to clarify, sometimes to intervene, sometimes to generate new perspectives, and always to serve as eyes and ears in our ongoing efforts at understanding the present and deliberating about the future. We may, in short, arrive at a social science that matters.

The development of social science seems to be constantly affected by conjunctures where we attempt to clarify to ourselves, and to others, what we can and cannot do with this kind of science. By way of concluding this book, I would like to develop two scenarios for clarification, the first a perpetuation of "science as usual," the second, an emergent "phronetic social science." In the first scenario, scientism, here understood as the tendency to believe that science holds a reliable method of reaching the truth about the nature of things, continues to dominate thinking in social and political science.[1] Epistemic science and predictive theory are regarded as the pinnacle of scientific endeavor in this scenario. The attempt

166

to substitute theory and rules for *phronesis* will persist. If this state of affairs continues, social and political research is likely to weaken further as a scientific activity. We are likely to continue to hear about the "crisis of social science." The Science Wars will continue with the kind of attacks and counterattacks described in chapter one, and with social science on the losing side. University administrators will continue to see sociology, political science, and other social science departments as appropriate and easy targets for cutbacks, when cutbacks are on the agenda. And all with good reason: the social scientists' era of glory in the 1960s and 1970s, when they attempted to be architects in the development of the "Great Society" and in other projects of the welfare state, has long since passed. These projects were built upon a natural science-inspired fallacy, which assumes a close association in social science between, on the one hand, theoretical, basic science (*episteme*) and, on the other, practical, applied science (*techne*).

The absence of this link between basic and applied social sciences does not mean that these sciences do not continue to play a role as *techne*. There remains a need for social sciences in the activities of the welfare society. These sciences help with registration, administration, control, and redistribution of resources among various social groups. But in the first scenario such a role will consist of a "headless" form of ad hoc social engineering no longer given credence by a superstructure of social-science theory. It will instead be dictated by a functional means-rationality defined by the ruling relations of power. This kind of practical social-science activity does not require advanced graduate and post-graduate specialized institutions of higher learning. The type of social engineering we are speaking of here primarily demands midlevel general-ists with an all-round Master's or Bachelor's degree: people who are flexible enough to administer and execute the kinds of measures dictated by whatever is considered instrumental at a given moment.

The second scenario replaces the view that the social sciences can be practiced as *episteme* with their role as *phronesis*. In this scenario, the purpose of social science is not to develop theory, but to contribute to society's practical rationality in elucidating where we are, where we want to go, and what is desirable according to diverse sets of values and interests. The goal of the phronetic approach becomes one of contributing to society's capacity for value-rational deliberation and action. The contribution may be a combination of concrete empirical analyses and practical philosophical considerations; "fieldwork in philosophy," as Pierre Bourdieu calls it.

A scenario of this kind will also involve the social sciences in their role as *techne*. However, when combined with the element of *phronesis*, it will be a *techne* "with a head on it," that is, a *techne* governed by value-rational deliberation. As mentioned earlier, it can be dangerous for individuals, groups, and societies when their capacity for value-rational deliberation is eroded. Today the erosion of such capacity seems to many to be rapidly taking place and coincides with the growing incursion of a narrow means-rationality into social and political life. Simultaneously, there is a marked need for discussion and reorientation of values and goals; for example, in relation to environmental risks, work, health, international security, and political stability. An evolution of the social sciences along the lines of this second scenario, that is, as phronetic sciences, could help counter the erosion of value-rationality and thereby help inhibit some of the destructive tendencies in society and in science.

Today, the dominant streak in social science continues to evolve along the lines of the first scenario, that of scientism. But scientism in social science is self-defeating because the reality of social science so evidently does not live up to the ideals of scientism and natural science. Therefore it is the second scenario, that of *phronesis*, which is more fertile, and worth working for. This is the scenario I have tried to unfold in this book by clarifying what phronetic social science is and how it can be practiced.

Notes

ACKNOWLEDGMENTS

1 The paper was later published as "Aristotle, Foucault, and Progressive *Phronesis*: Outline of an Applied Ethics for Sustainable Development," in Earl Winkler and Jerrold Coombs, eds., *Applied Ethics: a Reader* (Oxford: Basil Blackwell, 1993), pp. 11–27.

1 THE SCIENCE WARS: A WAY OUT

1 Alan D. Sokal, "Transgressing the Boundaries: Toward a Transformative Hermeneutics of Quantum Gravity," *Social Text*, 14: 1–2, Spring/Summer 1996.
2 Alan D. Sokal, "A Physicist Experiments with Cultural Studies," *Lingua Franca* 6: 4, May/June 1996. See also Babette E. Babich, "Physics vs. *Social Text*: Anatomy of a Hoax," *Telos* 107, 1996.
3 Steven Weinberg, "Sokal's Hoax," *The New York Review of Books*, August 8, 1996, p. 12.
4 Michael Holquist and Robert Shulman, "Sokal's Hoax: an Exchange," *The New York Review of Books*, October 3, 1996, p. 54.
5 Edward O. Laumann, John H. Gagnon, Robert T. Michael, and Stuart Michaels, *The Social Organization of Sexuality: Sexual Practices in the United States* (Chicago, IL: University of Chicago Press, 1994); Robert T. Michael, John H. Gagnon, Edward O. Laumann, and Gina Kolata, *Sex in America: A Definitive Survey* (Boston, MA: Little, Brown, 1994).
6 *The Economist*, May 13, 1995, p. 17.
7 R. C. Lewontin, "Sex, Lies, and Social Science," *The New York Review of Books*, April 20, 1995, p. 28.
8 *Ibid.*, p. 29.
9 Richard Sennett, "'Sex, Lies, and Social Science': an Exchange," *The New York Review of Books*, May 25, 1995, p. 43.
10 Edward O. Laumann, John H. Gagnon, Robert T. Michael, and Stuart Michaels, "'Sex, Lies, and Social Science:' an Exchange," *The New York Review of Books*, May 25, 1995, p. 43.
11 *Ibid.*
12 For more on the political and ideological background of the Science Wars, see Dorothy Nelkin, "What Are the Science Wars Really About?" *The Chronicle of Higher Education*, July 26, 1996.

13 Aristotle, *The Nicomachean Ethics*, translated by J. A. K. Thomson, revised with notes and appendices by Hugh Tredennick, introduction and bibliography by Jonathan Barnes (Harmondsworth: Penguin, 1976), 1140a24–1140b12, 1144b33–1145a11. See chapter five for more about *phronesis*.

14 Hans-Georg Gadamer, *Truth and Method* (London: Sheed and Ward, 1975).

15 Richard Bernstein, "Interpretation and Solidarity," an interview by Dunja Melcic, *Praxis International* 9: 3, 1989, p. 217.

16 My own attempts at developing the phronetic approach through practical research can be found in my books *Rationality and Power: Democracy in Practice* (Chicago, IL: University of Chicago Press, 1998) and, with Nils Bruzelius and Werner Rothengatter, *Mega Projects and Risk: Making Decisions in an Uncertain World* (Cambridge: forthcoming). See also chapter ten below.

2 RATIONALITY, BODY, AND INTUITION IN HUMAN LEARNING

1 Hubert and Stuart Dreyfus, *Mind over Machine: The Power of Human Intuition and Expertise in the Era of the Computer* (New York: Free Press, 1986, revised 1988). The description of the Dreyfus-phenomenology follows chapter one of the book, supplemented by discussions and interviews with Hubert and Stuart Dreyfus. The interviews indicate Stuart Dreyfus to be the actual architect behind the phenomenology, while Hubert Dreyfus has developed the phenomenology's philosophical–scientific prerequisites and implications. An excerpt of the interviews can be found in Bent Flyvbjerg, "Sustaining Non-Rationalized Practices: Body-Mind, Power, and Situational Ethics. An interview with Hubert and Stuart Dreyfus," *Praxis International* 11: 1, April 1991, pp. 99–113. For a critical discussion of the phenomenology, see Bent Flyvbjerg, *Rationalitet, intuition og krop i menneskets læreproces: Fortolkning og evaluering af Hubert og Stuart Dreyfus's model for indlæring af færdigheder* (Rationality, Intuition, and Body in Human Learning: An Interpretation and Evaluation of Hubert and Stuart Dreyfus's Skill Acquisition Model) (Aalborg: Aalborg University, 1990). See also Hubert and Stuart Dreyfus, "Making a Mind vs. Modeling the Brain: AI Back at a Branchpoint," in Margaret A. Boden, ed., *The Philosophy of Artificial Intelligence* (Oxford University Press, 1990); "What is Morality? A Phenomenological Account of the Development of Ethical Expertise," in James Ogilvy, ed., *Revisioning Philosophy* (New York: State University of New York Press, 1992); Charles Spinosa, Fernando Flores, and Hubert Dreyfus, "Disclosing New Worlds: Entrepreneurship, Democratic Action, and the Cultivation of Solidarity," *Inquiry* 38: 1–2, 1995; "Skills, Historical Disclosing, and the End of History: A Response to our Critics," *ibid.*

2 Helen A. Klein and Gary A. Klein, "Perceptive/Cognitive Analysis of Proficient Cardio-Pulmonary Resuscitation (CPR) Performance." Paper presented at the 1981 Meeting of the Midwestern Psychological Association, Chicago, here cited from Dreyfus and Dreyfus, *Mind over Machine*, pp. 200–1.

3 Patricia Benner, *From Novice to Expert: Excellence and Power in Clinical Nursing Practice* (Menlo Park, CA: Addison-Wesley, 1984), pp. 23–4. Benner utilizes

the Dreyfus model to provide an in-depth description of the learning process among nurses.

4 Herbert Simon, *Models of Man* (New York: Wiley, 1957), *The Sciences of the Artificial* (Cambridge, MA: MIT Press, 1969), *Models of Thought*, vols. I, II (New Haven: Yale University Press, 1979, 1989), *Models of Bounded Rationality*, vols. I, II (Cambridge, MA: MIT Press, 1982).

5 Dreyfus and Dreyfus, *Mind over Machine*, esp. chapters 3 and 4.

6 *Ibid.*, p. 25.

7 Flyvbjerg, "Sustaining Non-Rationalized Practices," p. 95.

8 *Ibid.*

9 *Ibid.* The interview reveals a disagreement between Hubert and Stuart Dreyfus regarding the body–mind problematic as it pertains to their model of learning. (All quotes in what follows refer to the interview, pp. 94–6.) Upon observing that intuition is central to their model, I asked the brothers where intuition resides in the body–mind. Hubert Dreyfus answered that it seems obvious to him that one cannot possibly think that chess intuition has anything to do with the body. "Intuition does not reside in the body or the mind," Hubert Dreyfus explains, "It resides in the fact that the brain can store whole gestalts." Chess is a perfect example, according to Hubert Dreyfus, because you do not even need perception. A blind person can become a chess master. Chess is a "totally mental activity," according to Hubert Dreyfus, who sees the distinction between mind and body as important because the mind can be analytical whereas the body cannot. According to Hubert Dreyfus it is always the mind that causes the trouble in relation to intuition. If a person does not become intuitive, it must be because the mind got in the way, says Hubert Dreyfus. But if you do become intuitive, "it isn't because the mind got out of the way and let the body do its thing," explains Hubert Dreyfus, "it's because the analytic mind got out of the way and let the intuitive mind do its thing." Stuart Dreyfus comments on these observations that his work with neural networks and connectionism is leading him to deny the split between mind and body. Stuart Dreyfus sees skilled behavior as "an activity in which there isn't any role for the mind as the mind is usually defined [the analytical Cartesian mind]. It's all 'body' if you think of the neurons as being part of the body and not part of the mind," says Stuart Dreyfus. See also Drew Leder, *The Absent Body* (Chicago, IL: University of Chicago Press, 1990); Chris Shilling, *The Body and Social Theory* (London: Sage, 1993); Bryan S. Turner, *The Body and Society: Explorations in Social Theory* (London: Sage, 1996); and George Lakoff and Mark Johnson, *Philosophy in the Flesh: The Embodied Mind and Its Challenge to Western Thought* (New York: Basic Books, 1999).

10 Dreyfus and Dreyfus, *Mind over Machine*, p. 28.

11 Whereas Dreyfus and Dreyfus use the term "experts" to describe performers at the highest level of skill acquisition, Pierre Bourdieu uses "virtuoso," a term which I find preferable for several reasons. Most important of these is that the concept of "expert" is usually linked to the type of analytical–rational decision-making, which characterizes the lower, rule-governed stages in the learning process. The Dreyfus's "expert," like Bourdieu's "virtuoso," acts in ways quite different from this. See chapter four for the description of Pierre Bourdieu's concept of "virtuosity."

12 For an interesting analysis of the relationship between narrative and scientific explanation, see Andrew Abbott, "What Do Cases Do? Some Notes on Activity in Sociological Analysis," in Charles C. Ragin and Howard S. Becker, eds., *What is a Case? Exploring the Foundations of Social Inquiry* (Cambridge University Press, 1992).

13 Sigmund Freud, "Delusions and Dreams in Jensen's *Gradiva*," in *The Standard Edition of the Complete Psychological Works of Sigmund Freud*, vol. IX (London: Hogarth Press, 1907), p. 8.; here quoted from Ronald W. Clark, *Freud: The Man and the Cause* (London: Granada, 1982), p. 116.

14 Hans-Jørgen Nielsen, *Fodboldenglen* (Copenhagen: Samlerens Forlag, 1979), pp. 28–30, translated from the Danish.

15 This discussion overlooks artificial intelligence simulated in neural networks.

16 Donald A. Schön, "The Crisis of Professional Knowledge and the Pursuit of an Epistemology of Practice," in C. Roland Christensen and Abby J. Hansen, eds., *Teaching and the Case Method* (Boston: Harvard Business School Press, 1987), p. 252.

17 Dreyfus and Dreyfus, *Mind over Machine*, revised paperback edition, p. xii.

18 *Ibid.*, p. 36.

19 I have developed this critique in Flyvbjerg, "Sustaining Non-Rationalized Practices" and "Rationalitet, intuition og krop."

20 Flyvbjerg, "Sustaining Non-Rationalized Practices," p. 111.

21 Friedrich Nietzsche, *The Gay Science* (New York: Vintage Books, 1974), p. 300 (§354).

22 Friedrich Nietzsche, *Twilight of the Idols* (Harmondsworth: Penguin, 1968), p. 34 (§11). Nietzsche implies that Socrates was himself aware of this "sickness" and that this was one reason why Socrates did not oppose his own death sentense (*ibid.*). Thus Nietzsche's overall view of Socrates is substantially more nuanced and ambivalent than the quote in the main text indicates; see also "Nietzsche's Attitude toward Socrates," Chapter 13 in Walter Kaufmann, *Nietzsche: Philosopher, Psychologist, Antichrist* (Princeton: Princeton University Press, 1974); and Alexander Nehamas, *The Art of Living: Socratic Reflections from Plato to Foucault* (Berkeley: University of California Press, 1998), pp. 128 ff.

23 Nietzsche, *The Gay Science*, p. 85 (§11).

3   IS THEORY POSSIBLE IN SOCIAL SCIENCE?

1 Richard J. Bernstein, *Beyond Objectivism and Relativism: Science, Hermeneutics, and Praxis* (Philadelphia, PA: University of Pennsylvania Press, 1985), pp. 16 and passim.

2 Three main sources of what follows are: Hubert Dreyfus, "Why Studies of Human Capacities modeled on Ideal Natural Science can never Achieve their Goal," revised edition of a paper presented at the Boston Colloquium for the Philosophy of Science, October 1982 (undated); Pierre Bourdieu, *Outline of a Theory of Practice* (Cambridge University Press, 1977); and Michel Foucault, *The Order of Things: an Archaeology of the Human Sciences* (New York: Vintage, 1973). Additional sources are indicated where relevant.

3 By "epistemic" is meant "well-founded" or "what must be regarded as

correct." Epistemic science is science which has achieved a paradigmatic and normal-scientific level in the Kuhnian sense, and which is thereby capable of explaining and predicting in terms of context-free knowledge. See also chapter five for a further discussion of the "epistemic science" concept.

4 Karl Marx, *Early Writings* (Harmondsworth: Penguin, 1975), p. 355.

5 Sigmund Freud, "Project for a Scientific Psychology," in *The Standard Edition of the Complete Psychological Works of Sigmund Freud*, vol. I (London: Hogarth Press, 1950), p. 295.

6 Ernest Jones, *Sigmund Freud: Life and Work*, vol. II (London: Hogarth Press, 1955); here cited from Ronald Clark, *Freud: The Man and the Cause* (London: Granada, 1982), p. 470.

7 In the following discussion, the term "science" is used in its epistemic meaning. The concept of science is further discussed in chapter five in connection with the discussion of Aristotle and his intellectual virtues.

8 Thomas S. Kuhn, *The Structure of Scientific Revolutions*, second revised ed. (Chicago: University of Chicago Press, 1970).

9 Thomas S. Kuhn, "What Are Scientific Revolutions," in Lorenz Kruger, Lorraine J. Daston, and Michael Heidelberger, eds., *The Probabilistic Revolution vol. I: Ideas in History* (Cambridge, MA: MIT Press, 1987), p. 9.

10 Steven Weinberg, "The Revolution That Didn't Happen," *The New York Review of Books*, October 8, 1998, pp. 48–52.

11 Thomas S. Kuhn, *The Essential Tension: Selected Studies in Scientific Tradition and Change* (Chicago, IL: University of Chicago Press, 1977), pp. xiii and xv.

12 See for example Richard Rorty, "A Reply to Dreyfus and Taylor," *Review of Metaphysics* 34, 1980, pp. 39 and passim; Bernstein, *Beyond Objectivism and Relativism*, pp. 172–4; Anthony Giddens, *Central Problems in Social Theory: Action, Structure and Contradiction in Social Analysis* (Berkeley, CA: University of California Press, 1979), p. 259.

13 See also Søren Brier, "Naturvidenskab, humaniora og erkendelsesteori: Er en holistisk sammentænking mulig?" (Natural Science, the Humanities, and Theory of Knowledge: Is a Holistic Unified Thinking Possible?), *Kritik* 79/80, 1987.

14 V. Y. Mudimbe and Bogumil Jewsiewicki, eds., *Open the Social Sciences: Report of the Gulbekian Commission on the Restructuring of the Social Sciences* (Stanford, CA: Stanford University Press, 1996), pp. 78–9.

15 Foucault, *The Order of Things*, p. 344.

16 The assertion as to the social sciences' instability and lack of success in becoming normal science should not be interpreted to mean that the development of social science is incidental or without significance for society. The point, rather, is that the social sciences' development and importance are not best understood in relation to their role as epistemic science, but in relation to the practical application of these sciences in society's institutions.

17 Richard Rorty, *Philosophy and the Mirror of Nature* (Princeton, NJ: Princeton University Press, 1979), p. 352. In his later work Rorty seems to think there is a difference between natural and social science. "[W]e have gradually become suspicious of essentialism as applied to human affairs, in areas such as history, sociology, and anthropology," Rorty now says while he maintains that "essentialistic habits of thought . . . pay off in the natural sciences." *Philosophical*

Papers, vol. II (Cambridge University Press, 1991), pp. 66–7. See also Herman J. Saatkamp, Jr., ed., *Rorty and Pragmatism: the Philosopher Responds to His Critics* (Nashville, TN: Vanderbilt University Press, 1995); Richard Rorty, *Contingency, Irony, and Solidarity* (Cambridge University Press, 1989); and Richard Rorty, *Philosophical Papers*, vol. I (Cambridge University Press, 1991).

18 Anthony Giddens, "Hermeneutics and Social Theory," in *Profiles and Critiques in Social Theory* (Berkeley, CA: University of California Press, 1982), p. 13.

19 *Ibid.*, pp. 7 and 11 and passim. For a critique of Giddens's double hermeneutics, see Rorty, *Philosophical Papers*, vol. I, p. 97.

20 Personal communication with the author. See also the following two books by Giddens, *Politics, Sociology and Social Theory* (Cambridge: Polity Press, 1995) and *Modernity and Self-Identity* (Stanford, CA: Stanford University Press, 1991).

21 Harold Garfinkel, *Studies in Ethnomethodology* (Cambridge: Polity Press, 1984), p. 32.

22 *Ibid*, p. 33.

23 Ethnomethodologists have argued that the natural sciences, too, ought to reflect their background skills more explicitly. However, as Hubert Dreyfus has pointed out, this demand indicates a lack of understanding of these sciences. It is one of Kuhn's main theses that the researchers' basic skills are external to normal natural science research in the sense that they are not reflected. This is precisely what defines "normal science." Basic skills are part of the accepted paradigm and are taken for granted. Skills being part of the paradigm is what makes possible relative stability and cumulative production of knowledge and this constitutes the strength of the natural sciences in relation to the ostensibly pre-paradigmatic social sciences. Background skills for researchers in the natural sciences "appear and should appear in the journals of the ethnomethodologists, not in *The Physical Review*," says Dreyfus in "Why Studies of Human Capacities," p. 5.

24 Giddens defines "practical consciousness" as "all the things which actors know tacitly about how to 'go on' in the context of social life without being able to give them direct discursive expression." See Anthony Giddens, *The Constitution of Society: Outline of the Theory of Structuration* (Cambridge: Polity Press, 1984), p. xxii.

25 Artificial intelligence as applied to digital computers is especially interesting because the form of intelligence allowed by the digital computer must hold itself rigorously to the analytical–rational (rule-based) model. Artificial intelligence thereby becomes the ultimate test of this model. The argument does not encompass artificial intelligence in neural network computers, which have been developed precisely in order to overcome some of the limitations of analytical–rational intelligence. Artificial intelligence on neural network computers is still too underdeveloped to be subjected to a genuine evaluation in these terms. For a broader view on the implications of artificial intelligence on thinking about human beings and social science, see Alan Wolfe, "Mind, Self, Society, and Computer: Artificial Intelligence and the Sociology of Mind," *American Journal of Sociology* 96: 5, 1991. See also Alan Wolfe, *The Human Difference: Animals, Computers, and the Necessity of Social Science* (Berkeley,

CA: University of California Press, 1993).

26 Here the term "human sciences" is used synonymously with "social sciences" meaning the study of human activity.

27 Foucault, *The Order of Things*, p. 344.

28 *Ibid.*, p. 364.

29 See also Edith Kurzweil, *The Age of Structuralism: Lévi-Strauss to Foucault* (New York: Columbia University Press, 1980).

4   CONTEXT COUNTS

1 The Dreyfus–Bourdieu argument can be found in the following two papers by Hubert Dreyfus, "Why Studies of Human Capacities, modeled on Ideal Natural Science can never Achieve their Goal," rev. edition of paper presented at The Boston Colloquium for the Philosophy of Science, October 1982 (undated), and "Defending the Difference: The Geistes/Naturwissenschaften Distinction Revisited," in Akademie der Wissenschaften zu Berlin, *Einheit der Wissenschaften*, Internationales Kolloquium der Akademie der Wissenschaften zu Berlin, Bonn, June 25–7, 1990 (Berlin: Walter de Gruyter, 1991), combined with Pierre Bourdieu, *Outline of a Theory of Practice* (Cambridge University Press, 1977), *The Logic of Practice* (Stanford, CA: Stanford University Press, 1990), and *An Invitation to Reflexive Sociology*, with Loic J. D. Wacquant (Chicago, IL: University of Chicago Press, 1992).

2 Dreyfus, "Why Studies of Human Capacities," p. 8.

3 Bourdieu, *Outline of a Theory of Practice*, p. vii.

4 *Ibid.*, pp. 5–6.

5 *Ibid.*, p. 5.

6 *Ibid.*, p. 6. In his discussion of structural analysis and hermeneutics, Anthony Giddens also invokes Lévi-Strauss and the gift example. Giddens says: "[W]hat counts as a 'gift' cannot be defined internally to structural analysis itself, which presumes it as an already constituted 'ordinary language concept'." Giddens sees Paul Ricoéur as correct when he argues that Lévi-Strauss's structural analyses of myth, far from excluding meaning as narrative, bound to the contexts of its reproduction, actually presuppose it. "Structural analysis presupposes hermeneutics," says Giddens in *Central Problems in Social Theory: Action, Structure and Contradiction in Social Analysis* (Berkeley, CA: University of California Press, 1979), p. 26. I return to the relationship between hermeneutics and structuralism in chapter nine.

7 Bourdieu, *Outline of a Theory of Practice*, pp. 8, 15.

8 Anthony Wilden, *The Rules Are No Game: The Strategy of Communication* (London: Routledge and Kegan Paul, 1987).

9 See also Antoine d'Autume and Jean Cartelier, eds., *Is Economics Becoming a Hard Science?* (Cheltenham: Edward Elgar, 1997).

10 These considerations apply to economics as an ideal science. The argument thus ignores economics' interest-specific character, that is, the relationship between economics and power.

11 *The Economist*, February 25, 1995.

12 Anthony Giddens, "Hermeneutics and Social Theory," in Profiles and Critiques in Social Theory (Berkeley, CA: University of California Press), p. 15.

13 Giddens, *The Constitution of Society*, Preface and p. 347.
14 Bourdieu, *Outline of a Theory of Practice*, pp. 21 and 20.
15 Dreyfus, "Why Studies of Human Capacities," p. 11.
16 *Ibid.*
17 An interesting example of social scientists grappling with the dilemma of prediction is attempts at understanding why the collapse of communist regimes in Russia and Eastern Europe caught the world by surprise. See, for example, the "Symposium on Prediction in the Social Sciences" reported in the *American Journal of Sociology* 100: 6, 1995 with contributions from, among others, James Coleman, Michael Hechter, and Timur Kuran.
18 Bourdieu, *Outline of a Theory of Practice*, p. 109.
19 Per Aage Brandt, "Kritikkens struktur" (The Structure of Critique), *Information*, April 22, 1988, p. 5.

5   VALUES IN SOCIAL AND POLITICAL INQUIRY

1 The distinction between instrumental rationality and value-rationality follows Max Weber's famous distinction between *Zweckrational* action and *Wertrational* action. Value-rationality is often called "substantive rationality." Both terms are used in the English translation of Max Weber, *Economy and Society* (Berkeley, CA: University of California Press, 1978); see, for instance, p. 85.
2 Richard Livingstone, *On Education* (Cambridge University Press, 1956), p. 99.
3 The argument is developed in *Rationalitetens Ufornuft* [Rationality Without Reason] and *Den Fatalt-Risikable Verden* [The Fatally-Risky World], *Information*, July 28–29, 1986. To Aristotle, people were animals with the possibility of a political existence; in the fatally-risky world, people are animals who put the life of the species at risk by the rationality of their own political strategies, for instance regarding ecology, genetics, and nuclear warfare. See also Bent Flyvbjerg, "Aristotle, Foucault, and Progressive *Phronesis*: Outline of an Applied Ethics for Sustainable Development," in Earl Winkler and Jerrold Coombs, eds., *Applied Ethics: A Reader* (New York: Basil Blackwell, 1993), pp. 11–27. My arguments about risk society were developed independently from those of Ulrich Beck, though less comprehensively. See for instance, *Risk Society: Towards a New Modernity* (London: Sage, 1992).
4 Peter Maas and David Brock, "The Power and Politics of Michel Foucault," interview in *Inside*, the Daily Cal's Weekly Magazine, April 22, 1983, p. 21.
5 *Ibid.*
6 *Ibid.*
7 Cf. also Richard Rorty's distinction between "irony" and "solidarity" in *Contingency, Irony, and Solidarity* (Cambridge University Press, 1989).
8 Richard Bernstein, "Interpretation and Solidarity," an interview by Dunja Melcic, *Praxis International* 9: 3, 1989, p. 217.
9 Aristotle, *The Nicomachean Ethics* (hereafter in this chapter abbreviated as *N.E.*) (Harmondsworth: Penguin, 1976). In the short space of this chapter, it is not possible to provide a full account of Aristotle's considerations about the intellectual virtues of *episteme*, *techne*, and *phronesis*. What follows are the bare essentials for understanding social and political science, based on a reading of

the original texts. A complete account would need to elaborate further the relations between *episteme*, *techne*, and *phronesis*, and the relationship of all three to *empeiria*. It would also need to expand on the relationship of phronetic judgments to rules, on what it means to succeed or to fail in the exercise of *phronesis*, and on the conditions which must be fulfilled if *phronesis* is to be acquired. For further discussion of these questions and of the implications of Aristotle's thinking for contemporary social science, see my discussion with Hubert and Stuart Dreyfus in "Sustaining Non-Rationalized Practices: Body-Mind, Power, and Situational Ethics," *Praxis International* 11: 1, April 1991, pp. 101 and passim. See also Hannah Arendt, *The Human Condition* (Chicago, IL: University of Chicago Press, 1958); Richard Bernstein, *Beyond Objectivism and Relativism: Science, Hermeneutics, and Praxis* (Philadelphia, PA: University of Pennsylvania Press, 1985); Hans-Georg Gadamer, *Truth and Method* (London: Sheed and Ward, 1975); Eugene Garver, *Machiavelli and the History of Prudence* (Madison, WI: University of Wisconsin Press, 1987); Agnes Heller, *Can Modernity Survive?* (Berkeley, CA: University of California Press, 1990); Carnes Lord and David K. O'Connor, eds., *Essays on the Foundations of Aristotelian Political Science* (Berkeley, CA: University of California Press, 1991); Alasdair MacIntyre, *After Virtue: A Study in Moral Theory* (Notre Dame, IN: University of Notre Dame Press, second edition, 1984); Alasdair MacIntyre, *Whose Justice? Which Rationality?* (Notre Dame, IN: University of Notre Dame Press, 1988); C. C. W. Taylor, "Politics," in Jonathan Barnes, ed., *The Cambridge Companion to Aristotle* (Cambridge University Press, 1995); and Ray Nichols, "Maxims, 'Practical Wisdom,' and the Language of Action: Beyond Grand Theory," *Political Theory* 24: 4, 1996.

10 *N.E.*, 1139b18–36.
11 *N.E.*, 1140a1–23.
12 Michel Foucault, "Space, Knowledge, and Power," interview with Paul Rabinow, in Paul Rabinow, ed., *The Foucault Reader* (New York: Pantheon, 1984), p. 255.
13 *N.E.*, 1140a24–1140b12.
14 Charles Taylor, *Sources of the Self: the Making of the Modern Identity* (Cambridge, MA: Harvard University Press, 1989), pp. 125, 148.
15 On the relationship between judgment and *phronesis*, see Richard S. Ruderman, "Aristotle and the Recovery of Political Judgment," *American Political Science Review* 91: 2, 1997.
16 *N.E.*, 1141b8–27.
17 For such an interpretation, with an unclear distinction between *phronesis* and *techne*, see Hubert and Stuart Dreyfus, "What is Morality: a Phenomenological Account of the Development of Expertise," in David Rasmussen, ed., *Universalism vs. Communitarianism* (Cambridge, MA: MIT Press, 1990). See also my discussion of this issue with the Dreyfus brothers in "Sustaining Non-Rationalized Practices," pp. 102–7.
18 Alessandro Ferrara, "Critical Theory and its Discontents: on Wellmer's Critique of Habermas," *Praxis International* 8: 3, 1989, p. 319.
19 *Ibid.*, p. 316. See also Alessandro Ferrara, *Justice and Judgement: the Rise and the Prospect of the Judgement Model in Contemporary Political Philosophy* (Thousand Oaks, CA: Sage, 1999).

20 Martha C. Nussbaum, "The Discernment of Perception: an Aristotelian Conception of Private and Public Rationality," in *Love's Knowledge: Essays on Philosophy and Literature* (Oxford University Press, 1990), p. 66. See also Daniel T. Devereux, "Particular and Universal in Aristotle's Conception of Practical Knowledge," *Review of Metaphysics* 39, March 1986.

21 *N.E.*, 1141b8–b27.

22 *N.E.*, 1142a12–29.

23 *N.E.*, 1141b27–1142a12.

24 Pierre Bourdieu, *In Other Words: Essays Towards a Reflexive Sociology* (Cambridge: Polity Press, 1990), p. 28; Robert N. Bellah, Richard Madsen, William M. Sullivan, Ann Swidler, and Steven M. Tipton, *Habits of the Heart* (Berkeley, CA: University of California Press, 1985), especially the methodological appendix, p. 297.

25 Pierre Bourdieu and Loic J. D. Wacquant, *An Invitation to Reflexive Sociology* (Chicago, IL: The University of Chicago Press, 1992), p. 128.

26 Bernstein, *Beyond Objectivism and Relativism*, p. 40; Stephen Toulmin, "The Recovery of Practical Philosophy," *The American Scholar* 57, 1988, p. 337; Richard Rorty, "Response to James Gouinlock," in Herman J. Saatkamp, Jr., ed., *Rorty and Pragmatism: the Philosopher Responds to His Critics* (Nashville, TN: Vanderbilt University Press, 1995), pp. 94–5; Richard Rorty, *Philosophical Papers*, vols. I, II (Cambridge University Press, 1991).

27 Rorty, "Solidarity or Objectivity?" in *Philosophical Papers*, vol. I, p. 25.

28 *N.E.*, 1144b33–1145all. For Aristotle, man has a double identity. For the "human person," that is, man in politics and ethics, *phronesis* is the most important intellectual virtue. Insofar as man can transcend the purely human, contemplation assumes the highest place. *N.E.*, 1145a6 and 1177a12.

29 Max Weber, *The Protestant Ethic and the Spirit of Capitalism* (London: George Allen & Unwin, 1985), p. 26.

30 *Ibid.*, p. 181.

31 Bellah *et al.*, *Habits of the Heart*, p. vi.

32 *Ibid.*, p. 3.

33 *Ibid.*, p. 297.

34 *Ibid.*, pp. 297–8.

35 *Ibid.*, pp. 301–2.

36 In the new 1996 introduction to the University of California Press paperback edition of *Habits of the Heart*, implications about power are discussed more explicitly. See also Robert N. Bellah, Richard Madsen, William M. Sullivan, Ann Swidler, and Steven M. Tipton, *The Good Society* (New York: Alfred A. Knopf, 1991).

6 THE POWER OF EXAMPLE

1 Nicolas Abercrombie, Stephen Hill, and Bryan S. Turner, *Dictionary of Sociology* (Harmondsworth: Penguin, 1984), p. 34. In the third edition of the *Dictionary* (1994), a second paragraph has been added about the case study. The entry is still highly unbalanced, however, and still promotes the mistaken view that the case study is hardly a methodology in its own right, but is best seen as subordinate to investigations of larger samples.

2 Plato, *The Dialogues of Plato* (New York: Bantam, 1986) pp. 196–202.

3 *Ibid.*, pp. 48–50.

4 *Ibid.*, p. 61.

5 Donald T. Campbell and J. C. Stanley, *Experimental and Quasi-Experimental Designs for Research* (Chicago, IL: Rand McNally, 1966), pp. 6–7.

6 Mattei Dogan and Dominique Pelassy, *How To Compare Nations: Strategies in Comparative Politics* (Chatham, NJ: Chatham House, second edition, 1990), p. 121. For a similar view, see Jared Diamond, "The Roots of Radicalism," *The New York Review of Books*, November 14, 1996, p. 6.

7 Harry Eckstein, "Case Study and Theory in Political Science," in Fred J. Greenstein and Nelson W. Polsby, eds., *Handbook of Political Science*, vol. VII (Reading, MA: Addison-Wesley, 1975); and Charles C. Ragin and Howard S. Becker, eds., *What is a Case? Exploring the Foundations of Social Inquiry* (Cambridge University Press, 1992). See also Jennifer Platt, "'Case Study' in American Methodological Thought," *Current Sociology* 40: 1, 1992.

8 Aristotle, *The Nicomachean Ethics* (Harmondsworth: Penguin, 1976), 1141b8 –27.

9 Hubert Dreyfus explicitly describes himself as an Aristotelian. We have already seen, in chapter five, that this is also the case for Bourdieu who refers to the *orthe doxa* of *Meno* quoted above in order to explicate what he means by practical knowledge and habitus. See Bent Flyvbjerg, "Sustaining Non-Rationalized Practices: Body-Mind, Power, and Situational Ethics. An Interview with Hubert and Stuart Dreyfus," *Praxis International* 11: 1, April 1991, p. 102 and Pierre Bourdieu and Loic J. D. Wacquant, *An Invitation to Reflexive Sociology* (Chicago, IL: The University of Chicago Press, 1992), p. 128.

10 Even in the natural sciences, Plato's ideas and the analytical–rational approach are now being reexamined. See chapter four and Hubert Dreyfus, "Why Studies of Human Capacities modeled on Ideal Natural Science can never Achieve their Goal," revised edition of a paper presented at the Boston Colloquium for the Philosophy of Science, October 1982 (undated).

11 *N.E.*, 1142a12, 1143a32–b17.

12 Donald T. Campbell, "Degrees of Freedom and the Case Study," *Comparative Political Studies* 8: 1, 1975, pp. 179, 191.

13 H. J. Eysenck, "Introduction," in Eysenck, ed., *Case Studies in Behaviour Therapy* (London: Routledge and Kegan Paul, 1976), p. 9.

14 Ragin and Becker, eds., *What is a Case?*

15 Anthony Giddens, *The Constitution of Society: Outline of the Theory of Structuration* (Cambridge: Polity Press, 1984), p. 328.

16 See also Ragin and Becker, eds., *What is a Case?* and Platt, "'Case Study' in American Methodological Thought."

17 On the relation between case studies, experiments, and generalization, see Allen S. Lee, "Case Studies as Natural Experiments," *Human Relations* 42: 2, 1989 and Barbara Wilson, "Single-case Experimental Designs in Neuro-Psychological Rehabilitation," *Journal of Clinical and Experimental Neuropsychology*, 9: 5, 1987. See also Mary Timney Bailey, "Do Physicists Use Case Studies? Thoughts on Public Administration Research," *Public Administration Review* 52: 1, 1992 and Larry J. Griffin, Christopher Botsko, Ana-Maria

Wahl, and Larry W. Isaac, "Theoretical Generality, Case Particularity: Quali-
tative Comparative Analysis of Trade Union Growth and Decline," in
Charles C. Ragin, ed., *Issues and Alternatives in Comparative Social Research*
(Leiden: E. J. Brill, 1991).

18 Einstein as quoted in Hubert and Stuart Dreyfus, *Mind over Machine: The
Power of Human Intuition and Expertise in the Era of the Computer* (New York:
Free Press, 1986), p. 41.

19 John Goldthorpe, David Lockwood, Franck Beckhofer, and Jennifer Platt,
The Affluent Worker, vols. I–III (Cambridge University Press, 1968–9). See
also Michel Wieviorka, "Case Studies: History or Sociology?" in Ragin and
Becker, eds., *What is a Case?*

20 W. I. B. Beveridge, *The Art of Scientific Investigation* (London: William
Heinemann, 1951), p. 101.

21 Mark Blaug, *The Methodology of Economics: or How Economists Explain* (Cambridge University Press, 1980).

22 Harry Eckstein, "Case Study and Theory in Political Science," in Fred J.
Greenstein and Nelson W. Polsby eds., *Handbook of Political Science*, vol. VII,
(Reading, MA.: Addison-Wesley, 1975), pp. 116, 131. See also Michael
Barzelay, "The Single Case Study as Intellectually Ambitious Inquiry," *Jour-
nal of Public Administration Research and Theory* 3: 3, 1993, pp. 305 and
passim.

23 John Walton, "Making the Theoretical Case," in Ragin and Becker, eds.,
What is a Case?, p. 129.

24 Eckstein, "Case Study and Theory in Political Science," pp. 103–4.

25 *Ibid.*, p. 80.

26 On the selection of cases, see also Charles C. Ragin, "'Casing' and the
Process of Social Inquiry," in Ragin and Becker, eds., *What is a Case?* and
Eleanor Rosch, "Principles of Categorization," in Eleanor Rosch and Barbara
B. Lloyd, eds., *Cognition and Categorization* (Killsdale, NJ: Lawrence
Erlbaum, 1978).

27 See also Michael Quinn Patton, *Qualitative Evaluation Methods* (Beverly Hills,
CA: Sage, 1980), pp. 302 and passim.

28 The example is based on a study by an occupational medicine clinic in
Denmark which found that brain damage was a problem even in an enterprise
which met all the regulations for safe ventilation. If the case study had not
found any brain damage among employees at this factory, one could conclude
that it is possible to solve the problem and then take another strategy, e.g.,
large samples, to identify workplaces where the problem still exists, followed
by the use of experiences from the model enterprise to mitigate the remaining
problems.

29 Robert Michels, *Political Parties: a Study of the Oligarchical Tendencies of
Modern Democracy* (New York: Collier Books, 1962).

30 W. F. Whyte, *Street Corner Society: The Social Structure of an Italian Slum*
(Chicago, IL: The University of Chicago Press, 1943). See also the articles on
"Street Corner Society Revisited" in *Journal of Contemporary Ethnography* 21:
1, 1992.

31 Harvard University is an example of an entire educational institution which to
a great extent has modeled both teaching and research on the basis of the

understanding that case knowledge is central to human learning. See for example C. Roland Christensen with Abby J. Hansen, eds., *Teaching and the Case Method* (Boston, MA: Harvard Business School Press, 1987) and Charles I. Cragg's classic article "Because Wisdom can't be Told," in *Harvard Alumni Bulletin*, October 1940.

32 Interview with Hubert Dreyfus, author's files.

33 Diamond, "The Roots of Radicalism," p. 6.

34 Francis Bacon, *Novum Organum*, in *The Physical and Metaphysical Works of Lord Bacon*, book I, p. xlvi (London: H. G. Bohn, 1853).

35 Charles Darwin, *The Autobiography of Charles Darwin* (New York: Norton, 1958), p. 123.

36 See Bent Flyvbjerg, *Rationality and Power: Democracy in Practice* (Chicago, IL: The University of Chicago Press, 1998).

37 Ragin, "'Casing' and the Process of Social Inquiry," p. 225.

38 Clifford Geertz, *After the Fact: Two Countries, Four Decades, One Anthropologist* (Cambridge, MA: Harvard University Press, 1995), p. 119.

39 Both Eckstein's "Case Study and Theory in Political Science" and Campbell's "Degrees of Freedom and the Case Study" contain several examples of this phenomenon. See also Michel Wieviorka, "Case Studies: History or Sociology?" in Ragin and Becker, eds., *What is a Case?*, pp. 159 and passim; and Allen Whitt, "Toward a Class-Dialectical Model of Power: An Empirical Assessment of Three Competing Models of Political Power," in *American Sociological Review* 44, 1979.

40 Campbell, "Degrees of Freedom and the Case Study," pp. 181–2.

41 Ragin, "'Casing' and the Process of Social Inquiry," p. 225; see also Charles C. Ragin, *The Comparative Method: Moving Beyond Qualitative and Quantitative Strategies* (Berkeley, CA: University of California Press, 1987), pp. 164–71.

42 Anthony Giddens, *Profiles and Critiques in Social Theory* (Berkeley: University of California Press, 1982), p. 15.

43 For more on narrative, see Seyla Benhabib, "Hannah Arendt and the Redemptive Power of Narrative," *Social Research* 57: 1, 1990; Joseph Rouse, "The Narrative Reconstruction of Science," *Inquiry* 33: 2, 1990; Paul A. Roth, "How Narratives Explain," *Social Research* 56: 2, 1989; Ann Fehn, Ingeborg Hoesterey, and Maria Tatar, *Neverending Stories: Toward a Critical Narratology* (Princeton, NJ: Princeton University Press, 1992); Hayden White, *The Content of the Form: Narrative Discourse and Historical Representation* (Baltimore, MD: Johns Hopkins University Press, 1990); Richard G. Mitchell, Jr. and Kathy Charmaz, "Telling Tales, Writing Stories: Postmodernist Visions and Realist Images in Ethnographic Writing," *Journal of Contemporary Ethnography* 25: 1, 1996; and David Rasmussen, "Rethinking Subjectivity: Narrative Identity and the Self," *Philosophy and Social Criticism* 21: 5–6, 1995. See also chapter nine.

44 Friedrich Nietzsche, *The Gay Science* (New York: Vintage Books, 1974), p. 335 (§373).

45 Pierre Bourdieu, *Outline of a Theory of Practice* (Cambridge University Press, 1977), pp. 8, 15.

46 D. A. T. Gasking and A. C. Jackson, "Wittgenstein as a Teacher," in K. T.

Fann, ed., *Ludwig Wittgenstein: the Man and His Philosophy* (Sussex: Harvester Press, 1967), p. 51.

47 Erving Goffman, *Behavior in Public Places: Notes on the Social Organization of Gatherings* (New York: Free Press, 1963).

48 Andrew Abbott, "What Do Cases Do? Some Notes on Activity in Sociological Analysis," in Ragin and Becker, eds., *What is a Case?*, p. 79.

49 William Labov, "Narrative Analysis: Oral Versions of Personal Experience," in *Essays on the Verbal and Visual Arts: Proceedings of the American Ethnological Society* (Seattle, WA: American Ethnological Society, 1966), pp. 37–9; here quoted from Alexander Nehamas, *Nietzsche: Life as Literature* (Cambridge, MA: Harvard University Press, 1985), p. 163.

50 *Ibid.*, pp. 163–4.

7   THE SIGNIFICANCE OF CONFLICT AND POWER TO SOCIAL SCIENCE

1 Jürgen Habermas, *The Philosophical Discourse of Modernity* (Cambridge, MA: MIT Press, 1987), p. 260. The following evaluation of Habermas's work concentrates on his concept for democracy. Other aspects of his authorship are not covered.

2 *Ibid.*, pp. 18–21, 302.

3 *Ibid.*, p. 294.

4 Jürgen Habermas, *The Theory of Communicative Action*, vols. I and II (Boston, MA: Beacon Press, 1984, 1987); *The Philosophical Discourse of Modernity*; *Moral Consciousness and Communicative Action* (Cambridge, MA: MIT Press, 1990); and *Justification and Application: Remarks on Discourse Ethics* (Cambridge, MA: MIT Press, 1993).

5 Jürgen Habermas, "Questions and Counterquestions," in Richard J. Bernstein, ed., *Habermas and Modernity* (Cambridge, MA: MIT Press, 1985), p. 196.

6 Habermas, *Philosophical Discourse of Modernity*, p. 294.

7 *Ibid.*, p. 315.

8 Habermas, *Theory of Communicative Action*, Vol. I, p. 10.

9 Habermas, *Philosophical Discourse of Modernity*, p. 316.

10 Habermas, "Questions and Counterquestions," p. 196.

11 Jürgen Habermas, *Communication and the Evolution of Society* (London: Heinemann, 1979), p. 97.

12 Habermas, *Moral Consciousness and Communicative Action*, p. 93.

13 *Ibid.*, pp. 120–1. See also Franklin I. Gamwell, "Habermas and Apel on Communicative Ethics," *Philosophy and Social Criticism* 23: 2, 1997.

14 *Ibid.*, p. 198.

15 Habermas, *Justification and Application*, p. 31; Habermas, *Moral Consciousness and Communicative Action*, pp. 65–6. See also Matthias Kettner, "Scientific Knowledge, Discourse Ethics and Consensus Formation in the Public Domain," in Earl R. Winkler and Jerrold R. Coombs, eds., *Applied Ethics: A Reader* (Oxford: Basil Blackwell, 1993).

16 See also Fred Dallmayr, "Introduction," in Seyla Benhabib and Fred Dallmayr, eds., *The Communicative Ethics Controversy* (Cambridge, MA: MIT Press, 1990), p. 5.

17 Habermas, *Moral Consciousness and Communicative Action*, p. 122.

18 Jürgen Habermas, *On the Relationship of Politics, Law and Morality* (Frankfurt: University of Frankfurt, Department of Philosophy, undated), p. 15. See also Jürgen Habermas, *Between Facts and Norms: Contributions to a Discourse Theory of Law and Democracy* (Cambridge, MA: MIT Press, 1996); and "Reconciliation through the Public Use of Reason: Remarks on John Rawls's Political Liberalism," *The Journal of Philosophy* 92: 3, 1995, with reply from John Rawls.

19 Habermas, *On the Relationship of Politics, Law and Morality*, p. 8. For further discussion of the role of law in Habermas's theory of communicative action, see also Bill Scheuerman, "Neuman v. Habermas: The Frankfurt School and the Case of the Rule of Law," *Praxis International* 13: 1, 1993 and Mathieu Deflem, ed., "Habermas, Modernity, and Law," special edition of *Philosophy and Social Criticism* 20: 4, 1994, with contributions from Peter Bal, Mathieu Deflem, Pierre Guibentif, Jürgen Habermas, Bernhard Peters, and David M. Rasmussen.

20 Michel Foucault, *The History of Sexuality*, vol. I (New York: Vintage, 1980), pp. 87–8.

21 *Ibid.*, pp. 82, 90.

22 *Ibid.*, p. 89.

23 Jürgen Habermas, "Burdens of the Double Past," *Dissent* 41: 4, 1994, p. 514.

24 Robert D. Putnam with Robert Leonardi and Raffaella Y. Nanetti, *Making Democracy Work: Civic Traditions in Modern Italy* (Princeton, NJ: Princeton University Press, 1993).

25 Habermas, *Moral Consciousness and Communicative Action*, p. 209.

26 *Ibid.*

27 Habermas, *Philosophical Discourse of Modernity*, p. 322.

28 Friedrich Nietzsche, *Beyond Good and Evil* (New York: Vintage Books, 1966), p. 15 (§8). Nietzsche adds elsewhere that to the extent that the philosopher's "conviction" is the basis of a "system" of thinking it corrupts the system. See *The Anti-Christ* (Harmondsworth: Penguin, 1968), p. 188 (Appendix A).

29 Some might argue that my claim that Habermas's universalism involves a leap of faith is misconstrued, since his fallibilistically conceived transcendental argument is subject to forms of indirect confirmation as Habermas illustrates through his concern with Lawrence Kohlberg and developmental psychology. To this I would answer that not only is this type of confirmation indirect, it is also partial and insufficient. As I will argue below, Habermas's emphasis of aspects of human development that confirm the transcendental argument, when seen in relation to aspects that do not, is unsustainable. For more on this point, and on the problematic character of Habermas's reformulation of Kantian critique, see also Kimberley Hutchings, *Kant, Critique and Politics* (London: Routledge, 1996) and Mitchell Dean, *Critical and Effective Histories: Foucault's Methods and Historical Sociology* (London: Routledge, 1994).

30 Bernard Crick, "Preface" and "Introduction" to Niccolò Machiavelli, *The Discourses* (Harmondsworth: Penguin, 1983), pp. 12, 17.

31 Niccolò Machiavelli, *The Prince* (Harmondsworth: Penguin, 1984), p. 96.

32 Michel Foucault, "The Ethic of Care for the Self as a Practice of Freedom,"

in James Bernauer and David Rasmussen, eds., *The Final Foucault* (Cambridge, MA: MIT Press, 1988), pp. 11 and 18.

33 Habermas, *The Philosophical Discourse of Modernity*, pp. 297–8.

34 The inseparableness of good and evil has been succinctly paraphrased by Nietzsche: "[I]t was God himself who at the end of his days' work lay down as a serpent under the tree of knowledge: thus he recuperated from being God. – He had made everything too beautiful. – The devil is merely the leisure of God on that seventh day," *Ecce Homo* (New York: Vintage Books, 1969), p. 311 (§2).

35 See also Joseph Heath, "The Problem of Foundationalism in Habermas's Discourse Ethics," *Philosophy and Social Criticism* 21: 1, 1995.

36 Richard Rorty, *Contingency, Irony, and Solidarity* (Cambridge University Press, 1989), p. 68.

37 *Ibid.*

38 Habermas, "Burdens of the Double Past" and "The Limits of Neo-Historicism," interview by Jean-Marc Ferry, *Philosophy and Social Criticism* 22: 3, 1996.

39 Habermas, "Burdens of the Double Past," pp. 513, 514.

40 Putnam *et al.*, *Making Democracy Work*; Bent Flyvbjerg, *Rationality and Power: Democracy in Practice* (Chicago, IL: University of Chicago Press, 1998).

41 Machiavelli, *Discourses*, pp. 111–12 (§I.3); text corrected for misprint.

42 Friedrich Nietzsche, *The Will to Power* (New York: Vintage Books, 1968), pp. 192–3 (§351).

43 Richard J. Bernstein, *The New Constellation: The Ethical–Political Horizons of Modernity/Postmodernity* (Cambridge, MA: MIT Press, 1992), p. 220.

44 *Ibid.*, p. 221.

45 Agnes Heller, "The Discourse Ethics of Habermas: Critique and Appraisal," *Thesis Eleven* 10/11, 1984–5, p. 7.

46 Albrecht Wellmer, *Ethik und Dialog: Elemente des moralischen Urteils bei Kant und in der Diskursethik* (Frankfurt: Suhrkamp, 1986), p. 63, my translation.

47 Hermann Lübbe, "Are Norms Methodically Justifiable? A Reconstruction of Max Weber's Reply," in Benhabib and Dallmayr, eds., *Communicative Ethics Controversy*; Benhabib, "Afterword," in Benhabib and Dallmayr, eds., *Communicative Ethics Controversy*, pp. 352–3.

48 Alessandro Ferrara, "Critical Theory and Its Discontents: On Wellmer's Critique of Habermas," *Praxis International* 8: 3, 1989. See also Richard J. Bernstein's debates with Richard Rorty and Fred Dallmayr in the journal *Political Theory*: Bernstein, "One Step Forward, Two Steps Backward: Richard Rorty on Liberal Democracy and Philosophy," and Rorty's rejoinder in "Thugs and Theorists: a Reply to Bernstein" (both in 15: 4, 1987); Bernstein's "Fred Dallmayr's Critique of Habermas" and Dallmayr's reply, "Habermas and Rationality" (both in 16: 4, 1988). See also Dallmayr, "The Discourse of Modernity: Hegel, Nietzsche, Heidegger (and Habermas)," *Praxis International*, 8: 4, 1989. In these debates, Bernstein defends Habermas's thinking.

49 See the following works by Habermas: *Between Facts and Norms*, esp. chapter eight; *Die Einbeziehung des Anderen: Studien zur politischen Theorie* (Frankfurt: Suhrkamp, 1996); and *Die Normalität einer Berliner Republik* (Frankfurt: Suhrkamp, 1995). See also Mikael Carleheden and Gabriels Rene; "An

Interview with Jürgen Habermas," *Theory, Culture and Society* 13: 3, August 1996, pp. 1–18.

50 Richard Rorty, "Unger, Castoriadis, and the Romance of a National Future," in *Philosophical Papers*, vol. II (Cambridge University Press, 1991), p. 190.

51 *Ibid.*

52 Milan Kundera, *Immortality* (London: Faber and Faber, 1991), pp. 155–6.

53 Richard Rorty, *Contingency, Irony, and Solidarity* (Cambridge University Press, 1989), p. 44.

54 Michel Foucault, *L'Impossible Prison* (Paris: Seuil, 1980), p. 317; here quoted from John Rajchman, "Habermas's Complaint," in *New German Critique*, 45, 1988, p. 170. See also David Ingram, "Foucault and Habermas on the Subject of Reason," in Gary Gutting, ed., *The Cambridge Companion to Foucault* (Cambridge University Press, 1994).

55 Vincent Descombes, "Je m'en Foucault," review of David Couzens Hoy, ed., *Foucault: a Critical Reader* (Oxford: Blackwell, 1986), in *London Review of Books*, March 5, 1987. For a good collection of articles in what has become known as the "Foucault/Habermas debate," see Michael Kelly, ed., *Critique and Power: Recasting the Foucault/Habermas Debate* (Cambridge, MA: MIT Press, 1994). See also Axel Honneth, *The Critique of Power: Reflective Stages in a Critical Social Theory* (Cambridge, MA: MIT Press, 1991), pp. 99 and passim and Samantha Ashenden and David Owen, eds., *Foucault contra Habermas: Recasting the Dialogue between Genealogy and Critical Theory* (Thousand Oaks, CA: Sage, 1999).

56 Michel Foucault, "Space, Knowledge, and Power," in Paul Rabinow, ed., *The Foucault Reader* (New York: Pantheon, 1984), p. 248. See also Foucault, "What is Enlightenment?" in Rabinow, ed., *The Foucault Reader* and Foucault, "Kant on Enlightenment and Revolution," *Economy and Society* 15: 1, 1986.

57 Michel Foucault, "What is Enlightenment?" and "Space, Knowledge, and Power," in Rabinow, ed., *The Foucault Reader*, p. 45.

58 *Ibid.*, pp. 45–6.

59 Habermas, *Philosophical Discourse of Modernity*, p. 276.

60 *Ibid.*, p. 294.

61 Habermas, "Questions and Counterquestions," p. 196; Habermas, *Communication and the Evolution of Society*, p. 97.

62 Michel Foucault, "Politics and Ethics: An Interview," in Rabinow, ed., *The Foucault Reader*, p. 374.

63 Friedrich Nietzsche, *The Gay Science* (Vintage Books: New York, 1974), pp. 284–5.

64 Paul Veyne, "The Final Foucault and His Ethics," in Arnold I. Davidson, ed., *Foucault and His Interlocutors* (Chicago, IL: University of Chicago Press, 1997), p. 230.

65 Foucault, "What is Enlightenment?" p. 46.

66 Michel Foucault, "Face aux gouvernements, les droits de l'Homme," a document written and read by Foucault at a press conference in June, 1981, on the plight of the Vietnamese boat people; first printed in *Libération* (June 30–July 1, 1984); here quoted from James Miller, *The Passion of Michel Foucault* (New York: Simon and Schuster, 1993), p. 316.

67 Foucault, "What is Enlightenment?" p. 46.

68 See also Mark Warren, *Nietzsche and Political Thought* (Cambridge, MA: MIT Press, 1988); and Richard Rorty, "Nietzsche, Socrates and Pragmatism," *South African Journal of Philosophy* 10: 3, 1991.

69 Michel Foucault, interview in "Le Retour de la morale," *Les Nouvelles* (June 28, 1984), p. 37; here quoted from Hubert Dreyfus and Paul Rabinow, "What is Maturity," in Hoy, ed., *Foucault*, p. 119. See also Foucault, "What is Enlightenment?" and "Space, Knowledge, and Power."

70 Foucault, "Space, Knowledge, and Power," p. 247.

71 Michel Foucault, "Nietzsche, Genealogy, History," in Rabinow, ed., *The Foucault Reader*, pp. 87–8.

72 For more on this point, see Dean, *Critical and Effective Histories*.

73 Habermas, *On the Relationship of Politics, Law and Morality*, p. 8, emphasis deleted.

74 Michel Foucault, *The History of Sexuality*, vol. I (New York: Vintage, 1980), p. 89.

75 Foucault, "Politics and Ethics," pp. 375–6.

76 Noam Chomsky and Michel Foucault, "Human Nature: Justice versus Power," in Fons Elders, ed., *Reflexive Water: The Basic Concerns of Mankind* (Souvenir: London, 1974), p. 171.

77 Foucault, "The Ethic of Care for the Self," p. 18.

78 *Ibid.* and Habermas, *The Philosophical Discourse of Modernity*, pp. 253, 294.

79 Michel Foucault, *Colloqui con Foucault* (Salerno, 1981); here quoted from Miller, *Passion of Michel Foucault*, p. 235.

80 Foucault, "What is Enlightenment?" p. 46.

81 Millicent Dillon, "Conversation With Michel Foucault," *The Threepenny Review*, Winter/Spring 1980, p. 5. For more on Foucault and prison reform, see Michel Foucault and Gilles Deleuze, "Intellectuals and Power: a Conversation Between Michel Foucault and Gilles Deleuze," in Donald F. Bouchard, ed., *Language, Counter-Memory, Practice: Selected Essays and Interviews* (Oxford: Basil Blackwell, 1977); Michel Foucault, "Michel Foucault on Attica: an Interview," *Telos*: 19, 1974; and Gilles Deleuze, "Foucault and the Prison," interview in *History of the Present*: 2, Spring 1986.

82 Jean-Louis Ezine, "An Interview with Michel Foucault," *History of the Present*, February 1985, p. 14. The interview first appeared in *Les Nouvelles Littéraires* in March 1975, just after the publication of Foucault's *Discipline and Punish*.

83 Lois McNay, *Foucault and Feminism: Power, Gender, and the Self* (Boston, MA: Northeastern University Press, 1992); S. Bordo and Alison Jaggar, eds., *Gender/Body/Knowledge* (New Brunswick, NJ: Rutgers University Press, 1990); Nancy Fraser, *Unruly Practices: Power, Discourse and Gender in Contemporary Social Theory* (Cambridge: Polity Press, 1989); Seyla Benhabib and Drucilla Cornell, eds., *Feminism as Critique: Essays on the Politics of Gender in Late Capitalist Societies* (Cambridge: Polity Press, 1987).

84 See, for example, the discussion in *Texas Law Review* 70: 4, 1992: Linda R. Hirshman, "The Book of 'A'"; Richard A. Posner, "Ms. Aristotle"; Martha C. Nussbaum, "Aristotle, Feminism, and Needs for Functioning"; and Linda R. Hirshman, "Big Breasts and Bengali Beggars: a Reply to Richard Posner and Martha Nussbaum." See also Martha C. Nussbaum, *Love's Knowledge:*

Essays on Philosophy and Literature (Oxford University Press, 1990); and Nancy Sherman, *The Fabric of Character* (Oxford University Press, 1989).

85 Habermas, *The Philosophical Discourse of Modernity*; *Moral Consciousness and Communicative Action*; and *Justification and Application*.

86 Jean L. Cohen, "Critical Social Theory and Feminist Critiques: the Debate with Jürgen Habermas," in Johanna Meehan, ed., *Feminists Read Habermas: Gendering the Subject of Discourse* (New York: Routledge, 1995), p. 57.

87 Mary P. Ryan, "Gender and Public Access: Women's Politics in Nineteenth-Century America," in Craig Calhoun, ed., *Habermas and the Public Sphere*, (Cambridge, MA: MIT Press, 1992) p. 262. See also Nancy Fraser, "What's Critical About Critical Theory? The Case of Habermas and Gender," in Benhabib and Cornell, eds., *Feminism as Critique*; Geoff Eley, "Nations, Publics, and Political Cultures: Placing Habermas in the Nineteenth Century," in Calhoun, ed., *Habermas and the Public Sphere*; Lorenzo C. Simpson, "On Habermas and Particularity: Is There Room for Race and Gender on the Glassy Plains of Ideal Discourse?" *Praxis International* 6: 3, 1986.

88 Question by Nancy Fraser to Jürgen Habermas in Habermas, "Concluding Remarks," in Calhoun, ed., *Habermas and the Public Sphere*, p. 466.

89 Habermas, "Concluding Remarks," p. 469.

90 *Ibid.*, p. 466.

91 *Ibid.*, pp. 466–7.

92 Eley, "Nations, Publics, and Political Cultures" and Ryan, "Gender and Public Access."

93 Paul Wapner, "Environmental Activism and Global Civil Society," *Dissent* 41: 23, 1994 and Charles Spinosa, Fernando Flores, and Hubert Dreyfus, *Disclosing New Worlds: Entrepreneurship, Democratic Action, and the Cultivation of Solidarity* (Cambridge, MA: MIT Press, 1997).

94 Eley, "Nations, Publics, and Political Cultures," p. 307.

95 Dankwart Rustow, "Transitions to Democracy: Toward a Dynamic Model," *Comparative Politics* 2, April 1970; Albert O. Hirschman, "Social Conflicts as Pillars of Democratic Market Society," *Political Theory* 22: 2, May 1994, p. 208.

96 Habermas, "Concluding Remarks," p. 467.

97 *Ibid.*

98 Jürgen Habermas, "Further Reflections on the Public Sphere," in Calhoun, ed., *Habermas and the Public Sphere*, p. 453.

99 For more on the view that Aristotle is one of the first philosophers to see political life as a conflict-ridden reality, see Bernard Yack, *Problems of a Political Animal: Community, Justice, and Conflict in Aristotelian Political Thought* (Berkeley, CA: University of California Press, 1993). On the relationship between Aristotle and Machiavelli, see Eugene Garver, *Machiavelli and the History of Prudence* (Madison, WI: University of Wisconsin Press, 1987).

100 For a more full development of this argument, see Hirschman, "Social Conflicts as Pillars of Democratic Market Society," pp. 206 and passim.

101 Jeffrey C. Alexander, "Bringing Democracy Back In. Universalistic Solidarity and the Civil Sphere," in Charles C. Lemert, ed., *Intellectuals and Politics: Social Theory in a Changing World* (Newbury Park, CA: Sage, 1991).

102 Ryan, "Gender and Public Access," p. 286.
103 *Ibid.*
104 Alexander, "Bringing Democracy Back In."
105 See also Spinosa *et al.*, *Disclosing New Worlds.*

8   EMPOWERING ARISTOTLE

1 Paul Rabinow, "Truth and Society," *History of the Human Sciences* 3: 1, 1990, p. 55.
2 Michel Foucault, "Theatrum Philosophicum," in *Aesthetics, Method, and Epistemology. Essential Works of Foucault 1954–1984*, vol. II, edited by James D. Faubin, series editor Paul Rabinow (New York: New Press, 1998), p. 343.
3 Lecture of February 15, 1984, C 69 (03) in the Foucault Archives, Paris. Foucault may also have mentioned *phronesis* in other material now in the Foucault Archives but not yet available to readers. I am indebted to Arpád Szakolczai for clarifying this point.
4 Paul Rabinow, "Introduction," in Michel Foucault, *Ethics: Subjectivity and Truth. The Essential Works of Michel Foucault 1954–1984*, vol. I, edited by Paul Rabinow (New York: New Press, 1997), pp. xiii–xiv.
5 Michel Foucault, "Space, Knowledge, and Power," interview conducted by Paul Rabinow, in Paul Rabinow, ed., *The Foucault Reader* (New York: Pantheon, 1984), p. 255. Like Gilles Deleuze, I see Foucault's interviews as an integral part of his work, because they enlarge the historical problematization of each of his books to cover the construction of present problems. See Deleuze, *Foucault* (Minneapolis, MN: University of Minnesota Press, 1988).
6 Foucault, "Space, Knowledge, and Power," p. 255.
7 Walter Kaufmann, *Nietzsche: Philosopher, Psychologist, Antichrist* (Princeton, NJ: Princeton University Press, 1974), pp. 382–4.
8 Even though Nietzsche's influence is obvious in Foucault's texts, Foucault does not mention Nietzsche often in his writings. Exceptions are the short essay "Nietzsche, Genealogy, History" in Paul Rabinow, ed., *The Foucault Reader* and the original preface to *Folie et déraison* (Paris, 1961). For more on the Nietzschean roots of Foucault's thought, see Leslie Paul Thiele, "The Agony of Politics: The Nietzschean Roots of Foucault's Thought," *American Political Science Review* 84: 3, 1990 and J. Scott Johnson, "Reading Nietzsche and Foucault: A Hermeneutics of Suspicion," *American Political Science Review* 85: 2, 1991 with reply by Leslie Paul Thiele.
9 Aristotle, *The Nicomachean Ethics* (Harmondsworth: Penguin, 1976), 1140a24–1140b12.
10 Michel Foucault, "Structuralism and Post-Structuralism," interview conducted by Gérard Raulet, in *Essential Works of Foucault 1954–1984*, vol. II, p. 450.
11 *Ibid.*
12 Michel Foucault, *The Use of Pleasure: The History of Sexuality*, vol. II (New York: Vintage Books, 1990), p. 9.
13 Foucault, *Use of Pleasure: History of Sexuality*, II and *The Care of the Self: The History of Sexuality*, vol. III (New York: Vintage Books, 1988).
14 Friedrich Nietzsche, *The Gay Science* (New York: Vintage Books, 1974), p. 282. See also Kaufmann, *Nietzsche: Philosopher, Psychologist, Antichrist,*

pp. 356–61 and Rabinow, "Introduction," p. xxx.

15 James W. Bernauer, "Michel Foucault's Ecstatic Thinking," in James W. Bernauer and David Rasmussen, eds., *The Final Foucault* (Cambridge, MA: MIT Press, 1988), p. 75.

16 Michel Foucault, "Final Interview," conducted by Gilles Barbadette and André Scala, *Raritan* 4: 1, 1985, p. 9.

17 Ronald Hayman, *Nietzsche: a Critical Life* (Harmondsworth: Penguin, 1982), p. 3.

18 Steven Riggins, "Michel Foucault," interview, *Ethos* 1: 2, 1983, p. 8.

19 Nietzsche, *Gay Science*, p. 81.

20 Friedrich Nietzsche, *On the Genealogy of Morals* (New York: Vintage Books, 1969), p. 59 (§2).

21 Foucault, "Nietzsche, Genealogy, History." On the writing of Foucauldian "histories," see also Mitchell Dean, *Critical and Effective Histories: Foucault's Methods and Historical Sociology* (London: Routledge, 1994).

22 Foucault, "Nietzsche, Genealogy, History," p. 76.

23 Nietzsche, *Genealogy of Morals*, p. 21 (§7). Nietzsche sometimes suggests that genealogy is his own invention. At other times he mentions the "English psychologists" David Hume, Paul Rée, and Herbert Spencer as also being involved in doing "moral genealogy," even if Nietzsche considered their efforts unsuccessful. Alexander Nehamas, *Nietzsche: Life as Literature* (Cambridge, MA: Harvard University Press, 1985), pp. 245–6.

24 Didier Eribon, *Michel Foucault* (Cambridge, MA: Harvard University Press, 1991), pp. 138, 139.

25 Foucault, "Nietzsche, Genealogy, History," pp. 76–7.

26 Friedrich Nietzsche, *Twilight of the Idols* (Harmondsworth: Penguin, 1968), pp. 106–7 (§2).

27 Nehamas, *Nietzsche: Life as Literature*, p. 104.

28 *Ibid.*, p. 112.

29 Maurice Florence, "Foucault," in *Essential Works of Foucault*, vol. I, p. 463. Maurice Florence is a pseudonym for Michel Foucault.

30 Michel Foucault, "My Body, This Paper, This Fire," *Oxford Literary Review* 4: 1, 1979, p. 27.

31 Michel Foucault, *Colloqui con Foucault* (Salerno, 1981), pp. 6, 32–3; here quoted from James Miller, *The Passion of Michel Foucault* (New York: Simon and Schuster, 1993), p. 211.

32 Some of the major works from an especially comprehensive literature include Robert A. Dahl, *Who Governs? Democracy and Power in an American City* (New Haven, CT: Yale University Press, 1961) and Dahl's updated reflections in "Rethinking *Who Governs?* New Haven Revisited," in Robert Waste, ed., *Community Power: Directions for Future Research* (Beverly Hills, CA: Sage, 1986). Floyd Hunter, *Community Power Structure* (Chapel Hill, NC: University of North Carolina Press, 1953) and *Community Power Succession: Atlanta's Policy Makers Revisited* (Chapel Hill, NC: University of North Carolina Press, 1980); the latter is especially interesting as Hunter's restudy of Coca-Cola's home town Atlanta. G. William Domhoff, *Who Really Rules? New Haven and Community Power Reexamined* (Santa Monica, CA: Goodyear Publishing Company, 1978) and *Who Rules America Now? A view for the '80's* (Englewood

Cliffs, NJ: Prentice-Hall, 1983).

33 Peter Bachrach and Morton S. Baratz, "Two Faces of Power," *American Political Science Review* 56, 1962 and "Decisions and Nondecisions: An Analytical Framework," *American Political Science Review* 57, 1963. Steven Lukes, *Power: A Radical View* (London: Macmillan, 1974) and "Power and Structure," in *Essays in Social Theory* (London: Macmillan, 1977).

34 At the state level, the following studies by Nicolas Poulantzas are classic: *Political Power and Social Classes* (London: New Left Books, 1973) and *State, Power, Socialism* (London: New Left Books, 1974). At the local level we may cite two works by J. Allen Whitt, *Urban Elites and Mass Transportation: The Dialectics of Power* (Princeton, NJ: Princeton University Press, 1982) and "Toward a Class-Dialectical Model of Power: An Empirical Assessment of Three Competing Models of Political Power," *American Sociological Review* 44, 1979.

35 For an assessment of other aspects of Lukes's work in relation to Foucault, see David Couzens Hoy, "Power, Repression, Progress: Foucault, Lukes, and the Frankfurt School," in Hoy, ed., *Foucault: A Critical Reader* (Oxford: Basil Blackwell, 1986). See also Stewart Clegg, *Frameworks of Power* (London: Sage, 1989), esp. pp. 86 and 182–3.

36 Steven Lukes, ed., *Power* (Oxford: Basil Blackwell, 1986), p. 17.

37 *Ibid.*, p. 5.

38 *Ibid.*, p. 9.

39 Michel Foucault, "The Ethic of Care for the Self as a Practice of Freedom," interview conducted by Raul Fornet-Betancourt, Helmut Becker, and Alfredo Gomez Müller, in Bernauer and Rasmussen, eds., *Final Foucault*, p. 11.

40 Michel Foucault, *Introduction: History of Sexuality*, vol. I (New York: Vintage Books, 1980), p. 94.

41 Michel Foucault, *Discipline and Punish* (New York: Vintage Books, 1979), p. 26.

42 Foucault, *Introduction: History of Sexuality* vol. I, p. 95.

43 *Ibid.*, p. 93.

44 *Ibid.*

45 See, for example, Michael Walzer, "The Politics of Michel Foucault," *Dissent* 30: 1, 1983.

46 Michel Foucault, "The Subject and Power," in Hubert Dreyfus and Paul Rabinow, *Michel Foucault: Beyond Structuralism and Hermeneutics* (Brighton: Harvester Press, 1982), p. 222. See also Michel Foucault, "Sex, Power, and the Politics of Identity," interview conducted by B. Gallagher and A. Wilson, in *Essential Works of Foucault*, vol. I, pp. 163–173.

47 Foucault, "Subject and Power," p. 222.

48 *Ibid.*, p. 217.

49 *Ibid.*

50 Clifford Geertz, *After the Fact: Two Countries, Four Decades, One Anthropologist* (Cambridge, MA: Harvard University Press, 1995), pp. 39–40.

51 Foucault, "Subject and Power," p. 217.

52 Foucault, *History of Sexuality*, vol. I, p. 82. Compare also: "[I]n studying . . . power relations, I in no way construct a theory of power," Foucault, "Structuralism and Post-Structuralism: An Interview with Michel Foucault,"

conducted by Gérard Raulet, *Telos* 16: 1, 1983, p. 107.

53 Michel Foucault, *Power/Knowledge: Selected Interviews and Other Writings 1972–1977*, edited by Colin Gordon (Brighton: Harvester Press, 1980), p. 199.

54 Foucault, *History of Sexuality*, vol. I, p. 85.

55 *Ibid.*, p. 92.

56 Foucault, *Discipline and Punish*, p. 194.

57 Foucault, *History of Sexuality*, vol. I, pp. 92 and passim.

58 *Ibid.*, p. 94.

59 Foucault, "The Ethic of Care for the Self as a Practice of Freedom," p. 12.

60 Foucault, "Subject and Power," pp. 210–11.

61 See also Miller, *Passion of Michel Foucault*, p. 234.

62 Friedrich Nietzsche, *The Will to Power* (New York: Vintage Books, 1968), p. 342 (§643).

63 Nietzsche, *Genealogy of Morals*, p. 77 (§2.12).

64 For an example of how this may be done in an empirical study, see chapter ten, "Interpretation over Truth," in Bent Flyvbjerg, *Rationality and Power: Democracy in Practice* (Chicago, IL: University of Chicago Press, 1998).

65 Foucault, *History of Sexuality*, vol. I, p. 102.

66 Michel Foucault, "Space, Knowledge, and Power," interview with Paul Rabinow, in Rabinow, ed., *The Foucault Reader* (New York: Pantheon, 1984), p. 249.

67 Foucault, *Discipline and Punish*, pp. 27–8.

68 See for example Aaron Wildavsky, *Speaking Truth to Power: The Art and Craft of Policy Analysis* (Boston, MA: Little, Brown, and Co., 1979).

69 Foucault, *Power/Knowledge*, p. 132.

70 Michel Foucault, "The Ethics of the Concern of the Self as a Practice of Freedom," interview conducted by H. Becker, R. Fornet-Betancourt, and A. Gomez-Müller, in *Essential Works of Foucault*, vol. I, p. 295.

71 Michel Foucault, "Questions of Method: an Interview," *I&C* 8, Spring 1981, p. 11.

72 Michel Foucault, "The Regard for Truth," interview conducted by François Ewald, *Art and Text* 16, 1984, p. 31.

73 Foucault, *History of Sexuality*, vol. I, p. 60.

74 Michel Foucault, "What is Enlightenment?" in Rabinow, ed., *The Foucault Reader*, pp. 45–7, emphasis in original. In an interview, Foucault remarked on his work: "[T]he questions I am trying to ask are not determined by a preestablished political outlook and do not tend toward the realization of some definite political project." From Michel Foucault, "Politics and Ethics," interview by Paul Rabinow, Charles Taylor, Martin Jay, Richard Rorty, and Leo Lowenthal in Rabinow, ed., *The Foucault Reader*, p. 375.

75 Michel Foucault, "Polemics, Politics, and Problematizations," interview conducted by Paul Rabinow, in *Essential Works of Foucault*, vol. I, p. 117.

76 *Ibid.* and Foucault, *Use of Pleasure: History of Sexuality*, vol. II, p. 9.

77 Foucault, "Politics and Ethics," pp. 373–4.

78 *Ibid.*, p. 374.

79 Foucault, "Structuralism and Post-Structuralism," p. 200.

80 Foucault, "Politics and Ethics," p. 374.

9 METHODOLOGICAL GUIDELINES FOR A REFORMED SOCIAL SCIENCE

1 It should be mentioned that Alasdair MacIntyre's Aristotle is substantially more Platonic than the Aristotle depicted by the others, and more Platonic than the interpretation given in this book. MacIntyre explicitly understands Aristotle "as engaged in trying to complete Plato's work, and to correct it precisely insofar as that was necessary in order to complete it." See MacIntyre's *Whose Justice? Which Rationality?* (Notre Dame, IN: University of Notre Dame Press, 1988), p. 94. See also MacIntyre's, *Three Rival Versions of Moral Enquiry: Encyclopaedia, Genealogy, and Tradition* (London: Duckworth, 1990).

2 Alexander Nehamas, *Nietzsche: Life as Literature* (Cambridge, MA: Harvard University Press, 1985), p. 63.

3 Michel Foucault, "The Subject and Power," in Hubert Dreyfus and Paul Rabinow, *Michel Foucault: Beyond Structuralism and Hermeneutics* (Brighton: Harvester Press, 1982), p. 217.

4 Donald T. Campbell, "Science's Social System of Validity-Enhancing Collective Belief Change and the Problems of the Social Sciences," in Donald W. Fiske and Richard A. Shweder, eds., *Metatheory in Social Science: Pluralisms and Subjectivities* (Chicago, IL: University of Chicago Press, 1986), pp. 128–9; Charles E. Lindblom and David K. Cohen, *Usable Knowledge: Social Science and Social Problem Solving* (New Haven, CT: Yale University Press, 1979), p. 84; Charles E. Lindblom, *Inquiry and Change: The Troubled Attempt to Understand and Shape Society* (New Haven: Yale University Press, 1990). The quote in the text is from Campbell.

5 Mary Timney Bailey, "Do Physicists Use Case Studies? Thoughts on Public Administration Research," *Public Administration Review* 52: 1, 1992, p. 50.

6 Action researchers typically identify with those under study; that is, researchers take on the perspective and goals of those under study and use research results as part of an effort to achieve these goals. This is not necessarily the case for phronetic research.

7 Michel Foucault, *Titres et travaux*, pamphlet printed in fulfillment of requirements for candidacy at the Collège de France (Paris: privately printed, 1969), pp. 4–5; here quoted from Didier Eribon, *Michel Foucault* (Cambridge, MA: Harvard University Press, 1991), p. 215.

8 Michel Foucault, "Nietzsche, Genealogy, History," in Paul Rabinow, ed., *The Foucault Reader* (New York: Pantheon, 1984), p. 89.

9 Henry Miller, "Reflections on Writing," in Miller, *The Wisdom of the Heart* (New York: New Directions, 1941), p. 27; quoted in slightly different form in C. Roland Christensen with Abby J. Hansen, "Teaching with Cases at the Harvard Business School," in Christensen with Hansen, eds., *Teaching and the Case Method* (Boston, MA: Harvard Business School Press, 1987), p. 18.

10 Clifford Geertz, *The Interpretation of Cultures* (New York: Basic Books, 1973), p. 6 and Clifford Geertz, *Local Knowledge: Further Essays in Interpretive Anthropology* (New York: Basic Books, 1983).

11 Foucault, "Nietzsche, Genealogy, History," p. 76.

12 Clifford Geertz, *After the Fact: Two Countries, Four Decades, One Anthropologist* (Cambridge, MA: Harvard University Press, 1995), p. 40. See also Geertz, "History and Anthropology," *New Literary History* 21: 2, 1990 and "Disciplines," *Raritan* 14: 3, 1995.

13 Friedrich Nietzsche, *The Anti-Christ* (Harmondsworth: Penguin, 1968), p. 182 (§59).

14 Friedrich Nietzsche, *Ecce Homo* (New York: Vintage Books, 1969), p. 256 (§10).

15 Friedrich Nietzsche in *The Wanderer and his Shadow* (§11), here quoted from Nietzsche, *The Anti-Christ*, p. 191 (Appendix C).

16 After Ludwig Wittgenstein had abandoned any possibility of constructing a philosophical theory, he suggested that Goethe's phrase from *Faust*, quoted in the main text, might serve as a motto for the whole of his later philosophy. See Ray Monk, *Ludwig Wittgenstein: The Duty of Genius* (New York: Free Press, 1990), pp. 305–6. The Foucault quote is from Michel Foucault, "Politics and the Study of Discourse," in Graham Burchell, Colin Gordon, and Peter Miller, eds., *The Foucault Effect: Studies in Governmentality* (Chicago, IL: University of Chicago Press, 1991), p. 72. On the primacy of practices in Foucault's work, see also Michel Foucault, "Questions of Method: an Interview," *I&C* 8, Spring 1981, p. 5; and Foucault, *Titres et travaux*, pp. 4–6, quoted in Eribon, *Michel Foucault*, pp. 214–6.

17 Foucault, "Politics and the Study of Discourse," p. 59. See also Foucault, "Questions of Method," pp. 6–7.

18 Michel Foucault, "Le Discours de Toul," *Le Nouvel Observateur* 372 (December 27, 1971–January 2, 1972), p. 15; here quoted from James Miller, *The Passion of Michel Foucault* (New York: Simon and Schuster, 1993), p. 191.

19 Friedrich Nietzsche, *The Will to Power* (New York: Vintage Books, 1968), p. 356 (§675).

20 For more on eventualization, see Andrew Abbott, "What Do Cases Do? Some Notes on Activity in Sociological Analysis," in Charles C. Ragin and Howard S. Becker, eds., *What is a Case? Exploring the Foundations of Social Inquiry* (Cambridge University Press, 1992).

21 Friedrich Nietzsche, *Beyond Good and Evil* (New York: Vintage Books, 1966), p. 55.

22 Aristotle, *The Nicomachean Ethics* (Harmondsworth: Penguin, 1976), 1141b8–1141b27.

23 Foucault, *Titres et travaux*, p. 7, quoted in Eribon, *Michel Foucault*, p. 216.

24 Bent Flyvbjerg, "Socrates Didn't Like the Case Method, Why Should You?", in Hans E. Klein, ed., *Case Method Research and Application: New Vistas* (Needham, MA: World Association for Case Method Research and Application, 1989). See also Alasdair MacIntyre, "Epistemological Crises, Dramatic Narrative, and the Philosophy of Science," *Monist* 60, 1977.

25 Richard Rorty, "Habermas and Lyotard on Postmodernity," in Richard J. Bernstein, ed., *Habermas and Modernity* (Cambridge, MA: MIT Press, 1985), p. 173.

26 Alasdair MacIntyre, *After Virtue: a Study in Moral Theory* (Notre Dame: University of Notre Dame Press, second edition, 1984), p. 215. For more on case study research, and on the relationship between case particularity and

theoretical generality, see chapter six.

27 Paul Rabinow and William M. Sullivan, "The Interpretive Turn: a Second Look," in Paul Rabinow and William M. Sullivan, eds., *Interpretive Social Science: a Second Look* (Berkeley, CA: University of California Press, 1987), p. 8. See also David K. Henderson, "Epistemic Competence and Contextualist Epistemology: Why Contextualism Is Not Just the Poor Person's Coherentism," *The Journal of Philosophy* 91: 12, 1994.

28 Pierre Bourdieu, *In Other Words: Essays Towards a Reflexive Sociology* (Cambridge: Polity Press, 1990), p. 9.

29 For more on context, see Daniel Andler, "The Normativity of Context," unpublished paper, Université Paris X, Nanterre, printed April 29, 1998; Craig Calhoun, "E. P. Thompson and the Discipline of Historical Context," *Social Research* 61: 2, 1994; Susan Engel, *Context is Everything: the Nature of Memory* (New York: W. H. Freeman, 1999); Richard F. Fenno, Jr., "Observation, Context, and Sequence in the Study of Politics," *American Political Science Review* 80: 1, 1986; and Benny Shannon, "What is Context?" *Journal for the Theory of Social Behaviour* 20: 2, June 1990, pp. 157–66.

30 MacIntyre, *After Virtue*, p. 216.

31 Friedrich Nietzsche, *Twilight of the Idols* (Harmondsworth: Penguin, 1968), p. 35 (§1).

32 Clifford Geertz, *Works and Lives: the Anthropologist as Author* (Stanford, CA: Stanford University Press, 1988), p. 114. See also Geertz, "History and Anthropology" with response by Renato Rosaldo; and Gerda Lerner, *Why History Matters* (Oxford University Press, 1997).

33 Geertz, *Works and Lives*, p. 9.

34 M. Novak, "'Story' and Experience," in J. B. Wiggins, ed., *Religion as Story* (Lanham, MD: University Press of America, 1975), p. 175; and Cheryl Mattingly, "Narrative Reflections on Practical Actions: Two Learning Experiments in Reflective Storytelling," in Donald A. Schön, ed., *The Reflective Turn: Case Studies in and on Educational Practice* (New York: Teachers College Press, 1991), p. 237. See also Abbott, "What Do Cases Do?"; Hannah Arendt, *The Human Condition* (Chicago, IL: University of Chicago Press, 1958); D. Carr, *Time, Narrative, and History* (Bloomington, IN: Indiana University Press, 1986); MacIntyre, *After Virtue*; Paul Ricoeur, *Time and Narrative* (Chicago, IL: University of Chicago Press, 1984); Ann Fehn, Ingeborg Hoesterey, and Maria Tatar, eds., *Neverending Stories: Toward a Critical Narratology* (Princeton: Princeton University Press, 1992); David Rasmussen, "Rethinking Subjectivity: Narrative Identity and the Self," *Philosophy and Social Criticism* 21: 5–6, 1995; and Mieke Bal, *Narratology: Introduction to the Theory of Narrative* (Toronto: University of Toronto Press, second edition, 1997).

35 MacIntyre, *After Virtue*, pp. 214, 216.

36 Mattingly, "Narrative Reflections on Practical Actions," p. 237.

37 For a discussion of the problems in moving beyond these dualisms, see Dreyfus and Rabinow, *Michel Foucault: Beyond Structuralism and Hermeneutics*, and Thomas McCarthy's considerations on hermeneutics and structural analysis in his introduction to Jürgen Habermas's *The Theory of Communicative Action*, vol. I (Boston, MA: Beacon Press, 1984), pp. xxvi–

xxvii. Other works of interest on this problem, which in my view is one of the more challenging in phronetic research, are James Schmidt, *Maurice Merleau-Ponty: Between Phenomenology and Structuralism* (New York: St. Martin's Press, 1985); T. K. Seung, *Structuralism and Hermeneutics* (New York: Columbia University Press, 1982); and Anthony Giddens, "Hermeneutics and Social Theory," in *Profiles and Critiques in Social Theory* (Berkeley, CA: University of California Press, 1982).

38 Pierre Bourdieu, *Outline of a Theory of Practice* (Cambridge University Press, 1977), p. 72.

39 Bourdieu, *In Other Words*, p. 10.

40 See also Diane Vaughan, "Theory Elaboration: the Heuristics of Case Analysis," in Ragin and Becker, eds., *What is a Case?*, p. 183.

41 *Ibid.*

42 Robert N. Bellah, Richard Madsen, William M. Sullivan, Ann Swidler, and Steven M. Tipton, *The Good Society* (New York: Alfred A. Knopf, 1991) p. 302.

43 Vaughan, "Theory Elaboration," p. 182.

44 Clifford Geertz, "Deep Play: Notes on the Balinese Cockfight," in Geertz, *The Interpretation of Cultures*.

45 Robert D. Putnam with Robert Leonardi and Raffaella Y. Nanetti, *Making Democracy Work: Civic Traditions in Modern Italy* (Princeton, NJ: Princeton University Press, 1993).

46 Stella Tillyard, *Aristocrats* (New York: Farrar, Straus, and Giroux, 1994).

47 For more on the actor/structure issue, see Bourdieu, *Outline of a Theory of Practice*; Bourdieu, *Homo Academicus* (Stanford, CA: Stanford University Press, 1988); James Coleman, "Social Theory, Social Research, and a Theory of Action," *American Journal of Sociology* 91, 1985; Randall Collins, "On the Microfoundations of Macrosociology," *American Journal of Sociology* 86, 1980; Gary Alan Fine, "On the Macrofoundations of Microsociology: Constraint and the Exterior Reality of Structure," paper presented at the annual meetings of the American Sociological Association, Atlanta, 1988; Anthony Giddens, *The Constitution of Society: Outline of the Theory of Structuration* (Cambridge: Polity Press, 1984); Paul Raymond Harrison, "Narrativity and Interpretation: On Hermeneutical and Structuralist Approaches to Culture," *Thesis Eleven* 22, 1989; Claude Lévi-Strauss and Didier Eribon, *Conversations with Claude Lévi-Strauss* (Chicago, IL: University of Chicago Press, 1991), esp. pp. 102–4; William H. Sewell, Jr., "A Theory of Structure: Duality, Agency, and Transformation," *American Journal of Sociology* 98: 1, 1992.

48 For more on the relationship between the public sphere and science, see Robert Bellah, "Professionalism and Citizenship: Are they Compatible?" Symposium on Redefining Leadership: New Visions of Work and Community, Wake Forest University, Winston-Salem, North Carolina, May 21, 1993.

49 Robert N. Bellah, Richard Madsen, William M. Sullivan, Ann Swidler, and Steven M. Tipton, *Habits of the Heart: Individualism and Commitment in American Life* (New York: Harper and Row, 1985), p. 307.

50 Friedrich Nietzsche, *On the Genealogy of Morals* (New York: Vintage Books,

1969), p. 119 (§3.12).

51 *Ibid.* See also Friedrich Nietzsche, *The Will to Power* (New York: Vintage Books, 1968): "There are no isolated judgments! An isolated judgment is never 'true,' never knowledge; only in the connection and relation of many judgments is there any surety" (p. 287 [§530]).

52 Richard Rorty, "Towards a Liberal Utopia," *Times Literary Supplement,* June 24, 1994, p. 14.

10   EXAMPLES AND ILLUSTRATIONS: NARRATIVES OF VALUE AND POWER

1 Ronald Abler, John Adams, and Peter Gould, *Spatial Organization: The Geographer's View of the World* (Englewood Cliffs, NJ: Prentice-Hall, 1971), p. 478.

2 Bent Flyvbjerg, *Rationality and Power: Democracy in Practice* (Chicago, IL: University of Chicago Press, 1998). See also Bent Flyvbjerg, *The Aalborg Study: Case Selection and Data Collection*, Research Report (Aalborg: Department of Development and Planning, Aalborg University, 1997).

3 Michel Foucault, "Nietzsche, Genealogy, History," in Paul Rabinow, ed., *The Foucault Reader* (New York: Pantheon, 1984), p. 77.

4 *Ibid.,* p. 76.

5 Flyvbjerg, *Rationality and Power*, p. 86.

6 *Ibid.,* pp. 86–7.

7 As a methodological footnote I should like to remark that in answering the question of who wins and who loses in the Aalborg Project, I carried out environmental and social impact audits using statistical and other quantitative analyses. This was necessary for relating process to outcome in the project. Here as elsewhere, the sharp separation often seen in the literature between qualitative and quantitative methods is a spurious one. The separation is an unfortunate artifact of power relations and time constraints in graduate training; it is not a logical consequence of what graduates and scholars need to know to do their studies and do them well. In my interpretation, phronetic social science is opposed to an either/or and stands for a both/and on the question of qualitative versus quantitative methods. Phronetic social science is problem-driven and not methodology-driven, in the sense that it employs those methods which for a given problematic best help answer the four value-rational questions. More often than not, a combination of qualitative and quantitative methods will do the task and do it best. Fortunately, there seems currently to be a general relaxation in the old and unproductive separation of qualitative and quantitative methods.

8 *Ibid.,* p. 110.

9 *Ibid.,* p. 113.

10 The alderman is the city council member with administrative responsibility for the Aalborg Project and for all other matters regarding planning and environment in Aalborg. The City Council has four aldermen/-women plus one mayor, each holding a powerful position with responsibility for a large budget and a large staff in each of five municipal main areas of policy and administration.

11 *Ibid.*, pp. 114–15.
12 Friedrich Nietzsche, *The Will to Power* (New York: Vintage Books, 1968), p. 342 (§643) and *On the Genealogy of Morals* (New York: Vintage Books, 1969), p. 77 (§2.12).
13 See Flyvbjerg, *Rationality and Power*, pp. 225–36, for the details of this conclusion.
14 "Better" is defined here simply as being more democratic and more effective in fulfilling the objectives of the Aalborg Project as ratified by the City Council.
15 I here understand a stakeholder to be an organization, group, or person with an interest in the outcomes of the research.
16 Michel Foucault, *Colloqui con Foucault* (Salerno, 1981); here quoted from James Miller, *The Passion of Michel Foucault* (New York: Simon and Schuster, 1993), p. 235.
17 Morten Rugtved Petersen, *Byfornyelse: Bypolitik og beslutninger*, Master's Thesis (Aalborg: Aalborg University, Department of Development and Planning, 1993), p. 44.
18 Foucault, *Colloqui con Foucault*; here quoted from Miller, *The Passion of Michel Foucault*, p. 235.
19 Bent Flyvbjerg, "90'ernes trafikplanlægning for miljø, sundhed og bæredygtighed" (Traffic Planning in the 90s for Environment, Health, and Sustainability), *Miljø og Teknologi: Nordisk Tidsskrift for Miljøteknik, -forvaltning og -politik* 6: 1, 1991, pp. 28–32; and Flyvbjerg, "Når demokratiet svigter rammes miljøet" (When Democracy Fails the Environment is Hurt), in Benny Kullinger and Ulla-Britt Strömberg, eds., *Planera för en bärkraftig utveckling: 21 nordiska forskare ger sin syn*, Stockholm: Byggforskningsrådet, 1993, pp. 187–97.
20 For the other six measures, see Flyvbjerg, "Når demokratiet svigter rammes miljøet," pp. 194–7.
21 The first results of the work on mega projects may be found in Bent Flyvbjerg, Nils Bruzelius, and Werner Rothengatter, *Mega Projects and Risk: Making Decisions in an Uncertain World* (Cambridge University Press: forthcoming); Nils Bruzelius, Bent Flyvbjerg, and Werner Rothengatter, "Big Decisions, Big Risks: Improving Accountability in Mega Projects," *International Review of Administrative Sciences* 64: 3, September 1998, pp. 423–40; and Mette K. Skamris and Bent Flyvbjerg, "Inaccuracy of Traffic Forecasts and Cost Estimates on Large Transport Projects," *Transport Policy* 4: 3, 1997, pp. 141–6.
22 See also Flyvbjerg, *Rationality and Power*, p. 237.
23 Michel Foucault, *Discipline and Punish: The Birth of the Prison* (New York: Vintage Books, 1979); Michel Foucault, *Introduction: The History of Sexuality*, vol. I, (New York: Vintage Books, 1980). For a brief introduction to Foucault's work, see Gary Gutting, ed., *The Cambridge Companion to Foucault* (Cambridge University Press, 1994). For a more extensive and in-depth introduction, see Paul Rabinow, ed., *Essential Works of Foucault 1954–1984*, vols. I–II (New York: New Press, 1997, 1998).
24 Graham Burchell, Colin Gordon, and Peter Miller, eds., *The Foucault Effect: Studies in Governmentality* (Chicago, IL: University of Chicago Press, 1991);

Mitchell Dean, *The Constitution of Poverty: Toward a Genealogy of Liberal Governance* (London: Routledge, 1991); Mitchell Dean, *Governmentality: Power and Rule in Modern Society* (Thousand Oaks, CA: Sage, 1999); Jacques Donzelot, *The Policing of Families* (New York: Pantheon, 1979); Jan Goldstein, ed., *Foucault and the Writing of History* (Oxford: Blackwell, 1994); Agnes Horváth and Arpád Szakolczai, *The Dissolution of Communist Power: the Case of Hungary* (London: Routledge, 1992); Giovanna Procacci, *Gouverner la misère: la question sociale en France (1789–1848)* (Paris: Éditions du Seuil, 1993); Nikolas Rose, *The Psychological Complex: Psychology, Politics and Society in England, 1869–1939* (London: Routledge and Kegan Paul, 1985); and Rose, *Powers of Freedom: Reframing Political Thought* (Cambridge University Press, 1999).

25 Ian Hacking, *Rewriting the Soul: Multiple Personality and the Sciences of Memory* (Princeton, NJ: Princeton University Press, 1995); Hacking, *Mad Travelers: Reflections on the Reality of Transient Mental Illness* (Charlottesville, VA: University Press of Virginia, 1998); and Joseph Rouse, *Engaging Science: How to Understand Its Practices Philosophically* (Ithaca, NY: Cornell University Press, 1996).

26 Pierre Bourdieu, *Acts of Resistance: Against the Tyranny of the Market* (New York: New Press, 1998) and *On Television* (New York: New Press, 1998).

27 Pierre Bourdieu, *Outline of a Theory of Practice* (Cambridge University Press 1977); *The Logic of Practice* (Stanford, CA: Stanford University Press, 1990). See also *The State Nobility: Grandes Écoles and Esprit de Corps* (Cambridge: Polity Press, 1996) and *Practical Reason* (Cambridge: Polity Press, 1997).

28 Bruno Latour, *Aramis, or the Love of Technology* (Cambridge, MA: Harvard University Press, 1996) and *Science in Action: How to Follow Scientists and Engineers Through Society* (Cambridge, MA: Harvard University Press, 1987). See also his *The Pasteurization of France* (Cambridge, MA: Harvard University Press, 1988) and *Pandora's Hope: Essays on the Reality of Science Studies* (Cambridge, MA: Harvard University Press, 1999).

29 Wendy Brown, *States of Injury: Power and Freedom in Late Modernity* (Princeton, NJ: Princeton University Press, 1995); Barbara Cruikshank, *The Will to Empower: Democratic Citizens and Other Subjects* (Ithaca, NJ: Cornell University Press, 1999); Éric Darier, ed., *Discourses of the Environment* (Oxford: Blackwell, 1998); François Ewald, *L'Etat providence* (Paris: B. Grasset, 1986); and Ewald, *Histoire de L'Etat providence: Les Origines de la solidarité* (Paris: Grasset, 1996).

30 Barry Hindess, *Discourses of Power: from Hobbes to Foucault* (Oxford: Blackwell, 1996) and Mitchell Dean and Barry Hindess, eds., *Governing Australia: Studies in Contemporary Rationalities of Government* (Cambridge University Press, 1998).

31 Robert D. Putnam with Robert Leonardi and Raffaella Y. Nanetti, *Making Democracy Work: Civic Traditions in Modern Italy* (Princeton, NJ: Princeton University Press, 1993). See also Bent Flyvbjerg, "Habermas and Foucault: Thinkers for Civil Society?" *British Journal of Sociology* 49: 2, June 1998, pp. 208–33.

32 Martin Duberman, *Stonewall* (New York: Dutton, 1993).

33 Sandra Lee Bartky, *Femininity and Domination: Studies in the Phenomenology of*

Oppression (London: Routledge, 1990); Judith Butler, *Gender Trouble: Feminism and the Subversion of Identity* (New York: Routledge, 1990); and Nancy Fraser, *Unruly Practices: Power, Discourse, and Gender in Contemporary Social Theory* (Minneapolis, MN: University of Minnesota Press, 1989). See further references to the feminist literature in chapter seven.

34 Naomi Wolf, *Promiscuities: A Secret History of Female Desire* (London: Vintage Books, 1997).

35 Paul Rabinow, *French Modern: Norms and Forms of the Social Environment* (Cambridge, MA: MIT Press, 1989); Rabinow, *Making PCR: A Story of Biotechnology* (Chicago, IL: University of Chicago Press, 1996); and Rabinow, *French DNA: Trouble in Purgatory* (Chicago, IL: University of Chicago Press, 1999).

36 Peter Miller, "Accounting and Objectivity: the Invention of Calculating Selves and Calculable Spaces," in A. Megill, ed., *Rethinking Objectivity* (Durham, NC: Duke University Press, 1994), pp. 239–64 and "Governing the Enterprise: The Hidden Face of Accounting," in T. Porter and D. Ross, eds., *The Cambridge History of Science*, vol. VII, *Modern Social and Behavioural Sciences* (Cambridge University Press, 1999).

37 Jonathan Crush, "Scripting the Compound: Power and Space in the South African Mining Industry," *Environment and Planning D: Society and Space* 12: 3, pp. 301–24; Raphaël Fischler, "Toward a Genealogy of Planning: Zoning and the Welfare State," *Planning Perspectives* 13: 4, 1998, pp. 389–410; Margo Huxley, "Planning as a Framework of Power: Utilitarian Reform, Enlightenment Logic and the Control," in S. Ferber, C. Healey, and C. McAuliffe, eds., *Beasts in Suburbia: Reinterpreting Culture in Australian Suburbs* (Melbourne: Melbourne University Press, 1994), pp. 148–69; Tim Richardson, "Foucauldian Discourse: Power and Truth in the Policy Process," *European Planning Studies* 4: 3, 1996, pp. 279–92; Tim Richardson and Ole B. Jensen, "Constructing Spaces of Mobility and Polycentricity: The ESDP as a New Power/Knowledge Rationale for European Spatial Planning," 13th Association of European Schools of Planning (AESOP) Congress, Bergen, Norway, July, 1999; and Oren Yiftachel, "Planning and Social Control: Exploring the Dark Side," *Journal of Planning Literature* 12: 4, May 1998, pp. 395–406.

38 Edward W. Soja, *Post-Modern Geographies: the Reassertion of Space in Critical Theory* (London: Verso, 1989); Soja, *Thirdspace: Journeys to Los Angeles and Other Real-and-Imagined Places* (Oxford: Blackwell, 1996); Soja, *Postmetropolis: Critical Studies of Cities and Regions* (London: Basil Blackwell, 2000); and James Ferguson, *The Anti-Politics Machine: "Development," Depoliticization, and Bureaucratic Power in Lesotho* (Cambridge University Press, 1990).

39 We basically employed the methodological guidelines described in chapter nine. See Fred Simon Lerise, *Planning at the End of the River: Land and Water Use Management in Chekereni Moshi District, Tanzania*, Ph.D. dissertation (Copenhagen: The Institute of Town and Landscape Planning, Royal Academy of Fine Arts, 1996); Tumsifu Jonas Nnkya, *Planning in Practice: Democracy in Tanzania*, Ph.D. dissertation (Copenhagen: The Institute of Town and Landscape Planning, Royal Academy of Fine Arts, 1996); and Nnkya,

"Land Use Planning and Practice Under the Public Land Ownership Policy in Tanzania," *Habitat International* 23: 1, March 1999, pp. 135–55.

40 National Land Use Planning Commission, *Guidelines for Participatory Village Land Use Management in Tanzania* (Dar es Salaam: Ministry of Lands and Human Settlements Development, 1998).

11   SOCIAL SCIENCE THAT MATTERS

1 Richard Rorty, "Pragmatism without Method", in *Philosophical Papers*, vol. I (Cambridge University Press, 1991), p. 65.

Index